UNDEAD TV

Essays on *Buffy the Vampire Slayer*

EDITED BY ELANA LEVINE AND LISA PARKS

Duke University Press   Durham and London   2007

© 2007 Duke University Press

All rights reserved

Printed in the United States of America on acid-free paper ∞

Designed by Heather Hensley

Typeset in ITC Galliard by Tseng Information Systems, Inc.

Library of Congress Cataloging-in-Publication Data appear on the

last printed page of this book.

CONTENTS

ACKNOWLEDGMENTS

The idea for this collection began soon after a conference entitled Console-ing Passions: Television, Video, and Feminism at the University of Notre Dame in 2000 when one of the conference organizers noted the intense scholarly interest in *Buffy the Vampire Slayer* in evidence at the conference. Since then many people have helped us to assemble this project and we are grateful to them all. Melissa Stevenson, a Ph.D. student at the University of California, Santa Barbara, served as an invaluable editorial assistant during the early stages of the book. Stacy Mitchell, Garrett Krnich, T. Q. Gaskins, and Amy Pocha, student research assistants, dug up important information about the series and diligently videotaped and archived episodes; Joe Palladino, a fan and a critic, shared our interest and gave us encouragement; and Melissa McCartney, Esq. gave us much needed assistance. Allison McCracken displayed great dedication to this project with her impressive compilation of *Buffy* materials and her enthusiastic participation throughout. Jane Espenson, the executive producer of *Buffy* and one of its writers, discussed the series with us at crucial points in the project's development. The anonymous readers for Duke University Press provided helpful feedback that has considerably strengthened the project. Ken Wissoker supplied us with enthusiasm and support throughout the long process of this book's development; we thank him for his stalwart commitment to scholarly research in television studies. Special thanks are due to our contributors, whose dedication to this project has been unflagging, whose passionate interest in *Buffy* has been sustaining, whose willingness to respond to requests quickly and effectively has been essential, and whose innovative and thought-provoking scholarship makes this book possible. Finally, Elana sends personal thanks to Michael Z. Newman and Ron Becker for their unwavering scholarly and personal support. And Lisa sends warm thanks to Anil de Mello, Moya Luckett, Constance Penley, Janet Walker, Jenny Thomas, Marion Mann, Beti Tomic, and Miha Vipotnik for their friendship, love, and support.

Elana Levine and Lisa Parks

INTRODUCTION

That's the beauty of the *Buffy*verse: death is no more permanent than a Fleetwood Mac reunion.

SEAN FESCHUK

Viewers of *Buffy the Vampire Slayer* were used to death. Week after week for seven years, Buffy the slayer and her "Scooby gang" of friends staved off their own deaths and those of the Sunnydale community and the world at large by battling demons, monsters, gods, politicians, clergymen, scientists, and vampires seeking to drain the lifeblood out of the living. Viewers had experienced the (temporary) death of Buffy herself and the more achingly permanent demises of such characters as Joyce, Buffy's mother, and Tara, the lover of Buffy's best friend Willow. Buffy's attraction to undead men had become legendary, as viewers had accompanied her through passionate relationships with the vampires Angel and Spike. Yet the end of *Buffy the Vampire Slayer* as a television series was still an affecting loss, one felt in homes, online, and in print. This time, the end was truly the end.

As fans privately made peace with the program's demise, so too did the popular press engage in a process of more public mourning. Some bemoaned the decline of a once-great show. Others celebrated the program's bold conclusion. Almost all emphasized the series' wider impact on both the television industry and the broader society, declaring that a program of such power would not simply disappear. As one writer stressed, "The show may have died last night, but its spirit, like its protagonist, will undoubtedly resurrect itself again."[1] Another emphasized the show's influence even in its very prose, a direct homage to Buffy's on-screen tombstone two years earlier: "*Buffy*'s passing is worth eulogizing, not just mourning, because *Buffy* changed the face of television a lot."[2] Over its seven-season run, *Buffy the Vampire Slayer* became a cultural phenomenon that epitomized trends in the production and reception of commercial television and offered provocative commentaries on matters of gender, sexuality, class, race, and age.

Buffy the Vampire Slayer tells the fantastical story of the teenage Buffy Summers's reign as "the chosen one," purportedly the "one girl in all the world" with the supernatural skill to slay vampires. Over the course of 144 episodes, Buffy and her friends battled myriad otherworldly embodiments of evil while they made their way through the many traumas and occasional joys of growing up, maturing from teens to young adults and facing the moral, emotional, intellectual, sexual, and spiritual quagmires of contemporary life. *Buffy the Vampire Slayer* dramatizes the travails of its title character but uses its metaphorical representations of life and death, good and evil, comedy and tragedy to speak about the power struggles inherent in many people's everyday lives in the Western world at the end of the twentieth century and the beginning of the twenty-first.

Like its beleaguered protagonist, the series has accomplished this cultural work from the margins. With its deliberately silly title and its placement (in the United States) on each of the two broadcast "netlets" (the WB and then UPN, as opposed to the four major national broadcasters), *Buffy the Vampire Slayer* never received the kind of legitimacy marked by prestigious awards or serious consideration from arbiters of high cultural taste. At the same time, however, the program inspired a passionate following from a broad range of viewers and, at least among such viewers, it became an exemplar of television's best. Many of its fans have proclaimed its uniqueness, and yet the series fits quite comfortably into long traditions of popular storytelling, building on the genres of science fiction, fantasy, horror, and melodrama. What is the legacy of such a series? Why has it been so influential to so many? In what ways can it live on as a special anomaly in television history, and in what ways might it

Fig. 1. Sarah Michelle Gellar is identified as Buffy on the cover of *Entertainment Weekly*, 8 October 2004.

be better characterized as a typical output of the commercial media industries of the late 1990s and early 2000s?

Undead TV seeks to answer such questions about the cultural impact of *Buffy the Vampire Slayer*. As we write this introduction after the program's end, it is clear that *Buffy*'s popularity and significance have persisted, that in many ways *Buffy*'s end was just a beginning. The show has been viewed in more than one hundred countries, from Poland to Portugal, Iceland to South Africa, and its ardent fan base is global in its span.[3] *Buffy*'s ongoing presence has been fostered by syndicated reruns in the United States and abroad, as well as by its release and impressive sales on DVD.[4] In online forums, fans still analyze the show and its characters. Scholars write books and articles about the program and stage academic conferences to explore its significance. *Buffy* merchandise still sells, and popular magazines still place the star, Sarah Michelle Gellar, on their covers. As the *Entertainment Weekly* issue of 8 October 2004 illustrates (fig. 1), Gellar remains linked to Buffy, even when promoting new film appearances.[5] There is no question that *Buffy the Vampire Slayer* continues to matter as both a commercial good and a cultural phenomenon. The chapters that follow seek to explain how and why *Buffy* has mattered, and continues to matter, in each of these respects. As a preface to that work, in this introduction we explore the implications of studying a television series once it has ended and ask how the study of this series in particular sheds light on the enterprises of television criticism and television itself.

THE AFTERLIFE

The active "afterlife" of *Buffy the Vampire Slayer* makes clear the program's popularity, but it also raises a broader set of questions about television and endings, whether we imagine them in terms of cancellation, replacement, or death. If American dramatic television had a cemetery, it would be overflowing with coffins by now, since nearly six decades' worth of series have ended. Yet one of the most distinctive features of commercial television series is that they rarely disappear.[6] Television series, like vampires, are made to return from the dead. Indeed, the American commercial television economy is predicated upon such revivals, re-emergences, and re-appearances.

Buffy the Vampire Slayer is a series that repeatedly plays with the question of closure, of finality, of ending, of death. In many respects, it is a series *about* termination and about resurrection, a point emphasized by the fact that it "ends" on one network only to begin on another. It thus provides a particularly clear instance through which to consider a television series' potentially interminable afterlife. From this perspective, the notion of a "final episode," an "end" to a series, is ultimately somewhat misleading, for it suggests the ending of something that doesn't really end. Instead, television series such as *Buffy* take on new manifestations and new meanings as they are repositioned in different cultural contexts and historical periods. The international distribution of American television programming makes this point especially clear, since markets around the world air the same programs according to different schedules and seasons.

Even within a single national context, a series' afterlife may parallel its first run. That is, a show may be syndicated and released on DVD even before its cancellation, as was the case with *Buffy*. Thus, what we are calling the afterlife does not necessarily "begin" when a show "ends," but rather may be conterminous with a show's initial phase of distribution. Furthermore, a show's afterlife, in ancillary products, in reissues, in global circulation, and certainly in the minds, emotions, and experiences of viewers, arguably begins during the show's initial broadcast phase and yet extends beyond it. Like *Buffy*, many series are now "over" or "dead"—that is, they have been canceled and there are no longer new episodes being produced—yet they persist in multiple ways.

The ongoing existence of a television series after its domestic first run suggests that the afterlife is an important moment of critical inquiry, since a television series can experience a range of fates during this period. In some cases, series are sold for enormous sums and earn much more revenue after cancellation than they did initially. For example, it is now believed that sales of television series on DVD will eventually match, and then better, the profits of broadcast and cable sales of off-network programming, multiplying a "dead" program's revenue streams.[7] As DVD sales have demonstrated, series that have sat unsold for years can become relevant and marketable once again. *The Ultimate Johnny Carson Collection* and *The Best of Bob Hope* have sold millions of units for their distributor, Respond 2 Entertainment, to name just two such cases.[8] The work of Joss Whedon, *Buffy*'s creator, has found a similar resurgence in such after-sales. In addition to *Buffy*'s impressive DVD performance, Whedon's short-lived series *Firefly* (Fox, 2002–3) has had great success on DVD, enough to have justified its revivification as a Hollywood feature film (*Serenity*, 2005). The resurrection of TV series can take on other forms, as well. Whedon's participation in the forthcoming feature film version of the 1970s TV series *Wonder Woman* (ABC, 1976–77; CBS, 1977–79) resurrects both the superheroine of the 1970s (herself a resurrection from her comic book past) and the Buffy character, since her place in the pantheon of superheroines will no doubt inform future representations of powerful women. Increasingly, a series' afterlife can have as much, if not more, economic and cultural impact as its initial domestic run.

To consider a television series as having an afterlife or as being "undead" is not to conflate television with liveness, but rather to recognize that the industrial structure of commercial television lends itself to the constant recovery of used, terminated, canceled, expired material for maximum return.[9] Derek Kompare sees this tendency as the structuring principle of commercial television. "What if television," he writes, "is not the ideal conduit for 'live,' new events, but is instead a machine of repetition, geared toward the constant recirculation of recorded, already seen events?"[10] Todd Gitlin has characterized this propensity for repetition as the "recombinant" property of commercial television, suggesting that this facet of the television industry's workings is "rooted deeply throughout all modern culture and thought" and is an inevitable byproduct of capitalism.[11]

While all American commercial television is subject to this sort of repurposing, we believe that *Buffy the Vampire Slayer* occupies a unique place within this capitalist economy. Unlike a series that simply recombines or repeats previous formulas, *Buffy* narrativizes the resuscitative patterns of commercial television by making interaction between the living and the dead a central programmatic premise. In so doing, the series connects to a deeply rooted, long-standing cultural conception of television as a technology that negotiates distance, including the purportedly infinite distance of death.[12] John Durham Peters argues that modern media (such as television) have been associated historically with two "key existential facts." These are "the ease with which the living may mingle with the communicable traces of the dead," and "the difficulty of distinguishing communication at a distance from communication with the dead."[13] *Buffy the Vampire Slayer* repeatedly stages and thematizes these "existential facts." The series' exploration of communication and communion between the living and the dead also reanimates a conception of television itself as a kind of portal for the undead. That is, the program's dramatic revivification of humans, whether in the form of vampires, demons, or monsters, spotlights at a metonymic level commercial television's own practice of recalling material thought to have long disappeared.

BUFFY BEFORE THE AFTERLIFE

The "life" of *Buffy the Vampire Slayer*, that is, its life as a first-run American broadcast network television series, began when Joss Whedon adapted his 1992 feature length screenplay of the same title into a TV pilot. After shopping it around the Big 3 networks with little success, Whedon's series finally landed on the new WB network in 1997. The series helped to build the WB's "Generation Y" audience and spurred a new cycle of youthful programming that included shows such as *Dawson's Creek* (WB, 1998–2003), *Charmed* (WB, 1998–2006), *Popular* (WB, 1999–2001), *Roswell* (WB, 1999–2001; UPN, 2001–2), *Smallville* (WB, 2001–6; CW, 2006–), and even a spin-off series, *Angel* (WB,

1999–2004). Initially focused on the unspoken horrors of high school, *Buffy* appealed both to young viewers, many of whom were in the midst of similar experiences, and to adult viewers for whom the "high school as hell" metaphor resonated meaningfully. To Whedon such material was ideal fodder for a series: "There's never a time when life is more like a TV show. Everything is so turgid when you're in high school. Everything is so powerful, so dramatic."[14] As one critic put it, "Where other high school series often wallow in teen angst to the point where even the loneliest, most pimply-faced outcast might get fed up with the characters' navel-gazing, *Buffy* took the emotional horrors of adolescence and made them into tangible ones."[15]

As the program evolved and its characters moved from high school on to college and working lives, its melancholic yet chirpy stories of love and loss, bravery and fear ignited an impassioned fandom and critical acclaim that garnered the series wide recognition in the United States and around the world. Renowned for its intricate narrative arcs, complex characters, witty writing, heavy use of metaphor, and satirical humor, the show also participated in broader social dialogues about teen alienation, feminist politics, media violence and sexuality, occult practices, drug use, and global militarization. The international security specialist Anthony H. Cordesman even used the show as the basis for a 42-page treatise called "Biological Warfare and the 'Buffy Paradigm,'" published by the Center for Strategic and International Studies in Washington. Claiming that the slayer "lives in a world of unpredictable threats where each series of crises only becomes predictable when it is over and is followed by a new and unfamiliar one," Cordesman used the show to rationalize a call for further U.S. militarization and preparedness, arguing that the world is stymied by a "Buffy syndrome" in which the threat of biological warfare is imminent and should be contained.[16]

As we write this introduction, military strategists are no doubt continuing their conjecture, and *Buffy the Vampire Slayer* has finished its seventh and final season. Though the series' first run has ended, as we have suggested, it already has a prosperous afterlife in multiple respects. Among these is the extensive parade of *Buffy* merchandise, with the show's identity affixed to everything from chess sets to velvet purses, light socket covers to action figures. This wave of *Buffy* product licensing has targeted a new generation of young consumers, and it is symptomatic of the maelstrom of media conglomeration underway across the global media industries. Indeed, when UPN acquired the show in 2001, *Newsweek* described the development as "the latest round in a slugfest between two of the world's largest media superpowers—AOL Time Warner, the WB's parent, and Viacom CBS, UPN's owner."[17] The show's producer, Twentieth Century Fox, not only negotiated a $102 million deal with UPN for two more first-run seasons (a sum unprecedented for a show with such a small, albeit highly valued, audience—roughly four million people per week), but also licensed syndicated episodes to FX, a cable network owned by Fox's parent company, News Corporation. There was even talk of Joss Whedon developing *Buffy the Vampire Slayer: The Animated Series* for the Fox Kids Network. The lucrative potential of these synergistic ties spurred industry speculation that Twentieth Century Fox had sold the series to UPN as part of a broader strategy by News Corporation to acquire that network, especially since Rupert Murdoch, the owner of News Corporation, was already buying up stations affiliated with UPN.[18] Although that eventuality has not come to pass, its very possibility is evidence that broadcast television production and distribution remain at the front of the ever-advancing march of media conglomeration. As one analyst put it, "The implication is that studios with network links will begin taking shows that are successful on one network and placing them on their owned network once they ripen into hits."[19]

Buffy's place in the changes that have befallen the commercial television industry since the mid-1990s has become particularly clear in the wake of the announcement in early 2006 that both the WB and UPN would cease operation in September 2006, to be replaced by a new, joint effort, the CW. As Meg James, a writer with the *Los Angeles Times*, postulated, "When the obituary is written of the WB network, the cause of death should probably read: complications resulting from *Buffy the Vampire Slayer*."[20] Post-mortems of the two "netlets" have cited *Buffy*'s move from the WB to UPN in 2001 as the incident that "set in motion a pitched battle for the coveted youth market that would eventually doom both networks."[21] While the end of the "netlets" succeeded the conclusion of the slayer's story by several years, it is arguable that *Buffy*'s life span was coterminous with, and perhaps even a foundational element of, an early phase of the post-network era. In this phase, multiple media conglomerates sought to enter the broadcast television business primarily through youth-targeted programming—and found that there was not enough such business to go around.[22] As one of the few series to participate in the histories of both "netlets," *Buffy* leaves a legacy that will be forever intertwined with this ultimately short-lived experiment in American broadcasting.

Buffy and the networks of which it was a part will also be remembered for being caught in the crosswinds of social controversy during its domestic first run. Moral conservatives scapegoated the show (as well as the singer Marilyn Manson, the video game Doom, and Goth subculture) for the Columbine High School shootings in April 1999.[23] Charged with glorifying violence and locating it within a high school setting, the program became a potential embarrassment for the WB instead of being its prized showcase series. As a result, Jamie Kellner, the CEO, pulled two episodes from the spring 1999 schedule. In the first of these, "Earshot," Buffy acquires a temporary ability to hear others' thoughts and discovers the murderous intentions of a member of the Sunnydale High community. Kellner also delayed the broadcast of "Graduation Day, Part 2," in which the students of Sunnydale take up arms against the evil Mayor Wilkins, who is a guest speaker at graduation and, it turns out, an "unholy big-ass snake thing," who is defeated only with the explosive destruction of the school. Though the WB aired the episodes at later dates, *Buffy*'s devoted fans, as well as Whedon, were outraged at what they saw as the network's censorship. Fans circulated videotapes of the episodes via online exchanges and even pooled funds to purchase a full-page ad in *Variety* condemning the WB for its actions.

Buffy's online presence in both industry-sponsored and fan-generated websites has offered audiences a multiply-mediated experience unavailable to viewers in previous historical periods. Though *Buffy*'s online presence is comparable to other cult TV hits such as *Xena: Warrior Princess* (syndicated, 1995–2001) and *The X-Files* (Fox, 1993–2002), its fan community has been exceptionally active in organizing and advocating for its interests within the entertainment industry. *Buffy*'s fans followed their first *Variety* ad with others that urged industry officials to award the series an Emmy, congratulated the show's producers on the one hundredth episode, and called for more *Buffy/Angel* crossover episodes when *Buffy* moved to UPN.[24] The program's online community has also served as a microcosm for the series' reception in the wider culture. In addition to the controversy over the episodes of school violence, viewers went online to discuss such issues as the show's ongoing development of the lesbian relationship between Buffy's best friend, Willow, and Willow's girl-friend, Tara. Audiences debated this story in message boards and discussion forums, alternately questioning the morality of a same-sex relationship and the consistency of Willow's lesbianism, and applauding Whedon's social pro-gressiveness in creating a tender and passionate romance between two girls on prime-time TV. The Willow/Tara plot drew broader interest as well, tapping into gay rights discourse and the responsibilities inherent in representing gay characters and themes, particularly when Tara was killed just after having sex with Willow. Fans who had been thrilled to see a sensitive portrayal of a long-term lesbian relationship were angered by the association between lesbian sex and violent death and joined together in public protest. This story—and espe-cially its controversial conclusion—generated grassroots activism to support gay and lesbian youth and to question media representations of sexuality.[25]

Like cult series such as *Twin Peaks* (ABC, 1990–91) and *The X-Files*, but even more intensely than these earlier shows, *Buffy* has been a scholarly phe-nomenon. Indeed, *Buffy the Vampire Slayer* may be the most studied television series in the medium's history. Academics in the fields of media and cultural studies, communication, English, philosophy, education, gender studies, and religious studies have taken up the program as an object of analysis. It is the subject of a host of scholarly books, including *Fighting the Forces: What's at Stake in "Buffy the Vampire Slayer"?*, *"Buffy the Vampire Slayer" and Philosophy*, *Why "Buffy" Matters: The Art of "Buffy the Vampire Slayer,"* and *Slayer Slang*, as well as an international online journal, *Slayage*.[26] It has been the focus of international scholarly conferences and college courses. This academic atten-tion has been paired with a substantial amount of journalistic criticism and popular, fan-targeted publishing. Add to this innumerable fan websites, fan fiction, fan videos, and fan art projects, and the outpouring of writing, think-ing, and speaking about the series becomes truly exceptional. *Undead TV* joins this substantial discourse on *Buffy* and participates in the ongoing analysis of the program's significance, focusing in particular on its status as a *television* program. By exploring *Buffy*'s place within the media industries and contem-porary popular culture, the essays in this collection join the many insightful investigations of the program's messages and themes and expand their focus. In the process, this book becomes part of the show's critical record, and thus it becomes as much a part of *Buffy*'s afterlife as are its DVD releases, its global syndication, and its treasured place in the lives of its viewers.

CRITICAL COMMUNION

In addition to allowing us to examine *Buffy*'s long-term impact, developing this book has also led us to reflect upon some aspects of television criticism. As a result, we hope that this volume will contribute to the dialogue on just what television criticism is, and what it should or could be. Throughout our work on this project, we have come to consider our own, and our contributors,' affective investment in the series, an investment that might best be described as a "critical communion" with the ethos of *Buffy*. Most of us readily acknowledge and in some cases revel in our emotional and political connection to the series and its characters. In this sense, all of us who have contributed to this collection can be considered fans, who, as Constance Penley has made clear, are often the most passionate—and most harsh—critics.[27] This means that the essays in this book sometimes find fault with the series' politics. Sometimes they question the program's role within a market-driven entertainment system. And sometimes they challenge popular readings of its narratives and themes—all without rejecting *Buffy*'s appeal. Throughout this collection, the contributors demonstrate how to be critical of television without denying its pleasures, how to take the medium seriously without betraying its entertainment value. What this work reveals is that television criticism can function as a kind of communion in that it demands regular connection to and affective engagement with a series and its world, it generates intellectual, emotional, and/ or spiritual resonances, and it trades on mediated yet intimate forms of contact and exchange. In other words, television criticism is a practice that involves communing with television shows, their characters, and their settings, as well as with the many others who create and consume them, all without sacrificing an analytical perspective.

This series sits at the crossroads of multiple critical issues, including the construction of the youth audience, teen stardom, generic hybridity, television narrative, media conglomeration, gender, sexual, racial, and ethnic representation, and the nature of television criticism itself. This volume examines these issues through two broad, and sometimes overlapping, foci: the show's position in the production and reception of commercial television culture and the representational politics of gender, sexuality, ethnicity and race, and age. The first four chapters explore some of the key stakes in the production and reception of *Buffy* as a commercial product. Mary Celeste Kearney's "The

Changing Face of Teen Television, or Why We All Love *Buffy*" grapples with *Buffy*'s generational address, querying the ways the program has been targeted to and read by differently aged audiences. Kearney's chapter focuses in particular on the marketing logic of the WB and the ways that the series fit that logic. She argues that the WB and *Buffy* actually targeted a multi-aged audience, but that they did so under the identity category of "youthfulness," an identity that transcends age and instead calls upon a "teen" sensibility to draw pre-teen and adult viewers valued by advertisers.

Susan Murray's "I Know What You Did Last Summer: Sarah Michelle Gellar and Crossover Teen Stardom" takes on the series' role in our convergent media environment. Murray explores the permutations of teen stardom in this technologically flexible commercial context. She sees Buffy's portrayer as emblematic of a new kind of star, one who effortlessly crosses media (from television to film to Internet and back again) and draws along with her a teen audience for whom boundaries between media have effectively dissolved. She argues that fans see stars such as Gellar as their key link between different characters and media, just as these young audiences have become proficient at traversing the Internet through a matrix of hyperlinks.

Annette Hill and Ian Calcutt's "Vampire Hunters: The Scheduling and Reception of *Buffy the Vampire Slayer* and *Angel* in the United Kingdom" takes up the vital question of the global circulation of television programming. One of *Buffy*'s most popular foreign markets is the United Kingdom, and Hill and Calcutt explain the specific circumstances within which viewers in the United Kingdom have engaged with *Buffy* and its spin-off, *Angel*, circumstances shaped by the structure of Britain's television system and its policies about content appropriateness for different audiences. They argue that the British TV system frames the viewing of *Buffy* in ways specific to the British context, and that fans' experiences of the show are thereby qualitatively different from viewers' experiences in other locales.

Amelie Hastie's "The Epistemological Stakes of *Buffy the Vampire Slayer*: Television Criticism and Marketing Demands" analyzes *Buffy* and the scholarly attention it has received as an example of the market demands central both to television production and to the production of scholarship *about* television. She examines the emphasis on a quest for knowledge via research in the series and some of its ancillary products, pointing out the particular appeals of such a focus for those who study and write about *Buffy*. But she also considers another implication of the connections between television programming and television scholarship by asking whether or not it is possible for scholarship about a commercial television product to avoid functioning as a merchandising tie-in for that very product. Ultimately, Hastie argues that television criticism—and scholarship on *Buffy* in particular—can attempt to resist these market logics, but only by being fully cognizant of them.

In the second half of the book, the focus shifts slightly to analyses of the politics of gender, sexuality, and race and ethnicity in the series. First is Cynthia Fuchs's "'Did Anyone Ever Explain to You What Secret Identity Means?': Race and Displacement in *Buffy* and *Dark Angel*." Fuchs considers the ways that these two series—one (*Buffy*) with a predominantly white cast and one (*Dark Angel*) with a more multicultural ensemble—represent race as an identity category constructed in relationship to another identity category, age. Although she delineates key differences between them, ultimately she argues that both series present race and youth as metaphorically related and as displaced by one another. In so doing, she engages with contemporary debates over the meaning of race and its function in fantasy and science-fiction-oriented television.

Allison McCracken's chapter, "At Stake: Angel's Body, Fantasy Masculinity, and Queer Desire in Teen Television," examines the character of Angel, tracing his visual and narrative function in *Buffy* and its spin-off series. She argues that Angel represents a new kind of mediated masculinity, and that his place in these on-screen worlds contributes significantly to their feminist perspective. While Angel seems to be the embodiment of normative white masculinity, his body is repeatedly subject to torture, and that torture is regularly linked to non-normative sexual practices. McCracken argues that instead of "demonizing" such practices, *Buffy* and *Angel* open up a fantasy space in which they are acceptable, pleasurable, and empowering for girls and queer viewers.

Jason Middleton's "Buffy as *Femme Fatale*: The Cult Heroine and the Male Spectator" analyzes the sexual politics of the series and its spin-off and ancillary products. Middleton focuses his analysis on comic books and science-fiction fan magazines that showcase the Buffy character and her portrayer. He argues that this sort of appropriation of the character reverses the somewhat progressive looking relations of the series in favor of a more conventionally patriarchal mode of figuring the female character and the actress who portrays her as objects of desire. Because the reading of *Buffy* invited by these texts challenges the more feminist, preferred reading of the series itself, Middleton argues that this reading position, while oppositional, is hardly progressive.

Finally, Elana Levine's essay "*Buffy* and the 'New Girl Order': Defining Feminism and Femininity" studies the program's much-discussed feminist stance by analyzing Buffy's status as a "New Woman," a character type with some feminist traits who has been visible on American television since at least the 1970s. Levine argues that although *Buffy* continues the television tradition of the "New Woman" in certain respects, the series uniquely shapes the meanings of both feminism and femininity in ways specific to its historical moment, a moment in which post-feminist and third wave feminist discourses converge and conflict. In this context, the series endorses a "new" form of feminism that nonetheless adheres to many long-standing feminist principles.

Across this book, the contributors engage with the series in ways that specify its significance as a commercial and cultural product. Their critical communion thus participates in *Buffy*'s ongoing existence, despite the end of its domestic, first-run life. By closely analyzing *Buffy the Vampire Slayer* as a complex media text, and by placing that text in relation to media industry imperatives, audience responses, and social and political developments, *Undead TV* seeks to expand our understanding of the life—and the afterlife—of this distinctive television program.

NOTES

The epigraph is from Feschuk, "In the End, Buffy Gave Us What We Wanted," *National Post* (Canada), 21 May 2003. Feschuk, a journalist, and his friend, Sean Twist, a custodian and a freelance writer, watched the final episode of *Buffy the Vampire Slayer* together in different cities and commented online to one another during it. This was one of Feschuk's remarks.

1. Hillary Frey, "Slain at Last: The Late Great *Buffy the Vampire Slayer*," *Slate*, 21 May 2003, http://slate.msn.com/id/2083387 (accessed 12 April 2007).
2. Anne Miller, "Bye-bye Buffy: 'Vampire Slayer' Changed TV and Gender Roles, One Vanquished Vampire at a Time," *Times Union* (Albany, N.Y.), 18 May 2003, 11.
3. "World's Fare," *Advertising Age*, 20 January 2003, 24.
4. *Buffy the Vampire Slayer* has been a key seller in Twentieth Century Fox's TV-on-DVD market, making the company the leader in this product category (with 42.4 percent of the market in 2002). Brett Sporich, "Laser-Sharp Profit: TV to DVD," *The Hollywood Reporter*, 12 June 2003, www.hollywoodreporter.com.
5. See also Joshua Rich and Missy Schwartz, "*Grudge* Report; She Scared up a $39 Million Opening. Does That Make Sarah Michelle Gellar a Movie Star?" *Entertainment Weekly*,

5 November 2005, 10. The first line of this story refers to Gellar as an "erstwhile vampire slayer."

6. Walter Benjamin notes that mass culture is predicated upon endless reproduction. We are interested here in exploring the specific ramifications of such a predication for commercial, series television. Benjamin, "The Work of Art in the Age of Mechanical Reproduction."

7. Sporich, "Laser-Sharp Profit."

8. Ibid.

9. Scholars have critiqued the construction of television as a quintessentially live medium as an ideologically motivated myth. See Feuer, "The Concept of Live Television"; and Caldwell, *Televisuality*.

10. Kompare, *Rerun Nation*, xi.

11. Gitlin, *Inside Prime Time*, 77.

12. Peters, *Speaking into the Air*; Sconce, *Haunted Media*; and Weber, *Mass Mediauras*.

13. Peters, *Speaking into the Air*, 149.

14. Bruce R. Miller, "Buffy Changes to Meet TV Demands," *San Diego Tribune*, 7 March 1997, www.trib.com/scjournal/ARC/1997/MAR/3_7_97/en3.html (accessed 19 April 2002).

15. Alan Sepinwall, "Say 'Goodnight,' *Buffy*," *NJ.com*, 18 May 2003.

16. Cordesman, "Biological Warfare and the 'Buffy Paradigm.'" For an interesting discussion of Cordesman's essay, see Phillips, "The 'Buffy Paradigm' Revisited."

17. Johnnie L. Roberts, "Rumble in the Media Jungle," *Newsweek*, 21 May 2001, 44.

18. Stephen Battaglio, "Buffy's Studio Shows Its Fangs," *Fortune*, 14 May 2001, 46.

19. Joe Schlosser, "Breaking a Taboo," *Broadcasting and Cable*, 30 April 2001, 46.

20. Meg James, "Buffy Fight May Have Slain Two Networks on the Edge," *Los Angeles Times*, 29 January 2006, C1.

21. Ibid.

22. Both netlets debuted with a significant amount of programming targeted to African American audiences but gradually decreased this portion of their schedules in favor of (white) youth-targeted fare. The first season schedule for the CW makes African American targeted programming an even smaller portion of the network lineup.

23. For further discussion of this issue, see Parks, "Brave New *Buffy*."

24. *Angel* remained on the WB throughout its first run.

25. "Fan Philanthropy: A *Buffy* Fan Site Reaches out to a Gay Youth Charity," *The Advocate*, 26 November 2002, 18; Mitchell, "Fans Slay Network"; Rundle, "Out of Bounds."

26. Wilcox and Lavery, *Fighting the Forces*; South, *"Buffy the Vampire Slayer" and Philosophy*; Adams, *Slayer Slang*; Wilcox, *Why Buffy Matters*; and *Slayage: The Online International Journal of Buffy Studies*, http://slayageonline.com (accessed 12 April 2007).

27. Penley, *NASA/TREK*.

1

Mary Celeste Kearney

THE CHANGING FACE OF TEEN TELEVISION,

OR WHY WE ALL LOVE *BUFFY*

For over a decade, the press has repeated ad nauseam the U.S. Census Bureau's projections that the teenage population will peak at close to 34 million by 2010. Not surprisingly, journalists who cite these figures often draw attention to the large amount of money teen consumers spend each year, estimated at $153 billion for 1999.[1] In turn, these phenomenal demographic and economic statistics have been used to explain the rampant juvenilization of American popular culture, particularly the increased proliferation of teenpics, such as *Scream*, teen magazines, such as *Cosmo Girl*, and teeny-bop musicians, such as *NSync.[2]

More specific to the world of television, numerous trade articles have appeared in recent years bearing titles such as "Smells Like Teen Demos," "Fountains of Youth," and "Media Taps into Zit-Geist" and connecting the teen population boom and teenagers' buying power with the greater number of teens depicted on TV.[3] Trade hype about teen-centered series was the most prolific from 1998 to 1999, largely due to the popularity of the WB's *Buffy the Vampire Slayer* and *Dawson's Creek*, and the resulting deluge of copycat series on both that and other networks. Virtually all press reports about this latest crop of "teen shows"[4] reveal some rendition of the logic exhibited by James Poniewozik, a reporter for *Time*: "The business motive behind these shows . . . is simple enough: . . . the large (about 31 million), fickle 12-to-19-year-old demographic draws ad money."[5]

Several crucial points remain obscured in such reasoning, however. Most significantly, teenagers watch *less* TV than any other age-based demographic. In fact, despite the large number of contemporary series featuring teens, the fifty-year tradition of teenagers' minimal TV consumption has continued. While adults over eighteen currently average almost 10 hours of television viewing per week, teenagers watch only about 6 1/2 hours.[6] Moreover, many reports show that today's teens are seeking out television entertainment less than ever before due to their involvement in other leisure activities, particularly surfing the web.[7] With so few teenagers watching TV, the teen audience has been spread extremely thin among the numerous programs that vie for its attention, so thin that *none* of the contemporary teen-centered series would make it on the air, and stay there, if they relied solely on teenage viewers.

Unlike many journalists covering television programming, TV executives recognize that appealing to the teen demographic alone is a risky proposition. As Sandy Grushow, the chair of Fox Television Entertainment Group, argues, "I . . . don't believe that targeting teens in and of itself is a sustainable business."[8] Jamie Kellner, the former CEO of the WB network, agrees: "You don't get as many dollars for teen viewers as adults 18–34."[9] As Kellner suggests, advertisers are similarly tentative about putting all of their eggs in the teen basket, and many have been rethinking their marketing strategies for this particular demographic due to teens' continued deprivileging of TV viewing and their increased interest in other media forms. For example, Frank Castiglione, the vice president of marketing for Mervyn's California, reports, "We're absolutely shifting media. . . . Traditional TV . . . [is] not the way to go."[10]

In order for teen shows to be viable, therefore, other age groups besides teenagers must watch them. Who, then, are the viewers who make up the teen show audience? To understand the construction of this audience more fully we must first move beyond the problematic assumption that media texts featuring characters of a particular age are consumed primarily by viewers of that same age, an assumption relied upon not only by most journalists, but also by scholars studying teen-centered TV series.[11] Although several media theorists have explored how spectatorial identifications cross the boundaries of sex, race, and sexuality, little attention has been paid to how viewers' televisual identifications may blur boundaries associated with age. Nevertheless, the widespread popularity of contemporary teen-centered series such as *Buffy the Vampire Slayer* suggests the prevalence of transgenerational identifications among many TV viewers.

Explorations of cross-generational forms of cultural identification necessitate thinking outside the age-specific frameworks of identity, taste, and desire upon which we have depended for far too long. The work of Philippe Ariès and Joseph Kett is useful in this regard, for these theorists demonstrate that although generation and life-stage status typically are linked to chronological age, such modes of identity are also, and perhaps primarily, socially constructed and thus have no essential, fixed meanings.[12] In other words, "childhood," "adolescence," and "adulthood" are empty terms that have been associated with different meanings at different times according to different social, political, and economic needs. As a result, the experiences, practices, and identities associated with these various stages of life are contingent, unstable, and mutable.

This chapter explores the shifting dynamics of aged-based consumer sensibilities and their relation to contemporary marketing and TV programming strategies in a post-network era. More specifically, I argue that in response to the audience fragmentation that resulted from changes within the television industry, the young WB network (founded in 1994) targeted a multi-aged market whose members shared a "youthful" sensibility. In order to capture this group for advertisers and merchandisers, the WB programmed a variety of teen-centered series whose appeals to youthfulness were collectively embraced by this multigenerational audience. Aired by the WB during its first five seasons and able to garner the broad multigenerational audience the new network needed to stay afloat during its infancy, *Buffy the Vampire Slayer* offers a somewhat unique opportunity to explore the WB's early programming strategies and to reexamine the teen show audience.[13]

RETHINKING THE MASS AUDIENCE

Given the profit-driven, consumer-oriented economy of the United States, American television networks ultimately desire to attract the largest audience possible for each of their shows in order to reach a significant mass of consumers for the advertisers to which the networks are beholden. The networks' traditional strategy for garnering a mass audience during prime time has been producing and programming series that appeal to family members with a shared viewing experience. Yet, with the increased penetration of cable and satellite delivery systems and the rise of new networks since the 1980s, the family audience has become too fragmented to sustain conventional broadcasting strategies. Instead, television programmers have turned to narrowcasting to appeal to smaller segments of the population categorized by demographic traits, such as sex and race. As John T. Caldwell notes, however, narrowcasting is a strategy dependent not just on smaller demographic segments, but also on the buying power of viewers within those groups: "Broadcasters began to value smaller audiences if the income-earning potential and purchasing power of those audiences were high enough to offset their limited numbers."[14]

Though extremely popular in the 1980s and early 1990s, narrowcasting ultimately was not the best answer to the problem posed by the fragmented TV audience. As Caldwell argues, "Audience growth was limited by narrowcast boundaries, which meant that advertisers and programmers had to find better ways to build distinctive audiences."[15] One of those strategies has been the creation of what Jim Collins calls a "coalition audience," whereby TV programmers develop series with "interlocking appeals" that are attractive to several different demographic segments.[16] The building of coalition audiences does not require doing away with narrowcasting strategies, but rather reconfiguring such an approach to produce the results generated by broadcasting. For example, instead of scrapping the traditional broadcasting goal of reaching a mass audience, the WB attempted to create a large coalition audience out of several smaller population segments, such as pre-teens and young adults. At the same time, the WB created this coalition by narrowcasting not to individuals who share demographic traits, but to those with a similar cultural sensibility: *youthfulness*.

A highly unusual development in American broadcasting, the WB's construction of a youthful coalition audience is not new when it is considered within the broader context of the global TV market. For example, in an article about British television in the 1980s, Simon Frith notes that programmers of that period tried

to devise a form of youth programming that could float quite free of any structural base. In this model "youth" became a category constructed by TV itself, with no other referent: those people of whatever age or circumstance who watched "youth" programmes became youth. . . ." "Youth," in this account, no longer described a particular type of viewer, who is attracted to a particular type of programme but, rather, describes an attitude, a particular type of *viewing behavior*.[17]

Though Frith does not relate this programming approach to advertising, it is important to note that because marketers attempt to ingrain an attitude of youthfulness in consumers of all ages in order to promote indiscriminate and frequent shopping, any network deciding to nurture a youthful viewing behavior among its various audience members is already more than halfway home. In other words, since consumers are encouraged to adopt a youthful sensibility in their commercial cultural practices, the TV industry can be somewhat assured that even viewers who are not chronologically young will gravitate toward programs that encourage a youthful viewing behavior.

READING UP

The advertising and media industries, however, are not solely responsible for the youthful identity and tastes shared today by individuals of different ages. One of the primary reasons for this common youthful sensibility is that the life stage of adolescence has been extended well beyond the teenage years that had been its defining feature for over half of a century. Indeed, adolescence now extends into both childhood and adulthood, thus blurring the boundaries traditionally associated with these stages of life. It is useful, therefore, to relate the extension of adolescence to the youthful attitude that marketers and media industries nurture in all consumers, for an exploration of this relationship helps to answer the question of why individuals chronologically categorized as children or as adults can be drawn to the same cultural texts, including *Buffy the Vampire Slayer*.

The extension of adolescence backward into childhood can be explained by a variety of social and physiological transformations over the last century. For instance, because of declines in infectious diseases, improvements in nutrition, and advancements in preventative healthcare, today's children mature physically at younger ages than those of previous generations, and therefore youth are entering pubescence—a traditional rite of passage into adolescence—earlier than ever before. In addition, there is much evidence to suggest that with the increasing number of divorces, single-parent families, and mothers who work outside the home, children are now forced to mature as social beings extremely early in life, often taking on household chores traditionally performed by parents.[18] A life stage called the "tweens" (typically ages nine to fifteen) has re-emerged in popular discourse, a phenomenon attributable both to an effort to offset adult fears about young people's early maturation and to attempts to cater to increasingly smaller segments of the youth consumer market.[19]

With reports from the late 1980s onward predicting that the number of tweens will soon become a 34-million-strong horde of teenagers, advertisers are extremely interested in attracting and grooming this demographic.[20] In addition to the vast numbers of these soon-to-be-teens, the collective amount of tweens' disposable income makes them quite appealing as consumers-in-training. In fact, youth income and thus buying power have risen substantially since the early 1990s as a result of an increase in two-income households and a (once) thriving economy. Moreover, since parents today tend to work longer hours and thus have less time for household chores, they often leave their children responsible for family shopping. Thus, contemporary youth spend a larger portion of their parents' money and influence family purchases to a greater degree than in previous generations. For example, it has been estimated that teenagers accounted for $48 billion of family consumption in 1999.[21] This phenomenon makes tweens a particularly lucrative market worth nurturing.

A primary strategy used by advertisers and merchandisers to attract tweens is appealing to their aspirations to grow up. As Peter Zollo, the president of Teenage Research Unlimited, reports, tweens have far greater age aspiration than do older teenagers. For instance, twelve- and thirteen-year-olds typically desire to be as much as five years older than they are, whereas eighteen- and nineteen-year-olds are fairly content with their current ages.[22] The aspirational desires of tweens directly affects their choice of cultural texts. Since tweens often fail to identify with the images and narratives of childhood targeted to younger children via popular culture, they are likely to seek out teen-oriented texts that help them feel more mature and "cool." As Nancy Dennis, the founder of Chickaboom girls' clothing, notes, "There's a real sophistication going on with this generation. . . . My daughter moved from Disney to *Buffy the Vampire Slayer* by age 7."[23]

This aspirational form of consumerism—popularly known as "reading up"—has been exploited rather well by merchandisers and advertisers who, since World War II, have used older teenagers as the primary role models for children. As Zollo notes, "Teens are important because they are trendsetters. . . . Younger children, being aspirational, look up to teens. . . ."[24] Evidence of the teen-as-role-model strategy can be seen in the magazine publication industry, which has used this approach to expand its readership. For instance, Alex Mironovich, the former publisher of *YM*, has argued, "Our philosophy is if we can get the 19-year-old we're pretty sure we'll get the 13- or 14-year-old as well because she's going to want to read up and find out what's going on. . . . If you get the older girls, you can get the young girls to read up."[25] Given the success of other media industries' reliance on tweens' aspirational consumerism, TV networks have programmed teen-centered series, such as *Buffy the Vampire Slayer*, in order to attract younger viewers and thus increase revenue from advertisers.

READING DOWN

At the same time that adolescence is now experienced by those traditionally categorized as children, this life-stage identity is being extended on the other end of the age spectrum by individuals over eighteen, who also are being encouraged to identify with teens and adopt a youthful sensibility. This extension of adolescence forward into adulthood is less the result of transformations in human physiology than changes in lifestyles, social practices, and economic conditions, as many contemporary adult-age individuals, particularly those of the middle class, are postponing the traditional rituals of adulthood. For instance, many middle-class individuals over eighteen are extending their educations past high school, which in turn delays their entrances into the full-time work force and extends their semi-dependent financial status. This phenomenon has led to an increasing number of young adults who are unable to afford the material goods that traditionally signified middle-class adulthood, particularly cars and homes.[26] In turn, because premarital sex is no longer taboo for the majority of Americans, young adults do not need to rely on the institution of marriage to legitimize their sexual activity, often cohabiting with their partners and postponing marriage, the traditional rite of passage into adulthood.[27] Moreover, the increased accessibility of cheap and effective contraception has allowed many individuals to postpone having children, the ultimate signifier of adult status.

But adolescence is not being extended only by those individuals over eighteen who *postpone* the onset of adult life. Since the postwar era, a significant number of adults have *rejected* the primary rituals and signifiers of adulthood. Woefully underresearched, this phenomenon is largely the result of an ongoing battle in American society by individuals who find the roles, practices, and institutions of normative middle-class adulthood oppressive. Rather than chart the entire history of this struggle, I want to draw attention to several groups of young Americans who have expressed their alienation from traditional adult society and thus helped to legitimize a form of youthfulness for people over the age of eighteen.

Though rarely self-identified as "youth" due to their goal of achieving parity with adult male citizens, feminists have comprised the largest and oldest group of Americans who reject traditional forms of adulthood, primarily through critiques of the patriarchal structure of the family and society, and by refusing to be confined to the domestic roles of wife and mother and thus excluded from the public sphere. In addition, the Beats of the 1950s and early 1960s rejected the various institutions and practices of bourgeois adulthood by privileging a bohemian, nomadic lifestyle that challenged the hegemony of white, middle-class careerism, domesticity, and sexuality. Often disparaged and criticized by older contemporaries as immature and irresponsible, the Beats have influenced virtually every American youth culture that emerged after them, leaving a trail of youth-oriented adults in their wake. Finally, homosexual, bisexual, and other queer individuals have posed perhaps the greatest challenge to normative notions of adulthood through their subversions of the monogamous, reproductive form of intimacy traditionally associated with heterosexual maturity.

By calling attention to individuals over eighteen who consciously postpone and reject the traditional rituals and signifiers of adulthood, I do not mean to suggest that adults who *do* engage in these practices cannot and do not have a youthful sensibility, for many do, and often well past their young adult years. In fact, *all* adults in contemporary American society are encouraged to adopt a youthful attitude, particularly with regard to consumerism.

Yet, adult engagement with youth-oriented cultural texts—"reading down"—is not broadly condoned. Indeed, in contrast to the childhood practice of reading up, a behavior that is commonly understood as psychologically and socially positive, in that it demonstrates a child's desire to develop a mature identity, reading down is typically constructed as socially inappropriate. Given the common assumption that taste matures with age, many conservative individuals also assume that adults find pleasure only in complex, well-crafted, and intellectually rigorous cultural texts. Reading down, therefore, often is understood as indicative of a lack of maturity, sophistication, and perhaps even intelligence, and, when seen as happening on a wide scale, it has been constructed as a profound social problem in need of repair.[28]

Considering the negative connotations associated with reading down, we might go so far as to theorize this practice as signifying deviance, especially when the youthful texts enjoyed by adults contain images of boys or girls that can be understood as appealing to erotic desire. Though many adults, especially parents, consume media representations of youth, excessive pleasure in such images, particularly outside the company of children, is not only considered socially unacceptable, it is seen as perverse. I do not mean to suggest that all forms of reading down are pedophilic, nor that pedophiles are the only people to be treated as deviant for consuming youthful texts. (Indeed, many an eyebrow has been raised when I have mentioned my pleasure in *Buffy the Vampire Slayer*.) Rather, I want to emphasize that because of the precariousness of the boundary separating children from adults—a boundary that, as James Kincaid has demonstrated, is heavily eroticized—any cultural practice or form that challenges that boundary is perceived as dangerous.[29]

Despite the taboo of reading down, the contemporary advertising, manufacturing, and retail industries seem to ignore the negative connotations associated with this practice and have been encouraging it since the 1940s. The reasons behind their approach are clear: on the one hand, these commercial enterprises have little concern about how consumers use the products they make, market, and sell; they only care that consumers buy and keep on buying. On the other hand, and more specific to my argument here, marketers and merchandisers are well aware that adults, especially those without children, have far more disposable income, and thus far more buying power, than youth. What adults may not have, however, are the *spending habits* of youth, that is, the tendency to consume indiscriminately, with a carefree attitude, and, most importantly, often. In order to cultivate this form of youthful consumerism in older individuals, the advertising and merchandising industries rely on the same strategy they use to attract tweens: presenting teenagers as role models. While all adults are bombarded everyday with messages that encourage us to look, think, act, and, most importantly, *buy* young, the teen-as-role-model strategy would appear to work best in attracting those individuals who have either postponed or rejected traditional forms of adulthood and thus continue to have a youthful sensibility.

CREATING A YOUTHFUL AUDIENCE

The extension of adolescence backward into childhood and forward into adulthood has, in turn, affected what has been known as the "youth market," which today might be described more accurately as the "youth*ful* market." Recognizing the tremendous population and spending power of this multi-aged group of consumers, the new TV networks that have emerged since the introduction of cable—Fox, UPN, the WB, and now the CW—have attempted to appeal to this market in order to build their audience base. Constructing itself as the hippest network of all, the WB, perhaps more than any other contemporary network, appealed to this multi-aged audience and worked to develop its members' youthful attitude for advertisers.

Although the WB offered a variety of sitcoms oriented toward African Americans and families in its early years, its founders—Bob Bibb, Lew Goldstein, and Jamie Kellner—soon realized that the demographic niche most likely to accept their new network would be youth, particularly tweens, who tend to adopt new trends quickly and, unlike older teens, watch a considerable amount of TV. Moreover, after recognizing the buying power of this ever-growing market, the WB's founders were further enthused about developing tweens as a loyal audience who would age along with the network. As Kellner argued, "You have to get them into the habit of watching your network [when they are young] or you won't have them later on."[30] Nevertheless, the ultimate objective of the WB executives was not to create a "teen network," as so many journalists assume. Instead, they set as their long-term goal the creation of a multigenerational coalition of youthful viewers between the ages of twelve and thirty-four. In order to attract this audience, the WB executives wisely relied on a dual approach: first, appeal to the tween demographic, and second, hope that older teens and young adults follow. As Goldstein, the co-president of marketing for the WB, argued, "When you get the teens, it gives a show that plasma it needs. It buys time for the adults to find it, too."[31]

Since youth marketing research indicates that, in comparison to boys, girls shop more frequently, adopt consumer trends earlier, spend larger amounts of their parents' money, stay at home to a greater degree, and watch more television, the WB narrowed its audience focus even more in order to appeal to female tweens.[32] In an effort to attract these girls, the WB looked to strategies that had helped Fox develop into a major network in the early 1990s.[33] One of Fox's most successful series during its initial broadcasting period was *Beverly Hills, 90210*, which prominently featured female teenagers and privileged girls' friendships alongside heterosexual relationships. This approach contributed to the show's popularity among girls, and helped bring Fox a market share that legitimized it as the fourth American broadcast network. Following Fox's success with *Beverly Hills, 90210*, other TV networks became entranced with girls, and by 1995 almost all of the networks had series featuring female adolescents: NBC introduced *Blossom* in 1991 and *Someone Like Me* in 1994; and ABC debuted *Phenom* in 1993 and *My So-Called Life* and *Sister, Sister* in 1994. Cable networks were jumping on the teen-girl bandwagon in the early 1990s also: HBO introduced *The Baby-Sitters Club* in 1991, while Nickelodeon debuted *Clarissa Explains It All* that same year, subsequently adding *The Secret World of Alex Mack* in 1994 and *The Mystery Files of Shelby Woo* in 1995. Attesting to the popularity of such programming in the early 1990s, five of these series had a minimum of a three-season run, a record last set by a girl-centered series (*The Patty Duke Show*) in the 1960s.

In addition to noting the success of girl-oriented programming on other networks, the WB executives recognized the privileging of girls in a wide variety of other cultural products and practices during the early 1990s. For instance, in 1991 a group of female youth joined forces to create a community that eventually became known as Riot Grrrl. Angered by their devalued position within the male-dominated independent music scene and society at large, riot grrrls championed the power of female youth and created a variety of independently produced cultural artifacts, particularly zines and musical recordings, that disseminated their "Revolution Girl-Style Now" message beyond their community.

In what seems now like only a matter of minutes, advertisers quickly expropriated and depoliticized Riot Grrrl's "girl power" battle cry, exploiting it as an enticing marketing slogan for selling more merchandise to female youth.[34] As a result, the media industries cashed in on the "girl power" craze by producing a variety of products directed toward younger females. For example, the film industry increased its production of girl-centered movies in the early 1990s, releasing such films as *Buffy the Vampire Slayer* (1992), *Poison Ivy* (1992), *Just Another Girl on the I.R.T.* (1993), *Mi Vida Loca* (1994), and *Clueless* (1995). Oddly enough, despite the popularity of *Sassy* magazine, which had been introduced in 1988, the publishing industry was a bit slow in joining the "girl power" frenzy, expanding its traditional lineup of *Seventeen*, *YM*, and *Teen* only slightly in the early 1990s with the introduction of *Sisters in Style* and *All About You*. And despite its hype about "women in rock" in the early 1990s, the recording industry similarly failed to see the lucrative nature of the female tween market until the Spice Girls emerged as international pop sensations in 1996, inspiring a slew of girl-friendly teeny-bop performers, such as Britney Spears.

The WB executives' decision to focus on female tweens as one of its initial target audiences must be considered part of this unique cultural moment. Though Gail Berman, one of the executive producers of *Buffy the Vampire Slayer*, has indicated that the series was picked up in 1997 by the WB because of the perception that "there were no TV shows out there pitched to young girls,"[35] the new network began airing its first girl-oriented series, *Sister, Sister*, a sitcom about twin African American teens, in 1995. Over the next few years, the network expanded its focus on female youth, as well as its dramatic lineup, introducing *Buffy* and *Dawson's Creek* in 1997, *Felicity* and *Charmed* in 1998, *Popular* in 1999, and *Gilmore Girls* in 2000. Presented with depictions of independent, assertive young females, and bombarded with promotions for these shows and their stars in virtually all media forms, including websites promoting the WB and its programming, many female adolescents became huge fans of the network's girl-centered shows.[36] For example, during the May 1997 sweeps, *Buffy the Vampire Slayer*, then in its first season, garnered a 3.4 rating among girls twelve to seventeen, compared to a 2.0 for teenage boys and a 1.4 for adults eighteen to thirty-four.[37] Though eventually moving to UPN for its final two seasons, *Buffy the Vampire Slayer* served as a keystone in the WB's girl-oriented lineup for over four years, helping to draw not only young female viewers but also the advertising money associated with that demographic, which was needed to support the fledgling network's operational structure.

Despite the WB's success in drawing girls as viewers during its initial programming period, it is important to note that the female tween audience was not the market that the WB was ultimately striving to capture for advertisers. As Cheryl Idell, a vice president of research for Western International Media argues, "Few advertisers would buy shows just to reach teen girls."[38] Given the desire of advertisers to attract eighteen- to thirty-four-year-olds, who tend to have more disposable income than both youth and older adults with children, the WB increasingly appealed to this particular demographic through the same youthful programming and hip marketing strategies that worked to attract female tweens. As Bibb, one of the WB's co-presidents of marketing, noted, "That's something we are very proud of—we have not closed the door to women 18–34, for example. My wife, for instance, doesn't feel like she is watching a teen network."[39]

The WB's attention to older viewers initially paid off well. In fact, the WB was the only broadcast network to show an increase in young adult viewers from 1997 to 1998, and by the 1998–99 season, the median age of the WB's viewers had risen to 26.6, up 2.4 years from the previous season.[40] And, more pertinent to my analysis here, by November 2000, part way into its fifth season, the eighteen- to thirty-four-year-old audience for *Buffy the Vampire Slayer* had increased 37 percent from the previous season.[41] Such statistics indicate that the WB was able to create a much larger audience by attracting and holding onto its younger viewers while appealing to older viewers as well. As Bibb and Goldstein have noted, "We are the only network that has a bond with viewers between the ages of 13 and 34 on a daily basis."[42]

But *how* did the WB attract the viewers who make up this multigenerational audience? The network's attempt to garner consumers of different ages was perhaps most evident in the commercials that accompanied its teen shows. In addition to promoting commodities typically directed toward younger viewers, such as inexpensive clothing, drugstore cosmetics, amusement parks, and video games, the commercials accompanying the WB's teen-centered series also featured products traditionally marketed to the older, and more wealthy, adult demographic, such as beer, cars, computers, and wrinkle creams. Commercials for household products, such as dish soap, medicine, telephone service, and cable television, suggest a transgenerational marketing approach, appealing not only to adults, but also to youth who either influence family purchases or are themselves responsible for such shopping.

Yet commercials are not the primary means for attracting viewers to a network. Thus, it is important to ask also: What type of series did the network program to reach such a broad viewing population, and how did those shows nurture the youthful consumer attitude privileged by advertisers? In order to answer these questions, it is useful to look more closely at *Buffy the Vampire Slayer*, a prime-time television series popular with both younger and older viewers.

BUFFY THE VAMPIRE SLAYER

Like the movie upon which it is based, *Buffy the Vampire Slayer* is a tongue-in-cheek homage to both horror classics and teen-oriented media fare that confounds the traditional gender and generational dynamics of hero narratives by positioning a blonde girl at the center of its plot. When adapting the film as a teen show, Joss Whedon retained much of his original screenplay's doom-and-gloom feel, as well as the film's generic hybridity. Whedon also incorporated many of the conventions of teen TV shows, especially the privileging of classmates and teachers rather than family members, and schools and teen hangouts rather than the domestic sphere. As a result, many critics reviewing *Buffy*'s TV debut shortsightedly reported that the series focused primarily on issues of concern to teenagers in articles bearing such titles as "*Buffy* Slays Them: Teens Wild about TV Show That's Metaphor for Their Lives."[43]

Such a narrow reading of the series' primary themes and audience obscures the appeal of a text that opens itself to multiple interpretations and transgenerational identifications. In order to understand that appeal, it is necessary to examine not only the *Buffy* text, but also the reasons individuals of different ages watch the show. Thus, in addition to analyzing the series' narrative and aesthetic strategies, I conducted an informal survey of *Buffy* fans in order to ascertain their interests and pleasures in the series.[44]

Given that *Buffy* centers on a girl and her similarly youthful friends as they move through their adolescent and young-adult years, it is not surprising that many tweens and teenagers would be drawn to this series. For example, one young fan noted that she identifies most with Buffy's character because "it seems all the things that she's gone through at the time i [*sic*] had too or I ended up going through."[45] Indeed, those segments of the show's early episodes that do not focus on Buffy's slaying duties demonstrate their narrative similarity to other teen-centered dramatic series, such as *Beverly Hills, 90210*, in which real-life teen experiences, such as schoolwork, dating, the prom, and graduation, are represented.

Yet, at the same time that *Buffy*'s realistic depiction of everyday teen activities may elicit teenagers' identification with experiences similar to their own, the series also provides a space for younger viewers' fantasies by appealing to their aspirational desires to be high schoolers and young adults. While fantasy is an aspect of TV reception overlooked by most journalists and scholars writing about young television viewers, Ien Ang argues that more attention must be paid to this form of identification, as it helps to explain viewers' pleasures in texts that do not reflect their experiences: "The pleasure of fantasy lies in its offering the subject an opportunity to take up positions which she could not do in real life: through fantasy she can move beyond the structural constraints of everyday life and explore other situations, other identities, other lives. It is totally unimportant . . . whether these are realistic or not."[46]

In addition to the larger slay-or-be-slayed horror narrative that grounds each episode's plot, the strategies used in *Buffy* to encourage younger viewers' fantasy identifications include casting beautiful actors and actresses, outfitting characters in trendy outfits, locating them in upper-middle-class locales, and, perhaps most importantly, depicting young people's social and cultural dominance of a community. In turn, many girls seem particularly drawn to Buffy's portrayal as a superhero. For example, when asked who her favorite character on *Buffy* is, one young female fan stated, "i've [*sic*] always liked buffy [*sic*] best—she's the hero."[47] Such comments suggest that girls find pleasure in Buffy's persona because it is a radical move away from not only the stereotypical teen-girl characters on TV, but also the reality of their own lives.

Although it is somewhat easy to understand why so many younger viewers are drawn to *Buffy*, the reasons its adult audience grew are less obvious; yet the series' narrative strategies provide a clue. Like those younger viewers who respond to *Buffy* as fantasy, many adults are drawn in by this narrative device as well and similarly use the show's representations of the supernatural to gain momentary escape from the banality of their everyday lives and the frailty of their own bodies. This reception practice is perhaps most noticeable in adult viewers' discussions of Buffy's role as an action hero. For example, a female fan in her late twenties reports: "I like the fantastic aspects of the show . . . like no girl can ever get in that big a fight without a single scrape!"[48] Yet, adult viewers' pleasures in *Buffy*'s fantastic characterizations and narratives are not determined solely by sex, as an older male fan demonstrates: "I'm a sucker for shows about women with superpowers. . . . I grew up loving shows like *The Bionic Woman*, *Wonder Woman*, and *Charlie's Angels*; and *Buffy* seems in many ways to be coming out of that tradition, except it's funnier and the writing is better."[49] Adult viewers' enjoyment of *Buffy*'s fantastic elements demonstrate that older individuals are not drawn to TV series featuring teenage characters simply because such programs inspire nostalgia for their own lost youth.

Fantasy is not the only narrative approach used in the series, however, as realism is often deployed as a means for establishing viewer identification. While there is little doubt that *Buffy* can be read as a text about youth, for those viewers with more life experience and cultural capital it can also be read as a program that deals with real-life issues that are virtually universal.[50] *Buffy*'s major narrative themes—friendship, community, morality, power, and conflicting roles and responsibilities—are not just teen concerns; they are concerns for us all. The operative metaphor of *Buffy*, therefore, is not "school is hell," as many early reviews of the series suggest, but rather "*life* is hell."[51]

In addition to *Buffy*'s narrative themes, the show's characterizations have been carefully constructed to appeal to adults, particularly those who have delayed or rejected traditional adulthood. For example, in contrast to competing series in the early prime-time programming schedule, which continue to be produced for families with young children, *Buffy* features very few adults, and the show tends to downplay parental figures and consanguine relationships. Indeed, Giles is the only regular character over twenty-one, and Buffy's divorced mother, Joyce, is the only parent who has a recurring role in the series. And though the series is populated with centuries-old vampires, these immortal figures function metaphorically for the youthful sensibility the WB cultivated in its viewers. In turn, Buffy is estranged from her father, and her sister, Dawn, did not appear until the series' fifth season. Perhaps most pleasurable for nontraditional adult viewers, *Buffy* focuses primarily on a group of similarly aged characters who are brought together through their shared knowledge of two secrets: Sunnydale's location on the Hellmouth, and Buffy's role in eliminating evil. This knowledge separates the characters from others in their community, thus necessitating their further reliance on and support of one another outside the conventional roles and practices associated with the family.

Moreover, contrasting dramatically with the cheery, wholesome depictions of family life on other early prime-time series, *Buffy* unabashedly explores identities and lifestyles rarely privileged, and often prohibited, by conservative adults. For example, alternative cultural practices and belief systems, such as magic and the occult, are presented in every episode. In addition, sexual innuendos are rife in the series, and non-normative sexual practices, such as sadomasochism and homosexuality, are regularly suggested, if not explicitly depicted. Several queer fans indicate that their interest in *Buffy* was aroused further by the positive portrayal of Willow's relationship with Tara. For instance, a lesbian fan who identifies strongly with Willow states, "This lesbian undertone has just hooked me in even more."[52]

Despite *Buffy*'s specific appeals to youth and nontraditional adults, as a program more about growing than growing up, *Buffy*'s serial format and focus on youthful characters allow for a metaphorical exploration of identity as unfixed and mutable, and thus it resonates with many contemporary viewers of different ages by allowing for cross-generational identifications. Moreover, the majority of the show's main characters do not have a singular, stable subjectivity, but rather several identities, including otherworldly roles that are not confined to a particular age group. For example, Buffy and Willow are not just students; they are also, respectively, a slayer and a witch. These multiple identities allow for more complex plot developments as well as more options for viewer identification and fantasy. As one fan notes, "I identify with virtually all of the characters on some level,"[53] while another, when asked about his primary pleasure in the series, responded succinctly with "the characters (don't ask me to name faves, cause [*sic*] there's a list)."[54]

Extending this theme of multiple, fluid identities, *Buffy* regularly features characters whose bodies or personalities are significantly transformed. While such morphings are de rigueur for the show's many vampires who alternate between human and monstrous form, each of *Buffy*'s main characters has been

Fig. 1. Xander is transformed into a soldier, "Halloween," 27 October 1997.

radically altered at some point in the series, offering them a different identity and perspective on the world around them, and thus affording viewers an opportunity for further identifications based on fantasy. For example, the physically weak Xander became a virile soldier in "Halloween" (season 2); Willow's vampish lesbian alter-ego appeared in "Doppelgängland" (season 3); and Giles reverted to his bad-boy teenage persona in "Band Candy" (season 3) (see figs. 1, 2, and 3).

While the characters' multiple, shifting identities appeal to many younger viewers who aspire to be grown up and often feel unanchored in the midst of conflicting desires and experiences, such representations also connect well with older individuals who recognize that part of adult life is taking on multiple roles and responsibilities. Indeed, Buffy's constant problem of balancing her personal desires and professional responsibilities, as well as her dual roles as lone hero and community organizer, resonates with many adult female viewers, particularly mothers who work outside the home. For example, one female viewer in her early forties notes: "Like Buffy, I have a million things going on in my life (none of which are life-and-death matters, fortunately!), and a bunch of different people I need to be responsive to. I empathize with her constant struggle to keep it all in balance and remain in control."[55] De-

Fig. 2. Willow becomes an evil vampire, "Doppelgängland," 23 February 1999.

Fig. 3. Giles is a bad-boy teen, "Band Candy," 10 November 1998.

spite women's identifications with Buffy in this regard, it is important to note that viewers' connections with the multi-tasked, multi-roled Buffy often blur the boundaries of sex and sexuality, as well as age. For instance, an adult gay male fan indicates that he identifies most strongly with the young heterosexual Buffy because she is a "young person burdened with responsibility beyond her years."[56]

In addition to employing narrative strategies that allow for transgenerational identifications, *Buffy*'s creators have included aesthetic elements that make the show's mise-en-scène resonate with viewers of different ages and sexes who share the youthful sensibility traditionally attributed to male adolescents. For example, each episode regularly features lengthy fight scenes that depict Buffy and other characters using a combination of karate, kung fu, jujitsu, and kickboxing. Historically dominated in the United States by adult males, the martial arts currently attract individuals from both sexes and all ages, largely due to the popularity of martial arts films from Hong Kong among American audiences. In turn, the American media industries have played a prominent role in increasing broader involvement in this type of sport over the last decade, as noted by a female student of kung fu who was inspired by women martial artists in movies and television series, such as *Buffy*: "There's a cool factor to it now, to be a woman and be strong and be able to be a crimefighter, even though I'm a quantitative analyst by day."[57]

Another production element that strongly informs *Buffy*'s youthful aesthetic is rock music. Unlike the film from which it was adapted, the TV series regularly deploys rock songs to ground its soundscape and set the mood of particular scenes. This technique is perhaps most noticeable in *Buffy*'s theme song, a hard-driving, high-energy, non-lyrical romp. In addition, when socializing in their favorite non-school hangout, the Bronze nightclub, Buffy and her friends enjoy the live music of rock performers, who help to reinforce the show's overall aesthetic as hip, cool, and youthful (not to mention "white").

Yet, like the martial artists represented on *Buffy*, the musicians appearing in the series are not only, or even predominantly, male, as rock convention would have it. In fact, the show regularly features female-powered bands, such as Cibo Matto, which works well to highlight *Buffy*'s subversion of the traditionally male horror and action genres, while also speaking to a cultural moment when female rock musicians have been gaining more control in an industry

Fig. 4. Spike's contemporary rock chic.

historically dominated by men. In turn, just as the number of young female fans of the martial arts, slasher films, and comic books has increased in the last two decades, altering the traditional gender dynamics of youth culture, so too has the number of girls who consume rock. Yet, like these other pop culture forms, rock music is no longer enjoyed primarily by teenagers. Rather, as the baby boomer fans of over-fifty musicians such as Bonnie Raitt and Mick Jagger attest, rock is now the soundtrack of several generations, the members of which are often well past their teens.

In addition to using rock music to increase *Buffy*'s appeal among viewers of different ages, the show's producers use rock fashion to imbue the mise-en-scène with an alternative form of youthfulness rarely seen outside MTV by television viewers. For example, several of *Buffy*'s evil characters, particularly Spike and Faith, are outfitted in contemporary rock chic, an androgynous style that merges several different periods of rock fashion, particularly punk and goth, and includes tattoos, dark makeup, workboots, black and leather clothing, and excessively bleached or darkly dyed hair (see fig. 4). Those who attire themselves in rock fashion are typically assumed to be teenagers; however, many nontraditional adults display an adherence to rock style and thus may identify closely with *Buffy*'s similarly adorned characters. At the same time, other viewers may use the show's rock aesthetic as fantasy, trying on identities that they feel are either too youthful or too deviant to explore in their everyday lives.

CONCLUSION

By featuring teen-centered series such as *Buffy the Vampire Slayer* that combine aesthetic elements typically associated with youth culture and narrative themes that speak to specific age groups but also allow for cross-generational identification, the WB successfully appealed to and further developed its viewers' youthful sensibility. As the journalist James Collins noted, "There are adolescents, and then there are the adolescent-at-heart, a demographic group whose members the WB . . . serves brilliantly."[58] The network's cultivation of this broad coalition of youthful viewers made it extremely attractive to marketers who were trying to reach such consumers through the television medium. Indeed, the upfront advertising dollars spent on the WB increased phenomenally over the network's short history, rising from $170 million for the 1996–97 season to $450 million for the 1999–2000 season, a 137 percent increase in only four years.[59] While the WB's ratings did not fare as well in comparison, the network's strong appeal among viewers and advertisers alike is evidence that it became a legitimate contender among contemporary television networks, at least for a time.

As I have demonstrated through textual analysis, ratings statistics, viewer feedback, and comments from the WB's top executives, the success of this young network, contrary to popular belief, was not due solely, or even primarily, to its ability to attract the burgeoning teenage demographic. Rather, in light of teens' limited TV use, tweens' aspirational consumerism, the eighteen to thirty-four market's attractiveness to advertisers, and the transgenerational nature of youthful identity, the WB effectively used its programming to construct a large and lucrative audience base composed of differently aged, yet similarly identified, viewers. An effect of both the extension of adolescence and the fragmentation of the television audience in the latter half of the twentieth century, the WB's multigenerational coalition of viewers demonstrated that it does not take families to create a mass audience.[60]

1. For example, Lisa Reilly Cullen, "Ride the Echo Boom to Stock Profits," *Money*, July 1997, 98–104; and Greg Johnson, "When Teens Talk, Companies Listen," *Los Angeles Times*, 30 May 1999, C1 and C14.

2. See Michiko Kakutani, "Adolescence Rules!" *New York Times Magazine*, 11 May 1997, 22; and Robin Rauzi, "The Teen Factor: Today's Media-Savvy Youth Influence What Others Are Seeing and Hearing," *Los Angeles Times*, 9 June 1998, F1.

3. Gary Levin, "Smells Like Teen Demos," *Variety*, 6 October 1997, 35+; John Consoli, "Fountains of Youth," *Mediaweek*, 24 May 1999, 1B; and Leonard Klady and Dan Cox, "Media Taps into Zit-Geist," *Variety*, 22–28 February 1999, 1.

4. I use "teen show" to refer to TV series that feature teenage characters as protagonists, not those watched by teens, a second definition of the term often conflated with the first. This chapter also draws attention to programs that construct viewers as teenagers, a third meaning for "teen show" that is rarely addressed.

5. James Poniewozik, "Their Major Is Alienation: Meet the Class of 1999," *Time*, 20 September 1999, 77.

6. Michael Schneider and Susanne Ault, "Teeny-Bop Crop Goes Plop," *Variety*, 17 April 2000, 41.

7. See Becky Ebenkamp, "Special Report: Upfront Markets; Tipping the Balance," *AdWeek East*, 10 May 1999, S4; and "Media Use Is a Full-Time Job for Kids," *Youth Markets Alert*, February 2000, 1+.

8. Quoted in Schneider and Ault, "Teeny-Bop Crop Goes Plop," 41.

9. Quoted in John Consoli, "The Teens Are Alright," *Mediaweek*, 27 November 2000, 6.

10. Quoted in Ebenkamp, "Special Report," S4.

11. For example, see Susan Murray's chapter in this volume. One of the few scholars to note the media industries' construction, rather than simply reflection, of a youthful sensibility is Luckett, who argues that the teen lifestyle was marketed to all consumer demographics in the 1960s, not just to teenagers. Nevertheless, she leaves unquestioned the common assumption that teenage girls comprised the target market, as well as audience, for 1960s TV series featuring female adolescents. See Luckett, "Girl Watchers."

12. Ariès, *Centuries of Childhood*; and Kett, *Rites of Passage*.

13. As my interests here are related specifically to the WB's strategies for building a coalition audience, my analysis of *Buffy the Vampire Slayer* does not include the series' last two seasons on UPN, nor the latter network's programming practices.

14. Caldwell, *Televisuality*, 9.

15. Ibid., 296.

16. Collins, "Postmodernism and Television," 342.

17. Frith, "Youth/Music/Television," 75. Like my own, Frith's analysis of the TV industry's construction of youthful adult viewers differs from the analyses of Joshua Meyrowitz and Neil Postman, who argue that television does not require the advanced conceptual skills associated with print media and thus disrupts the age-based hierarchy of traditional informational flows, producing "child-like" adults and "adult-like" children and contributing to the disappearance of childhood and adulthood as distinct life stages. In addition to their problematic assumptions about television's "primitivism" and TV viewers' uncritical reception, neither Postman nor Meyrowitz considers adolescence in his analysis of shifting life-

stage identities. See Postman's *The Disappearance of Childhood*; and Meyrowitz's *No Sense of Place*.

18. Zollo, *Wise Up to Teens*, 13, 88–89.
19. A "tween" is someone who is nearly, or has just become, a teenager. First used in the 1950s, the term experienced a revival in the 1990s. See the *Oxford English Dictionary On-Line*, http://www.dictionary.oed.com.
20. See Debra Phillips Ebenkamp, "Tween Beat," *Entrepreneur*, September 1999, 126.
21. "Teen Spending Increased in 1999," *Youth Markets Alert*, February 2000, 8.
22. Zollo, *Wise Up to Teens*, 184–85.
23. Quoted in Phillips, "Tween Beat," 126.
24. Zollo, *Wise Up to Teens*, 15.
25. Quoted in Peirce, "*YM*," 486.
26. The U.S. Census Bureau reported in 1997 that two-thirds of adults who are twenty-five to thirty-four cannot afford a median-priced home in their area. See D. James Romero, "Adulthood? Later, Dude!" *Los Angeles Times*, 21 March 1997, E8.
27. The U.S. Census Bureau reported in 2001 a 71 percent increase in unmarried partners between 1990 and 2000, with such partnerships making up 5 percent of all American households. This data is available online at http://www.census.gov.
28. For example, see Postman, *The Disappearance of Childhood*.
29. Kincaid, *Child-Loving*, 6–7.
30. Quoted in Consoli, "The Teens Are Alright," 6.
31. Quoted in T. L. Stanley, "Net Gains," *Mediaweek*, 11 October 1999, 72.
32. Zollo, *Wise Up to Teens*, 8–9 and 94.
33. The similarities between the early programming strategies of the WB and Fox are not surprising given that Bibb, Goldstein, and Kellner founded the Fox network in 1986.
34. See Nina Munk, "Girl Power!" *Fortune*, 8 December 1997, 132–40.
35. Quoted in John Dempsey, "Femme Leads Earn Piece of the Action," *Variety*, 14 July 1997, 28.
36. For example, the WB created a website specifically devoted to *Buffy the Vampire Slayer* (http://www.buffy.com). This website was no longer operating at the time of publication.
37. Dempsey, "Femme Leads Earn Piece of the Action," 28.
38. Quoted in Consoli, "Fountains of Youth," 27.
39. Quoted in "Event-Like Promos Build Loyal Young Core for WB," *Advertising Age*, 1 February 1999, S1.
40. Stanley, "Net Gains," 72; and "MediaOne Looks to 'Star Power' for Upgrades," *Multichannel News*, 22 February 1999, 34.
41. Joe Schlosser, "Weblets Now Neck and Neck," *Broadcasting and Cable*, 6 November 2000, 24.
42. Quoted in "Are You Watching the WB? Your Customers Are!" *Brandweek*, 21 June 1999, 4. Nickelodeon, a cable network, appeals to a youthful, intergenerational market also. See Murray, "'TV Satisfaction Guaranteed!'"; and Hendershot, "Nickelodeon's Nautical Nonsense."
43. Phil Kloer, "Buffy Slays Them: Teens Wild about TV Show That's Metaphor for Their Lives," *Atlanta Journal and Constitution*, 28 April 1998, C1. See also Dempsey, "Femme Leads Earn Piece of the Action"; and Jeff Jarvis, *Buffy the Vampire Slayer* TV series review, *TV Guide*, 25 April 1997, 12.

44. I conducted an informal survey of *Buffy* fans during the summer of 2000 by posting notices on The Bronze threading board, which was part of the WB's *Buffy* website. In addition, I surveyed members of the Buffy Adult Discussion listserve (bad@listserv.unc.edu), as well as other *Buffy* fans with whom I am acquainted.

45. BTSR, email correspondence with the author, 21 August 2000. The identities of respondents to my *Buffy* fan survey are protected by these non-identifying labels.

46. Ang, "Melodramatic Identifications," 162.

47. BASF, email correspondence with the author, 19 August 2000.

48. BASA, email correspondence with the author, 19 August 2000.

49. BASB, email correspondence with the author, 5 September 2000.

50. A Freudian analysis of adult viewers' pleasures in *Buffy* might argue that the series restages the unresolved traumas of such viewers' own childhood experiences.

51. See T. L. Stanley, "*Buffy* to Slay Small Screen," *Mediaweek*, 17 February 1997, 9–10; and Hannah Tucker, "High School Confidential," *Entertainment Weekly*, 1 October 1999, 23.

52. BASA, email correspondence with the author, 19 August 2000.

53. BASY, email correspondence with the author, 1 September 2000.

54. BTSP, email correspondence with the author, 19 August 2000.

55. BASH, email correspondence with the author, 23 August 2000.

56. BASB, email correspondence with the author, 5 September 2000.

57. Quoted in Lorraine Ali, "Coming to a Gym Near You," *Newsweek*, 11 December 2000, 76.

58. James Collins, "The Youth Brigade," *Time*, 26 October 1998, 90.

59. Stanley, "Net Gains," 72; and Mark Berman, "Teen Angles," *Mediaweek*, 31 May 1999, 24.

60. I am extremely grateful to the fans who shared with me their interests, pleasures, and, in some cases, disappointments in *Buffy the Vampire Slayer*. Their comments help to remind me of how much astute cultural criticism happens outside the academy. I also thank this collection's editors and anonymous readers, who provided valuable feedback for the revision of this chapter.

2

Susan Murray

I KNOW WHAT YOU DID LAST SUMMER:

SARAH MICHELLE GELLAR AND CROSSOVER TEEN STARDOM

Besides youth, does a thoughtful and powerful teenage vampire slayer have anything in common with a manipulative New York debutante, a chatty sorority girl, a frightened high school beauty queen, or a ditsy cartoon character come to life? She does when all of these roles are played by Sarah Michelle Gellar. While these five female characters have been constructed by a number of different writers, exist in various narrative and temporal worlds, and reside in both film and television, they collectively construct Gellar's teen star persona. Yet the connection between Gellar, the actress, and Buffy, the character, is perhaps the strongest conflation of her off-screen and on-screen identities, since the unrelenting narrative presence of weekly television and the voraciousness of the program's fans constantly re-assert it. As Gellar's persona travels from the broadcast television text of *Buffy* (the initial site of her stardom) to other media forms and texts, she carries with her traces of the Buffy character, while project-ing and collecting other on-screen motives, desires, and personality traits. For example, one cannot help but think of Gellar's network affiliation and various roles when she asks her on-screen boyfriend Ryan Phillippe (who also played her sexually interested stepbrother in *Cruel Intentions* [1999]) to take her down to "Dawson's Beach" in Kevin Williamson's *I Know What You Did Last Summer* (1997).

Gellar, however, is not unique in her ability to maintain such an intertexual persona while acting in both film and television, since the media's obsession with the "new" teen audience has stimulated an overall alteration of teen and young adult stardom. In 1986, Thomas Doherty wrote:

[Teens in the 1950s] were impossible to ignore: a statistical anomaly in population distribution had converged with unparalleled economic prosperity to produce the nation's first generation of true teenagers. They were distinct from previous generations of American young people in numbers, affluence and self-consciousness: there were more of them, they had more money, and they were more aware of their unique status.[1]

Although describing the baby-boomer teens of the mid- to late 1950s, Doherty's observations apply equally well to the teens of today. The most recent generation of teenagers—commonly labeled "echo boomers" in reference to their relation and resemblance to postwar boomer teens—have become the entertainment industry's most highly sought after consumer demographic and have thereby altered the state of the millennial media landscape. During the explosion of teen-targeted media in the late 1990s, many teen stars developed successful careers in both film and television. Consequently, many producers have used the crossover appeal of stars such as Gellar, Jennifer Love Hewitt, Seth Green, Brandy, Katie Holmes, James Van Der Beek, and Michelle Williams to their advantage, highlighting and exploiting their stardom in one medium to attract the new teen audience to the star's appearance in another. This cross-pollination has led the teen audience to expect their stars to be highly intertextual and highly flexible in their embodiment of heterogeneous character traits.

This chapter analyzes the marketing strategies and spectator positionings surrounding the late 1990s phenomenon of teen-targeted stardom in the context of post-network television and the New Hollywood by concentrating on Sarah Michelle Gellar and other teen stars. As distinctions between traditional networks and cable stations blur, as film studios become increasingly involved in television production, and as the Internet develops into a central media marketing tool, stars often act as the primary point of identification for viewers. In many cases, they also are the most visible ligature that ties together multimedia marketing and merchandising campaigns. Some of the marketing strategies employed to cultivate these synergistic relationships have been used previously in media products targeted to adults, yet at the end of the twentieth century and the beginning of the twenty-first, stars in their teens and early twenties have become uniquely adept at traversing the aesthetic and industrial conditions of different media while retaining their large and lucrative fan bases. This is due, in part, to the entertainment industry's recent focus on the intensely media-literate female teen audience, but it is also related to shifts in the development of stardom.

TARGETING THE TEEN MARKET

Since the "discovery" of teenagers and their buying power in the 1950s, the media's interest in the demographic has swelled periodically. These moments have resulted in distinct eras of teen stardom, such as the 1970s stardom of Leif Garrett and Shaun and David Cassidy, or the 1980s fame of the Brat Pack and the MTV pop star. But the 1990s manifestation of teen stardom reached epic proportions only during the latter half of the decade, when media conglomerates recognized that there were 31 million teens in the United States who had an estimated $140 billion dollars a year of spending money at their disposal.[2] Throngs of twelve- to seventeen-year-olds were attending films such as *Clueless* (1995), *Romeo and Juliet* (1996), and *Scream* (1996), tuning into television series such as *Buffy* and *Dawson's Creek*, and listening to pop music acts such as the Backstreet Boys. By 1999, the entertainment industry was so obsessed with twelve- to seventeen-year-olds that it began referring to them as, simply, "the demographic."

Teen girls have become the most prized segment of the demographic. Certainly, the media industries are also interested in attracting teen boys. But industry wisdom claims that teen girls are responsible for getting the boys into theaters in the first place, by bringing them as their companions.[3] As for television, industry logic assumes that boys are less interested in hour-long dramas such as *Buffy* and *Dawson's Creek* and are more likely to tune into the masculine soap opera of professional wrestling.[4] In addition, girls have proven themselves to be highly involved and dedicated consumers and viewers. When the blockbuster film *Titanic* was released in 1997 teenage girls represented a major portion of the film's repeat viewings, with some of them seeing the film four or five times and thereby "generating an estimated 30 to 40 percent of [its] $580 million U.S. gross."[5] In fact, a year after *Titanic*'s release, *The Guardian* reported that half of all women under the age of twenty-five had already seen *Titanic* twice.[6] A key draw for such films has been the teen star. As Melanie Nash and Martti Lahti posit, "The single most important aspect of the enormous appeal of [*Titanic*] to its primary audience, young girls, [was] the star presence of Leonardo DiCaprio."[7]

A late 1999 *New York Times Magazine* cover story on Hollywood's teen actors described the new teen demographic in terms similar to those Doherty used to describe the 1950s teen market: "The teen-age children of the baby-boom generation happen to form the largest audience of teenagers in history. Hollywood, of course, has always cared about the young, but it is the numbers that have made teenagers a late-'90s obsession."[8] A newer development has been the industry's focus specifically on girls: "There is a huge viewership, spearheaded by teenage girls, who will pretty much see or watch anything as long as the actors and actresses look like teenagers too."[9] Certainly, young women have always been a staple audience for the media industries, since they have tended to be one of the more active groups in terms of their engagement with extratextual materials, ancillary products, and the fashions and beauty aids that have been Hollywood byproducts since the silent era.[10] Yet, the advent of websites and chat boards have taught those in the industry something new about the ways and priorities of the fan culture of girls, in particular, girls' interest in stars who are like them.

Perhaps the foremost example of the online presence of girls' fan culture is the one that surrounded ABC's teen program, *My So-Called Life*. In 1994–95 when news of the possible cancellation of *MSCL* led fans to initiate a highly visible campaign to save the program, many girls wrote in their online posts that the character of Angela (played by Claire Danes) was the first television teen character with whom they could identify. They claimed that unlike the characters and stars they saw on shows such as *Beverly Hills 90210*, Angela was a genuine representation of their current state as female adolescents.[11] They found particularly significant the fact that Danes was actually a young teen herself. Although ABC did not choose to renew the show, the fans' desire for teen actors and actresses was sated by many of the teen-targeted programs that followed. I argue that the girls' attraction to teen and young adult stars in the case of *MSCL*, as well as that of *Buffy*, can be best understood as a complex process of negotiated identification, following Jackie Stacey's theories of female spectatorship.[12] According to Stacey, a fan may recognize parts of herself in a star, but also consider the star as an idealized other. Stacey asserts that the acknowledgment of this difference and sameness is what keeps a spectator engaged with a particular same-sex star. I would add that, for many teens, age, along with gender, can be an integral point of recognition. This was certainly the case for the majority of *MSCL*'s fans. They felt that they could give more credence to *MSCL*'s representation of the female adolescent experience because they knew (through extratextual materials) that Danes was the same age as her character, Angela. Teen actors and actresses provide teen media with an air of authenticity and a hook for audience identification.

The fact that a performer's age can affect his or her reception is only one lesson that the entertainment industry has learned from online teen culture. In the years following the *MSCL* campaign, the online practices of teen fans have been carefully tracked and cultivated by many network-owned websites. For instance, upon entering the *Dawson's Creek* official site, a visitor could acquire not only background information, pictures, and clips of members of the cast, but could also keep a viewing diary to be filled out at the end of each episode (which she could choose to keep private or make public). The site suggested that, in the diary, the viewer recall which characters she most identified with during this particular installment and what she liked and disliked about the various plotlines. This diary not only encouraged the viewer to be highly aware of her own position as an active spectator, but also provided the show's producers with invaluable information about what types of storylines, stars, characters, and settings are important to the demographic. The diaries that were made public on the site in February 2000 were all written by individuals who identified themselves as adolescent girls. Not surprisingly, most of the diary entries focused on the direction of the romantic relationship between the two main characters, Joey and Dawson, providing the network and producers with valuable information about the audience's desires.

It is difficult to judge just how much fan opinion influences program plot and product development. However, it is clear that these sites have proven productive for networks, since they have invested heavily in their creation and upkeep. The WB's home page for *Buffy* was a painstakingly detailed interactive site that replicated the show's mise-en-scène and emotional tone. Besides housing all the requisite links to chat rooms, boards, and star photos, the site included an innovative component—an online interactive game based on the show's narrative. This free ancillary product allowed fans to enter virtually into the text, taking verisimilitude and identification to another level. It also encouraged the core audience's consistent involvement with the website and the program narrative. Of course, a viewer's return to the website is another opportunity for the network to hawk mugs, t-shirts, posters, and CDs.

Producers of teen television programs have helped extend the narrative of their programs and stars into more traditional ancillary products. Some of them have entered into lucrative deals with clothing manufacturers; the labels become their "official clothing providers." For example, *Dawson's Creek* entered into a deal with American Eagle Outfitters, which provided the show with the characters' wardrobes. In exchange, the programs' stars, such as James Van Der Beek and Katie Holmes, appeared in their catalogs and website. This particular form of product placement centers on the girls, since according to reports such as one done by the Ban Youth Poll, a New York company that specializes in teenage marketing and research, "teenage girls spent $15.1 billion on clothing in 1992, at a per-person average of $1,200."[13] Although the producers of *Buffy* did not enter into a deal with a specific company, the WB sold (at its studio stores and website) tank tops, baby-Ts, necklaces, and backpacks bearing the show's logo, along with stationery, school folders, watches, and "locker posters" that displayed images of Gellar as Buffy. (UPN benefited from later additions to the *Buffy* line, including action figures and comic books.) Gellar herself became the new face of Maybelline cosmetics in an effort by the cosmetics company to draw the female teen market to its products (see figs. 1a and b). The fans' apparent obsession with teenage stars has also influenced the print media, as many publishers that have witnessed the popularity of teen films, television, and Internet activities have begun to produce magazines to appeal to the girls' insatiable desire for images of and information on their favorite stars.

MEDIA CONGLOMERATION, INTERTEXTUALITY, AND STAR LINKING

Born between the mid-1980s and the early 1990s, the current generation of teenagers grew up interacting with cable television, computers, video games, VCRs, and DVD players in an environment of increasing media conglomera-

Figs. 1a and b. Sarah Michelle Gellar's Maybelline print ads.

tion. As a consumer group, their sensibilities were stimulated and nourished by the synergistic imperatives of media and toy companies. The boys played with Teenage Mutant Ninja Turtle action figures while watching the accompanying Saturday morning television show; the girls went to see *The Little Mermaid* (1989) and begged for the McDonald's Happy Meal that contained its ancillary toys. In other words, this generation was trained by what Marsha Kinder has labeled the "supersystem," a multimedia-based blockbuster economy centered on pop culture figures that generates intertextual references and product convergence.[14]

In children's media of the 1980s, the figures that tied together multimedia promotional campaigns were most often fictional cartoon personae, such as the Ninja Turtles, who necessarily never stepped out of the narrative world and characteristics created for them. Yet, the commercial ties inherent to the characters' very existences prepared today's teens to become savvy readers and consumers of intertextual star texts. In her research on children's media, Kinder found that transmedia intertextuality participates in positioning young spectators to "recognize, distinguish, and combine different popular genres and their respective iconography that cut across movies, television, comic books, commercials, video games and toys."[15] In addition, the generation reared on transmedia intertextuality is less likely to privilege one medium over another. It is this childhood training that makes this generation of teens such a receptive audience for particular types of products and stars resulting from media oligopolies. In an interview for PBS's *Frontline* documentary "Merchants of Cool," the media scholar Robert McChesney uses a strong, but perhaps apt, simile to describe how integral teens are to the project of conglomeration: "[The entertainment companies] look at the teen market as part of this massive empire that they're colonizing. You should look at it like the British empire or the French empire in the 19th century. Teens are like Africa. You know, there's this range that they're going to take over, and their weaponry are films, music, books, CDs, Internet access, clothing, amusement parks, sports teams."[16] The confluence of media conglomeration and the development of the Internet has spawned an intricately linked decentralization of media production and practice. Recent corporate mergers, further deregulation, and a focus on technological convergence have made this situation all the more palpable.

While many spectators may not be aware of the industrial alliances that exist behind any one production, their interaction with extratextual materials may lead them through a maze of information, products, and services arising out of such alliances. For teenage female fans specifically, the search for extratextual material usually centers on a particular star or collection of stars from a favored media text. Thus, if a girl is an active fan of *Buffy* with access to a computer, she will likely interact with official and fan websites and boards that center on Gellar. This will lead her to find information not only on the television program *Buffy*, but also on Gellar's films, such as *I Know What You Did Last Summer* and *Scooby Doo* (2002). It can also work conversely, with web users interested in a teen-targeted film being directed to television series featuring the films' stars.

America Online's teen chat boards and events were popular online gathering spots for youth interested in teen stars when *Buffy* was on the air. These spaces were not organized according to program or film titles, but were grouped according to stars' names. As a result, the spaces were often used to talk about the stars' various roles, to debate their authentic identities (such as whether or not Gellar "is really Jewish"), and to analyze what their most recent projects say about the direction of their careers and their appeal to audiences. In these spaces, the stars' film and television characters intermingle.

Participants in these online gathering spots study these multiple personae as evidence of the stars' true, off-screen identities. For example, Katy, a pre-teen, wrote the following to Gellar on an AOL board:

> I have never missed a [*Buffy*] episode. I cried for two days when you died in the season finale! I love you more than anything [*sic*] even my boyfriend . . . You and Angel made an OK TV couple but you and Freddy are perfect! I saw *Cruel Intentions*. I never would have thought a spunky character could go so bad. In *Scream 2* and *I Know What You Did Last Summer* I cried when you died. I've seen a couple old shows of *All My Children* and you are so good! Umm . . . Oh yeah and I have millions of books about you and stuff! I love you![17]

Many of these posts, such as Katy's, say nothing about the fans' preference for seeing stars, such as Gellar, on film versus television, and instead focus on the star as a text unto itself; a text that moves across media, acquiring deeper and often contradictory facets as it extends itself through numerous characterizations.

Message boards in a number of fan sites dedicated to *Cruel Intentions* contained posts from fans that did not address the film at all. Instead, they focused on either Gellar or *Buffy*. Such linkages do not just track the ties between production companies and studios that are actually financially inter-invested; they also establish interrelationships among various media. Moreover, the structure and weekly presence of network television help to reassert continually the co-mingling of Buffy, the character, with Gellar, the actress. As a result, Gellar's star persona has become so soaked with her slayer character that it is difficult for fans to see her films without bringing with them their image of Buffy. Therefore, fans may view the character of Kathryn in *Cruel Intentions* as carrying traces of the slayer or, perhaps, may constantly compare the characteristics of Kathyrn and Buffy.

While the television character of Buffy may be the primary point of identification for many young fans of Gellar, these fans have also been trained by their interaction with multimedia forms to become highly media-literate viewers who expect to encounter intertextual references.[18] Media producers have recognized this and have written scripts that encourage this type of reading. *Scream*, one of the first films of the 1990s to engage intensely the new teen audience, is an apt example of this, as it is peppered with self-referential play, knowing asides, and deconstructions of its own generic form. Following the success of the *Scream* series, teen-geared films and television programs have been structured to contain similar intertextual moments. In fact, *Buffy*'s success is often attributed to its tendency to include such references. The program's pop culture nostalgia, co-mingling of genres, ironic settings, and self-aware dialogue demand that viewers engage their knowledge of other texts in order to enjoy fully reading and re-reading it. This type of text prepares viewers to anticipate fluidity in their interactions with the media. When these TV and filmic intertextual moments are coupled with viewers' experience on the Internet, they can then make sense of Gellar's and other teen television stars' movements across media through the analogy of *linking*. Just as a website is set up with links to other pages, Gellar's primary star image and character, Buffy Summers, is now linked to other media texts and characters through her films, games, products, fan sites, and publicity materials. A viewer may depend more heavily on one site (such as the television program) than on others, but he or she is aware that the other sites lie in wait for his or her engagement. Certainly, the importance of star-based extratextual materials has long been recognized by the film and television industries. As early as the silent era, the film industry learned that such materials extend spectators' involvement in the cinema to spaces outside the filmic event, as well as bringing them back to the box office. Yet, the current state of media ownership requires that extratextual materials and star personae lead the spectator to multiple sites in *various media* in order to promote a range of products.

Star linking also contributes to a leveling of the traditional hierarchy of entertainment media that posits film as the pinnacle of an actor's career. Traditionally, an actor or actress would either begin his or her career in television and eventually leave it when he or she found success in film, or begin his or her career in film and only use television as a venue for guest appearances or publicity junkets. The television teen actors and actresses of today tend to use film as a way to expand their audiences and their career potential, yet they remain committed to the medium in which they first attained stardom. This is done not out of a sense of loyalty, but rather as a way to remain connected to their audience base. The television performer's forays into film are particularly alluring to audiences during the summer, when network shows are on hiatus and the average teen is on summer vacation, since it is an opportunity for fans to see their favorite television star in fresh, big-screen material.

Certainly a star's persona can be altered to conform to the needs of the film at hand, yet for many teen stars the characters they play in films end up being conceived as simply extensions of the overall construction of their highly intertexual star image. The film is an opportunity for fans to see the teen star in a new setting, with new motives and desires. In the case of Gellar, the dramatic structure of *Buffy* provides a certain level of continuity for the viewer and the star in their moves between media. The tone of Gellar's acting and the basic tenor of some of her characters' development remain somewhat stable in many of her films, although that becomes less so as Gellar's film career continues.[19] This may be a byproduct of the closing gap between television and film narrative and aesthetics. As Justin Wyatt suggests, the New Hollywood's "movement toward high concept . . . favors the aesthetics of television: the reliance on character types, the strict genre parameters, and, of course, the modular structure."[20] If this is the case, the similarities among media will help make a viewer's transition from television to film and back an easy one. Furthermore, the star in high concept products is key to the development of the concept itself and much of the resulting marketing and merchandising hinges on his or her image. Thus, if a star's persona has already been established by his or her work in television, the studio and/or production company can reactivate that persona, capitalizing on its status as a pre-sold commodity. Neal Moritz, producer of *I Still Know What You Did Last Summer* (1998), has remarked that the "recognizability of these [teen] actors makes them valuable. They have a built-in awareness, and they're a proven commodity."[21] Thomas Schatz argues that the pre-sold product is a significant component of the horizontally integrated New Hollywood system. He also suggests that the intertextuality inherent in such products and their campaigns has led "younger, media literate audiences to encounter a movie in an already-activated narrative process."[22] Since they have been trained to read media in this type of environment, teens are more amenable to the marketing and narrative practices enacted by media conglomerates. Therefore, they are more likely to follow readily their favorite stars from television to film.

A television network can also benefit from a star's work in another medium, as his or her continued exposure may bring new viewers and additional publicity to his or her program. Even though the WB allowed UPN to purchase the series after its fifth season, the WB has repeatedly acknowledged that *Buffy* was the first of its programs to bring in its core teen audience. The network cashed in on Gellar's high visibility in films, commercials, and on the web for five years, certainly an aim for UPN in acquiring the series. After all, at the WB, Gellar, along with such *Dawson's Creek* stars as Michelle Williams, James Van Der Beek, and Katie Holmes, became a physical manifestation of the network's aims and image. By 1999 the network was boasting on its company website that it had "established itself as a branded network targeted to young adults and teens. . . . The WB's goal of being the destination network for the 12–34 demographic coincides with the network's fourth consecutive season of being number one with female teens."[23] This success has certainly been helped along by the crossover popularity of so many of its stars.

The network's reliance on its stars could be seen quite dramatically in its promotional campaigns of the late 1990s. In these spots, the stars of *Dawson's Creek*, *Buffy*, *Felicity*, *Charmed*, *Popular*, and *Roswell* act like a popular, yet friendly, high school clique as they pose, hang out, and playfully hug each other in a shadowy WB warehouse. The content of the individual programs is not addressed by these spots; rather, it is the stars themselves who are the representatives of the overarching industrial narrative of the WB. The spots remind viewers (and advertisers) that they tune into the network to see this stable of high-profile teen stars. (In fact, stars of programs such as *The Steve Harvey Show*, which achieved higher ratings than *Felicity*, were not included in the promotional campaigns, since they do not attract the teen audience so desired by advertisers.)[24] As in Hollywood films of the studio era, certain television actors function as markers of "house style" for a network, as well as serving as the primary selling points in the acquisition of new sponsors. Still, this does not mean that the network remains the *sole* point of identification for the star, since linking produces a multifaceted persona for a performer such as Gellar.

Historically, television stardom has been considered by many media scholars to be more about the production of celebrities than about the traditionally glamorous and rare version of stardom thought to be present in film.[25] Yet, the versatility and intertextuality of teen media stars points to a potential breakdown of these demarcations. The fluidity and frequency of their movements across media put into question the privileging of one form of stardom over another. This shift stems from the larger industrial movement toward convergence, which is creating an environment in which ownership and media form will become increasingly interlocked. Stars who no longer signify a house style of a particular film studio but who still tend to represent the intentions and images of networks will be the most visible manifestation of generic formations and audience identification. They are also less likely to be identified as belonging solely to one medium.

CONCLUSION

In an article in 2001 on television programming and teens, the *New York Times* tracked the viewing habits of Lily Rothman, a wealthy, white, fifteen-year-old New Yorker. "Fiercely loyal, opinionated, even obsessive" in her program choices, Rothman claims *Buffy* as her long-standing favorite show. She writes online fan fiction, goes to chat rooms and boards as soon as she has finished watching an episode, and speaks to some of her fellow fans over the phone. "I have so much in common with the people I meet through *Buffy*," she says. "I can't pinpoint why, exactly, but we tend to like the same music and the same books and the same movies."[26] Rothman's media affinities are just the kind of information contemporary media companies are trying to track and harness. Television series such as *Buffy* can become a nexus of teen media consumption and thus help shape group tastes, interests, and involvement outside of the initial textual site. In their transmedia movements, stars of such programs can amplify and/or hasten this process.

The intricate relationships that have developed among film, television, and publishing during these years of massive conglomeration, along with technological developments such as cable television and the Internet, have further complicated the processes and relationships between fans, texts, and stars. Although the roots of these relationships can be traced back to the struggle to define television stardom in the 1940s and 1950s, the contemporary media industries have demanded new institutional and cultural developments. The new teen star's ability not only to straddle both media, but also to engage in cross-promotion and outside advertising (and, in a couple of cases, their own production companies), while reminiscent of the careers of some early television stars, is also a product of the confluence of developing marketing techniques and the renewed fascination with the teen audience on the part of the media industries. The further study of such stars will reveal the definitional contours of media stardom as well as the shifting interrelationships among producers, audiences, and media texts in this new media age.

NOTES

1. Doherty, "Teenagers and Teenpics, 1955–1957," 298.
2. "Merchants of Cool," *Frontline*, PBS and 10/20 Productions, 2001.
3. Tim Kiska, "Buffy Still Slays Us: Sarah Michelle Gellar Builds a Network, Homes for Needy and an Adult Life—All by Age 22," *The Detroit News*, 4 October 1999, E1.
4. Lynn Hirschberg, "Desperate to Seem 16," *The New York Times Magazine*, 5 September 1999, 44.
5. Nash and Lahti, "'Almost Ashamed to Say I Am One of Those Girls,'" 64.
6. Emma Forest, "Inside Story: The Future Is Female," *The Guardian*, 16 December 1998, 6.
7. Nash and Lahti, "'Almost Ashamed to Say I Am One of Those Girls,'" 64.
8. Hirschberg, "Desperate to Seem 16," 42–49.
9. Ibid., 74–79.
10. See, for example, Hansen, *Babel and Babylon*; and Studlar, *This Mad Masquerade*.
11. Murray, "Saving Our So-Called Lives: Girl Fandom, Adolescent Subjectivity, and *My So-Called Life*."
12. Stacey, *Star Gazing*.
13. Francine Prose, "A Wasteland of One's Own," *New York Times Magazine*, 13 February 2000, 68.
14. Kinder, *Playing with Power in Movies, Television, and Video Games*.
15. Ibid., 47.
16. "Merchants of Cool," *Frontline*.
17. Katy Porter, Teen Boards: Sarah Michelle Gellar, www.aol.com.
18. Buffy was not Gellar's first prominent role, as she played Erica Kane's daughter on *All My Children* for close to three years and won an Emmy for her performance. However, most teen girls associate Gellar with the Buffy role.
19. Gellar's more recent roles, such as *The Grudge*, show a significant movement away from the character of Buffy; however, she is still cast as a woman in danger who must defend herself against supernatural forces.
20. Wyatt, *High Concept*, 195.
21. Annette Cardwell, "Generation Next: Recent Hits Have Studios Screaming for More Teen Flicks," *Boston Herald*, 23 September 1998, 55.
22. Schatz, "The New Hollywood," 34.
23. "About Us: Who's Who: Jamie Kellner," AOL-Time Warner website, http://www.aoltime warner.com/about/whos_who/turnerbroad/Kellner.html.
24. Joe Flint, "Whitewash," *Entertainment Weekly*, 30 July 1999, 24. *The Steve Harvey Show* was also one of the few WB series that featured people of color; the absence of people of color in these promotional spots suggests the race-based narrowness of the WB's representations (and target audiences?), as well as its age-specific focus.
25. See Langer, "Television's 'Personality System,'" 353; Ellis, *Visible Fictions*; and Marshall, *Celebrity and Power*.
26. Julie Salamon, "Teenage Viewers Declare Independence," *New York Times*, 13 March 2001, E1.

3

Annette Hill and Ian Calcutt

VAMPIRE HUNTERS: THE SCHEDULING AND RECEPTION OF

BUFFY THE VAMPIRE SLAYER AND *ANGEL* IN THE UNITED KINGDOM

n a televised viewers' feedback program, a senior executive responded
to public criticism of the scheduling and censorship of imported cult
TV in the United Kingdom. Key examples included *Buffy the Vampire
Slayer* and its spin-off series, *Angel*. The executive stated, "The problem is, with some of the series we acquire from the States, in the
States they go out at eight o'clock or nine o'clock. We don't have that
option here because we want to be showing history documentaries
or some other more serious programming at eight or nine o'clock."[1]
TV channels in the United Kingdom do not perceive programs such
as *Buffy* and *Angel*, which have garnered critical and ratings success
in the United States, as appropriate for a similarly prominent time
slot. Although peak time programs can include entertainment shows,
these are generally productions made in the United Kingdom, such as
lifestyle shows or dramas.

This chapter analyzes the circumstances within which British viewers are able to see *Buffy* and *Angel*, and the implications of those circumstances for their experiences as audience members and fans. First,
we outline the British TV system in general, and the different missions
and purposes of the relevant TV channels. We also address the specifics
of scheduling *Buffy* and *Angel*, including the role of censorship and
the editing of episodes. The way certain channels understand their

role as broadcasters, in particular for a young or "family" audience, has implications for how *Buffy* and *Angel* are presented. Our study concentrates on *Buffy* as it reached the fourth season, a time when its growing success spawned the spin-off *Angel*. In the second section, we explore the consequences of the scheduling and censorship of these programs in relation to the viewing experience, specifically through online fan communities. The experience of being a fan of *Buffy* or *Angel* in the United Kingdom highlights culturally specific fan activity. We focus on the British context for the scheduling and reception of *Buffy* and *Angel* as a case study that illuminates different broadcasting attitudes to, and viewer experiences of, cult TV. Because of their passionate fan bases and these kinds of scheduling considerations, cult TV series such as *Buffy* and *Angel* offer an especially revealing case of contemporary transnational reception practices.

BROADCASTING *BUFFY* AND *ANGEL* IN THE UNITED KINGDOM

The main network television channels in the United Kingdom perceive themselves as catering to a mass audience. BBC1, the public service broadcasting channel funded by a license fee, aims to inform, educate, and entertain a mass audience, while also catering to regional and minority interests. ITV, a commercial channel funded by advertising, aims primarily to entertain a mass audience, but it is also required by the Independent Television Commission (ITC) to inform and educate viewers. Prime-time television on the two main network channels (those broadcast over the airwaves) is primarily home-grown product, offering a range of genres, in particular soaps and drama, that can regularly attract over ten million viewers (a market share of more than 40 percent). BBC1 and ITV have been engaged in a scheduling and ratings war and in recent years have moved main night-time news bulletins to incorporate more popular entertainment programs during prime time. The ratings war has yet to affect significantly the early prime-time, or family, slot, which is devoted to the news; teatime, or late afternoon, news bulletins are a time-honored tradition in the United Kingdom, and the public often structures its daily routines in relation to these news bulletins.[2]

Buffy and *Angel* have been shown on minority network channels (BBC2, Channel 4), and a pay-TV channel (Sky One). The minority network channels have felt the impact of the ratings war on BBC1 and ITV, and they have been competing to attract surplus viewers by consolidating their niche programming during prime time. In an increasingly fragmented and competitive TV market, minority network channels in the United Kingdom have worked hard to establish clear channel identities, especially during prime time. This connects with the scheduling of imported cult TV as these channels primarily schedule such series during the teatime slot, perceiving U.S. science fiction and fantasy drama as suitable for family viewers and younger viewers who are not necessarily the target audience for these minority channels.

It is rare for imported programming other than feature films to be shown in prime time on BBC1, thus it is unsurprising that an imported show such as *Buffy* appears on BBC2. What is surprising is that BBC2 airs cult TV at all. The main audience for BBC2 consists of upwardly mobile, educated, older viewers, aged forty and over, and the majority of programs (lifestyle, factual) reflect this niche audience. Its prime-time programs attract up to three million viewers. Thus, although BBC2 airs *Buffy*, it would be unlikely to feature it in a prime-time slot, as this is reserved for more "serious," mature programming.

Unlike BBC2, Channel 4 is funded by advertising rather than a license fee. However, like BBC2, its remit is to cater to minorities, in particular to focus on new programming from independent producers that highlights innovation and experimentation. Its prime-time programs attract up to three million viewers. Channel 4 prides itself on taking risks, and showing films and TV programs uncut.[3] Its main audience is young (ages sixteen to twenty-four) and upwardly mobile, and youth audiences perceive the channel as catering specifically to them. It is not surprising that Channel 4 acquired *Angel*. Many American imports are shown in prime time, such as *ER* and *Friends*, with soaps, news, and factual and lifestyle programs airing earlier in the evening. However, what is surprising is that Channel 4 adopted BBC2's approach to imported cult TV and classified *Angel* as children's programming.[4]

Content regulation in the United Kingdom follows specific guidelines, outlined by the BBC, the ITC, and the Broadcasting Standards Commission (BSC). The guidelines are based on government policy regarding the content of all network, satellite, cable, and digital channels in the United Kingdom. The ITC licenses and regulates all television services, other than license-funded services by the BBC. The ITC is funded by fees from its licensees, and it is independent of the government Department for Culture, Media, and Sport, although the DCMS does appoint members of the commission. The ITC sets standards for program content and monitors output, ensuring that broadcasters comply with these standards and applying penalties (in the form of warnings, fines, and, in extreme cases, loss of license) if they do not. The BSC is an independent organization that assesses complaints based on its codes for taste and decency, which include codes for portrayals of violence and sex; it also researches public attitudes regarding standards.[5] The BBC has its own monitoring system for content regulation, but it works closely with the BSC and the ITC to ensure that the BBC's codes are similar, if not identical, to existing broadcast regulation. Broadcasters are expected to comply with television regulation, and research by the BSC and the ITC suggests that the British public expects broadcasters to adhere to current guidelines: two-thirds of the public believe that there is an appropriate amount of broadcast regulation in the United Kingdom.[6]

The guidelines ensure that programming before the nine o'clock watershed should not contain material that could be considered offensive to a family audience. Although 70 percent of homes in the United Kingdom do not contain children, "the earlier in the evening a program is placed the more suitable it is likely to be for children to watch on their own."[7] In the United Kingdom, 61 percent of the public believes it is necessary to protect children and other vulnerable groups by using content regulation.[8] Thus, programming featured in the teatime slot must be suitable for children.

While the BBC is aware of the audience's diverse views on what will and will not cause offense, material shown in the early prime-time slot will be unlikely to contain scenes of violence, sexual innuendo, or offensive language. These editorial values also apply to acquired material. As *Buffy* is made for a niche American audience watching after eight o'clock in the evening, adjustments must be made to fit the program in a family slot. Although "the BBC will try to ensure that editing interferes as little as possible with the original intentions of the film maker," in the case of *Buffy*, substantial editing occurs in order for it to be shown in the United Kingdom.[9] Channel 4 must adhere to the ITC program codes, which mirror the BBC's in terms of the nine o'clock watershed. The ITC's Family Viewing Policy "assumes a progressive decline throughout the evening in the proportion of children viewing, matched by a progression towards material more suitable for adults."[10] Thus, Channel 4's decision to show *Angel* in early prime time ensured that it had to edit the series to fit the time slot.

Non-network TV (cable, satellite, or digital) in the United Kingdom treats imported cult TV differently from broadcast channels. British Sky Broadcasting's Sky One is a general entertainment channel available by subscription on cable, satellite, and digital TV. Sky has a significant ownership connection with Fox through Rupert Murdoch's News Corporation and regularly acquires some of the Fox network's most popular TV shows for transmission in the United Kingdom, such as *The X-Files* and *The Simpsons*.[11] Sky One was launched in 1989, and by 2001 approximately 40 percent of the viewing public had access to it. Its prime-time programs can attract up to one million viewers (and more for special events), and it caters to a niche audience of young adults (sixteen to thirty-five). Its identity is mainly based on the channel's ability to acquire the first airing of American imports before they appear on broadcast TV. When Sky One showed new episodes of *Buffy* and *Angel*, it was only a few weeks behind the American air dates, but it was months ahead of broadcast screenings in the United Kingdom. Sky is expected to adhere to the ITC Family Viewing Policy, but the watershed is at eight o'clock rather than at nine for premium encrypted subscription channels. Sky One mirrored the American treatment of *Buffy* and *Angel* by showing new episodes during prime time.

Thus, the fans' ideal platform for watching American cult TV is Sky One. However, because it is a pay TV, minority channel, most cult TV fans watch their favorite programs on network broadcasting channels. Neither BBC2 nor Channel 4 perceives imported cult TV as suitable for prime time, preferring to rely on home-grown factual, lifestyle, and dramatic genres to attract its niche adult audience. By classifying *Buffy* and *Angel* as children's programming, network TV in the United Kingdom is unable to respond to the expectations of fans, who are predominantly prime-time viewers ages sixteen to thirty-five.

SCHEDULING AND CENSORING

The scheduling of imported cult TV on British network television can be problematic for viewers. Imported cult TV, in particular American science fiction and fantasy, is usually scheduled between 5:00 and 8:00 PM. The 8:00–10:00 PM time slot is frequently used for leisure and drama shows made in the United Kingdom. Cult classics that originated in the United Kingdom, such as *Thunderbirds*, *Space 1999*, and *Doctor Who*, are also shown in this tea-time slot, having attracted a cult audience since their original broadcasts in the 1960s and 1970s.[12] Contemporary U.K. productions that attract a cult follow-ing tend to be comedy or comedy-drama hybrids, such as *League of Gentlemen* (BBC2) and *Father Ted* (Channel 4). A rare example of a peak-time show in the United Kingdom that resembled *Buffy* and *Angel* was Channel 4's *Ultraviolet*, a modern vampire thriller, which attracted a cult reputation after only one short season.

In the United Kingdom *Buffy* was first seen on Sky One. At the time of *Buffy*'s initial broadcast, January 1998, Sky One's prime-time and daytime pro-gramming was dominated by imports from various American sources, includ-ing network shows such as *ER* and *Friends*, plus series from syndicated outlets such as *Star Trek: Voyager*, *Stargate SG-1*, and *Xena: Warrior Princess*. Apart from *The Simpsons*, Sky One's most popular genres were science fiction and fantasy. Given that Sky One aired aforementioned properties such as *The X-Files* and *Xena*, it is clear why *Buffy* was seen to suit its channel profile. Ac-cording to the Broadcasters' Audience Research Board, over 400,000 viewers, mainly ages sixteen to thirty-four, watched *Buffy* on Sky One.[13] According to Sam Rowden, the head of Sky One Acquisitions, "*Angel* was a 'must-have' as an acquisition because of the following that had already built up around *Buffy*. It is equally well produced, though darker and more sinister, but the storytell-ing strength is still there and consequently so are the fans. We committed to this series even before it started airing in the U.S."[14]

It was almost a full year before the first episode of *Buffy* appeared on broad-cast network (that is, non-cable or satellite) television in the United Kingdom. The BBC acquired non-pay-TV rights to *Buffy* and premiered it on 30 Decem-ber 1998. On BBC2 *Buffy* sat between a diverse and changeable schedule of pro-gramming—from drama, sports, current affairs, and documentaries to com-edy—including shows that originated in the United Kingdom and those that were acquired from overseas. Like Sky One, BBC2 often buys cult TV series and tries to allocate a 6:00–8:00 PM slot for them, but the exact scheduling of cult TV shows is highly volatile (due to preemptions from live sports coverage and the like). *Buffy*'s BBC2 stablemates were science fiction series such as *Star Trek: Voyager* and archived reruns such as previous incarnations of *Star Trek*, *Battlestar Galactica*, and *Doctor Who*.

Despite the eventual ratings success of *Buffy* on both Sky One and BBC2 (see below), the chronicle of *Buffy*'s own spin-off series, *Angel*, in the United Kingdom is unusual for British television. Sky took the lead by acquiring first U.K. transmission rights to *Angel* and followed the American model by broadcasting it directly after *Buffy* on the same channel. The later time slot (9:00 PM) suited its darker theme and ensured that the occasional but important crossover story lines with *Buffy* remained synchronized. This proved successful in the United States, with similar national ratings (3.55 and 3.58) for *Buffy* and *Angel* in the 1999–2000 season, and it was successful for Sky One: *Buffy* regularly attracted 70,000 viewers and *Angel* 60,000, placing them in the top ten shows for Sky One. Although fans expected *Angel* to make its later network appearance on BBC2, Channel 4 instead snatched the rights. Channel 4 is more inclined to show imports in prime time (usually at 10:00 PM), but with very few exceptions these are mainstream American hits such as *ER* and *Friends*. A rare prime-time genre import for Channel 4 was *American Gothic*, again shown in a 10:00 PM slot. Channel 4 returned to this tactic in 2005–6 by acquiring the ABC shows *Invasion* and *Lost*, the latter being a rare example of a major ratings hit that has cult TV characteristics.

Channel 4's other cult shows have included *Babylon 5* and *Stargate SG-1*. The former, a cerebral space opera not necessarily suitable for children, was shown at various times, including weekend afternoons and early evenings during the week. Not only were devotees missing the early broadcasts, but these were occasionally censored to suit the time slot. Only after protests from a vociferous body of fans was a late-night repeat added, which went some way to appeasing the protesters. *Stargate SG-1*, a syndicated American series, is also occasionally cut for violence. It is shown normally at 8:00 PM on Sky One, apparently uncut, but it is shown again in a range of daytime and early evening times on Channel 4. Unlike *Babylon 5*, there have been no late night uncut reruns.

A similar fate has befallen *Angel*, which started on 15 September 2000, at 6:00 PM. Some of Channel 4's thinking is revealed by Annette Maye, the program executive for acquired series: "C4 decided to acquire *Angel* as we saw it as a series with lots of potential to appeal to a wide range of audiences. It fits with C4's identity in bringing the best of U.S. series to the U.K. and also we saw it as cutting edge drama for teens."[15] Certain *Buffy* and *Angel* episodes contained shared story lines, but Channel 4 decided not to make its *Angel* episodes co-incide with BBC2's *Buffy* transmissions. "We have no plans to liaise with BBC about running both episodes together," said Maye. "They are different but complementary shows."[16]

The scheduling of imported cult TV has consequences for viewers and reveals some of the structuring factors that shape transnational reception. In the case of *Buffy*, the BBC first paired it with *Star Trek: the Next Generation*, showing *Buffy* after *Star Trek* at 6:45 PM on Wednesday evenings. During the first season, *Buffy* rarely made it into the top ten programs on BBC2, and it averaged just over three million viewers, slightly less than *Star Trek: TNG*. This was a much earlier time slot, targeted at a different age group compared to the Sky One transmissions a year earlier. By the end of season 1, fans were vocal about BBC2's scheduling and censoring of *Buffy*. Although it was possible to spot one or two slight trims made to Sky's prime-time broadcasts of *Buffy* in the United Kingdom, such censorship appeared to be minimal and infrequent. In its earlier slot on BBC2, however, its cuts were more noticeable by fans — even if they had not seen the original versions. Edits usually applied to violent fight scenes, often accompanied by music, which would jump when trims occurred. Fans staged a successful campaign to show a late-night unedited version, thus illustrating the type of consumer activism described by Jenkins in relation to other cult TV series such as *Twin Peaks*.[17]

Teatime episodes continued to be shown but also cut. Examples include "Where the Wild Things Are" (season 4) in which sex scenes between Buffy and Riley were shortened. Because of such cuts, the 6:45 slot is unpopular with fans, but some of the remaining material is found to be too explicit for other kinds of viewers. Complaints about another sexually charged scene in "Harsh Light of Day" (broadcast at 6:45 PM, 12 October 2000) were upheld by the BSC, which ruled that the sex scene had exceeded acceptable boundaries for broadcast at a time when young children could be watching. Sophie Turner Laing, an acquisitions editor for the BBC, explained why BBC2 would not drop the teatime slot for *Buffy*: "The original early evening transmission will remain an appointment to view for a large part of the audience, and particularly for fans at the younger end of the spectrum. We have a responsibility to this audience and therefore episodes are occasionally edited to ensure they remain suitable for the audience available to view at that time."[18] The idea of an appointment to view assumes that a specialized audience will tune to a particular channel at a given time, especially to see a show. However, in a Gallup survey, 44 percent of British viewers claimed that what most annoyed them about watching TV was not being home for their favorite show.[19] In the case of *Buffy*, a teatime slot may be suitable for the younger fans, but not for viewers ages sixteen to twenty-four, who are the core audience for this series.

The establishment of the show as an appointment to view was further complicated by frequent interruptions. BBC2 rarely interrupts a season of its successful programs that originate in the United Kingdom. Yet *Buffy* was taken off the air in mid-season on fourteen occasions between December 1998 and October 2000, usually to show sporting tournaments. The BBC's attitude to *Buffy* is evidence of the network's lack of concern with the often complex story arcs of cult TV shows and with the desire of cult TV fans to follow each season with little interruption, both of which are complications of transnational reception practices.[20]

Despite the teatime scheduling of *Buffy*, it gradually attracted a core following of viewers ages sixteen and older, as intended by the makers of the program. When *Buffy* returned to BBC2 in November 1999 it was more popular than *Star Trek: TNG*. In February 2000, *Buffy* was the eighth most popular BBC2 program with 3.59 million viewers; *Star Trek: TNG* barely made it into the top thirty. During the summer of 2000, *Buffy* was rarely out of the top three BBC2 programs, rivaling very successful and highly marketed homegrown programs such as *The Naked Chef* and *Gardener's World*, and attracting up to and over four million viewers, a high figure for a cult TV series.

The growing success of *Buffy* on BBC2 in this teatime slot accompanied online activity among fans. Key members of the BBC online message board titled *Buffy*/Cult TV criticized the BBC for censoring *Buffy*, complained about its marketing of *Buffy* as a children's program, and lobbied for an 8:00 PM slot, which was seen as the ideal time for the show based on its scheduling in the United States. The BBC acknowledged that *Buffy* "is targeted at our younger adult audience (18–24)" but argued that "as a public service broadcaster we have to try and cater for the varied interests of our diverse audience . . . therefore it is not possible to please all our viewers."[21] Fans were bemused by the BBC's logic: "It seems to me the 6:45 timeslot is now weirder than ever! To me they are totally contradicting themselves."[22] This type of response from the

BBC is illustrative of the way in which "fan response is assumed to be unrepresentative of general public sentiment and therefore unreliable as a basis for decisions."[23]

When Channel 4 bought the rights to *Angel*, *Buffy*'s fans had to watch *Angel* on a different channel, on a different day, at a different time. It was originally given a 6 PM start time, with no late night repeat; later episodes were combined into double bills, starting at 5:25 PM. *Angel*'s darker tone resulted in heavier cuts. Regarding *Angel*'s first Channel 4 broadcast, Christopher Andrews reported that "several notable edits were made, especially to the opening scene which was practically non-existent due to censors' edits for violence and language. It is thought that a total of 1 minute and 22 seconds were cut from the opening episode."[24]

One fan website discovered that the episode "Room with a View" was one of the most affected by cuts: examples included shots of beatings, blood, choking with a noose, violent exorcism, and knives: "Angel's second fight with Griff was greatly cut, especially the neck breaking at the end."[25] Similar to the BBC's position on certain episodes of *Buffy*, the tone of the censored episodes were seen as too dark for some viewers. In its January 2001 report, the BSC upheld a complaint against "In the Dark"; the ITC received over eighty complaints about the series and reprimanded Channel 4 for airing *Angel* at a time when children might be watching.

Fans dubbed Channel 4's treatment of *Angel* "the *Angel* Massacre."[26] Over one thousand fans signed a petition criticizing Channel 4 for its "outrageous scheduling"; some wrote in with suggested new schedules that would accommodate a later screening. A viewer feedback program, *Right to Reply*, gave a fan of *Angel* the opportunity to argue that Channel 4 had "sucked the life" out of the program: "In the first episode, Angel stumbles across a pair of vampires terrorizing two girls. But we don't actually see the girls being attacked because part of the fight scene has been cut out. So, when we suddenly see a close-up of one girl with blood pouring out of her head, it doesn't make any sense. . . . The first episodes of *Angel* are the least violent in the series; I dread to think how much will be cut out in future programs."[27] Jay Kandola, the head of series acquisition for Channel 4, echoed the BBC by arguing that: "*Angel* is one of those rare series which appeals to both an older and younger audience. Channel 4 has to make minimal cuts to make sure that it can be viewed by all of its fans and not just some."[28] In its first week of transmission, *Angel* was number 27 in the top Channel 4 programs for that week. By its second week, it had dropped to number 53.

When Channel 4 changed the schedule to an earlier slot, a news bulletin on the BuffyUK.org website summed up fan response to the scheduling:

> Question, what do you do when you are trying to establish a slot for a high profile drama that's currently annoying both fans and the easily offended? If your answer is: "put it on even earlier and show TWO episodes" then maybe Channel 4 has a job for you! . . . Even worse, in a strange manifestation of cosmic symmetry, BBC2 is skipping *Buffy* that same week, on account of . . . snooker. When we hoped BBC2 and Channel 4 would collaborate on scheduling. This isn't quite what we meant.[29]

Channel 4 was compelled to drop three episodes entirely (episodes 11, 12, and 14: "Somnambulist," "Expecting," and "I've Got You Under My Skin") because they had "been deemed unsuitable for family viewing and therefore [had to be removed] from the present schedule."[30] Belatedly acknowledging the unsuitable teatime slot for *Angel* and reacting to fan pressure, Channel 4 dropped the early evening transmission and began airing new episodes at 11 PM in double bills (beginning 3 December 2000), starting with "Eternity" and "Five by Five." Although this was an attempt to appease fans, the new scheduling did not solve the problem of poor synchronicity with BBC2's *Buffy*. Fan response is evident in the ratings for season 4 of *Buffy* and season 1 of *Angel*, which show fluctuating viewing figures. Although *Buffy* started off with 3.6 million viewers on BBC2 in January 2001, the number of viewers dropped to 2.6 million in February, barely placing it in the top thirty. On Channel 4, ratings for *Angel* fluctuated between 400,000–800,000 viewers for the new late-night slot.

In the late 1990s and early 2000s, one fan strategy for dealing with unreliable scheduling and heavy editing of cult TV was to purchase home videos or DVDs. In order to watch their favorite programs uncut and in the right order, almost two hundred thousand fans in the United Kingdom bought the first three seasons of *Buffy*, and almost fifty thousand have purchased the fourth season of *Buffy* and the first season of *Angel* as of this writing.[31] However, fans in the United Kingdom have continued to face potential censorship in their access to these videos and DVDs. The first boxed set for *Angel*, like *Buffy*, was certified as only suitable for viewers ages fifteen and over by the British Board of Film Classification. The second *Angel* boxed set released in the United Kingdom (12 February 2001) was classified as suitable for viewers ages eighteen and over. This ensured that episodes were uncut, but the rating was controversial among younger fans: "This could be bad for a lot of fans—I myself am only seventeen so won't be able to get it, and considering the state Channel 4 has made of the episodes, the boxed set was a lot of people's only hope."[32]

Although fans can purchase and build video and/or DVD archives of *Buffy* and *Angel*, the scheduling and censorship of both series is clearly important to the viewing experience, as the majority of viewers watch network TV, despite the fact that episodes can be almost a year behind those aired in the United States. The difference between the ratings for season 4 of *Buffy* and season 1 of *Angel* on network TV highlights how important complementary programming and cross-promotion are for fans of cult TV. With sympathetic scheduling, network ratings for *Angel* in the United Kingdom could have equaled those of *Buffy*, as evident in the United States and pay TV in the United Kingdom. However, the "*Angel* Massacre" ensured this was not the case. The broadcasts of *Buffy* and *Angel* are not supplementary but essential to the viewing experiences of fans in the United Kingdom. Indeed, in the next section we argue that fan experience of these shows in the United Kingdom is connected to, not separate from, the national context of the British TV system.

WATCHERS GO ONLINE

Henry Jenkins's argument that "fandom constitutes a basis for consumer activism" is particularly applicable to the circumstances of *Buffy* and *Angel* in the United Kingdom.[33] As Jenkins notes, "Network executives and producers are often indifferent, if not overtly hostile, to fan opinion."[34] In the United Kingdom this indifference has led to the creation of an online community that is primarily a forum for complaints and for sharing information on the availability of the shows across all media. Thus, the treatment of *Buffy* and *Angel* by programmers in the United Kingdom has led to an online fan community that specifically seeks out other fans in the United Kingdom. The sites offer these fans an opportunity to talk about the experience of watching *Buffy* and *Angel* in the United Kingdom, an experience that both emphasizes the negative side to cult TV fandom and celebrates being a fan. One fan summed it up when he or she explained, "People say, 'So what do you spend all your time on the internet doing then?' I reply about the BuffyUK site & they say, '*Buffy!*' Unless you have watched it I really think people have a bad misconception of the show."[35] The networks' treatment of both series in the United Kingdom has done little to contradict the misconception that *Buffy* is not "mature, quality programming," and fans seek to validate their status by participating in message boards and discussions that celebrate rather than denigrate being a fan of *Buffy* and/or *Angel*.

The fan community in the United Kingdom may choose to visit TV industry sites, such as BBC.co.uk/buffy, Skyone.com, and Channel 4.com, or fan-based sites, such as The Watcher's Web, unofficiallybuffy.uk, Slayed.co.uk, and BuffyUK.org. All of these sites provide news, scheduling information, merchandise, and discussion forums. Sites in the United Kingdom have the added complication of dealing with an imported series. For example, as the news about the shows' story lines originates from the United States, the more attentive web pages for fans in the United Kingdom, such as Earshot (BuffyUK.org), add "spoiler alerts" to news items in case readers do not want story lines revealed ahead of time.

Perhaps because of the circumstances surrounding viewership of *Buffy* and *Angel* in the United Kingdom, there was a flourishing demand for *Buffy*chat. Two of the most frequented and updated sites were BBC Online's *Buffy*/Cult TV message board and the fan-organized BuffyUK.org. We want to focus on these two sites to illustrate how being a fan of *Buffy* and *Angel* in the United Kingdom is different from being a fan in other countries.[36] Discussion by fans on BBC Online highlights the experience of watching *Buffy* in the context of television regulation in the United Kingdom and attitudes toward American cult TV. Discussion by fans on BuffyUK.org highlights how fans in the United Kingdom successfully seek out each other in order to validate their status as cult TV fans.

BBC Online Cult TV acts as an auxiliary to cult shows such as *The X-Files* and *Star Trek: The Next Generation*. Once at the *Buffy* site, one can find profiles of the key characters, information about episodes, and a lively message board. The *Buffy* site was so popular that the BBC opened a second site for reviews of *Buffy*, as opposed to general chat about *Buffy* (the site had over twenty-five thousand hits as of this writing). Although Sky One and Channel 4 both have sites that profile *Buffy* and *Angel*, there is little sense of a community on these corporate sites, as fans either visit the BBC site or fan-based sites such as BuffyUK.org. The Sky site simply does not have enough users to generate a fan community. Channel 4 gives little attention to online discussion, instead using its site as a promotion for programs. It is difficult to find the chat forum for *Angel* and if, as we did, one stumbles across it in a fan site such as BuffyUK .org, then one will only find a handful of people trying to generate a discussion or, in most cases, air grievances.

Those fans who do visit the BBC Online site have often been unhappy with spoilers inadvertently posted by BBC staff members who are unfamiliar with the shows. Thus, fans spend much time in this chat forum complaining about the BBC ("me moaning about the BBC again"), Channel 4 ("I hate Channel 4"), and cuts to particular episodes ("cuts to 'Enemies'"). This does not allow much room for actual *Buffy*chat as the regulars are generally policing the site or leaving the site to become members of fan-based online communities. The type of discussion that does take place at BBC Online consists usually of reviews of new episodes or topics relating to viewers' favorite episodes, characters, and dialog. Some sense of a community does emerge in these posts, as fans exchange musings and personal likes and dislikes.

The BBC's goal in hosting these boards is to facilitate chat and interest in the series from all kinds of fans, young and old. Thus, the following post would seem particularly well-suited to the BBC's mission as a provider of television for the entire family: "I am writing on behalf of my daughter who is 4 and would like to join you in saying how great she thinks *Buffy* is. A little young I know, but we have all been dragged in to the series. Unfortunately, I missed a few eps, so fill me in, how did Willow get to be a witch?"[37] However, such discussion also captures the conflicts that arise from the BBC's scheduling policies. Responses to this post ranged from support for to condemnation of this parent for allowing her daughter to watch a show aimed at more mature viewers. Although the BBC seeks just this type of family user and viewer, to many fans of *Buffy* and *Angel*, such posts only serve to demonstrate the BBC's mishandling of the two series and misconceptions about their core audiences. As this example illustrates, many viewers fail to find the fan community they seek at the site controlled by the BBC.

Alternatively, the fan-based site BuffyUK.org illustrates the type of fan activity that occurs in an environment more supportive of cult TV fans and their interests, in this case specific to the United Kingdom. The Stakehouse, the meeting place for fans of *Buffy* and *Angel*, is moderated by fans, not by an entity such as the BBC, so there are few spoilers or trolls (users who ignore house rules) to interrupt fan chat. The "*Buffy* on TV" discussion area has eight forums that cover the main interests and concerns of fans, ranging from BBC, Sky, and *Angel* on Four forums, to Spoiler, Box Set, and News forums, plus the WB forum for those fans in the United Kingdom who have managed to obtain contraband copies of the latest episodes from the United States. Thus, the Stakehouse manages to solve the fans' main problem with the BBC *Buffy*/Cult TV site, its lack of attention to the specific viewing conditions for fans in the United Kingdom. The Stakehouse allows fans to go to the forum that matches their viewing circumstances and engage in chat that is based on episodes of *Buffy* and *Angel* that they have actually seen.

There is also a strong social community at BuffyUK.org, with seven different rooms to visit within the socializing forum of the Stakehouse. There is a stakehouse within the Stakehouse where fans can get to know each other. This is by far the most popular room, with over thirty-five thousand posts. Core fans arrange to meet offline at conferences, film screenings, and live gigs such as that of Four Star Mary, which is featured in some episodes of *Buffy*. There is even a BuffyUK community projects room, including a parachute jump for charity and an enterprising suggestion that fans start up their own BuffyUK lottery syndicate.

Fan sites such as BuffyUK.org are more creative and more organized around fan interests than industry sites and are a product of fans' desire to share experiences and perceptions of *Buffy* and *Angel* in a supportive and understanding online environment. Even though *Buffy* ceased production in 2003 and *Angel* in 2004, BuffyUK.org continues to be updated with news about the latest projects of the cast and crew. The types of fan productions to be found at BuffyUK.org are common practices for cult TV fans. However, BuffyUK .org also highlights how different being a fan of *Buffy* and *Angel* is in the United Kingdom compared to other countries. Because of the time difference between the showing of *Buffy* and *Angel* in the United States and on network and pay TV in the United Kingdom, and because of the denigration of American cult TV in the United Kingdom, viewers have to work hard at being fans and engaging in fan activities that are about the shows, rather than about scheduling or censorship.

Since the airing of the final episodes of *Buffy* and *Angel*, high-speed broadband Internet connections have become more common and cult TV fans have increasingly turned to file-sharing software such as BitTorrent to download new episodes of their favorite shows almost immediately after transmission in the United States. However, there is still a divide between people with broadband and those with unfeasibly slow connections or no Internet access. Users must also have a good deal of technical knowledge and, at the time of this writing, organizations such as the Motion Picture Association of America (MPAA) are attempting to crack down on copyright-infringing, file-sharing activity. Official TV and movie downloads are becoming more widely available in both the United States and the United Kingdom, but unlike free-to-view TV, a fee is sometimes charged and access to overseas users is usually denied. Therefore viewers in the United Kingdom who want to use official broadcaster downloads still have to wait several weeks or months for the episodes to appear on local broadcasters' Internet services.

CONCLUSION

The circumstances within which British viewers are able to see *Buffy* and *Angel* affect their experiences as audience members and fans. The wave of popularity relating to *Buffy* spread across the Atlantic to the United Kingdom, but it has been difficult for viewers to enjoy this experience fully because of many months' delay and scheduling issues. A show that is readily and freely available in the United States becomes a comparatively hard-to-find commodity abroad. Network television channels are out of step with the expectations of cult TV viewers. While fans lobbied TV schedulers to show *Buffy* and *Angel* uncut in an appropriate and regular time slot, their complaints were largely ignored. This is because the TV environment in the United Kingdom foregrounds home-grown factual, lifestyle, and drama programs in prime time. Imported cult TV is relegated to an earlier time slot, which means that under current content regulation it must be suitable for a family audience. Imported cult TV is generally treated better by pay television channels, and in related merchandising, because these media companies have realized the significance of niche audiences in a multi-channel environment and because they rely on imported products as staple prime-time entertainment.

Fans in the United Kingdom have thrived despite and perhaps because of the difficulties in watching *Buffy* and *Angel* on network TV. Their experience illuminates different national attitudes toward cult TV and its fans. Fans seek out British websites in order to communicate with other fans who have similar viewing experiences. Websites that are designed and moderated by fans in the United Kingdom are the most popular platform for *Buffy*chat. Only the forums run by fans manage to cope with the complexities of variable transmissions in the United Kingdom. And only the forums run by fans manage to validate fan status by providing a platform for the fan productions and discussions traditionally associated with cult TV.

NOTES

1. Janey Walker, the managing editor of commissioning at Channel 4, quoted on *Right to Reply*, Channel 4, original airdate 11 October 2000.
2. Gauntlett and Hill, *TV Living*.
3. See for example their statement about not editing feature films to fit required time slots. Channel 4, www.channel 4.com.
4. Since the initial writing of this article, another minority network channel, Five, acquired the rights to show the first network transmission of the third and fourth seasons of *Angel* in the United Kingdom, but as with Channel 4, the scheduling was in erratic late-night time slots.
5. The ITC and the BSC merged into one organization, Ofcom, in 2004.
6. Independent Television Commission and Broadcasting Standards Commission, *The Public's View 2002* (ITC/BSC, 2003).
7. British Broadcasting Commission, *BBC Producers' Guidelines* (BBC, 2000), 77.
8. Broadcasting Standards Commission, *BSC Regulation: The Changing Perspective* (Broadcasting Standards Commission, 2000), 1.
9. Channel 4, www.channel 4.com.
10. Independent Television Commission, *ITC Program Code* (Independent Television Commission, 2001), 4.
11. In the United States, Twentieth Century Fox TV produced *Buffy* and *Angel* for transmission on the WB and UPN networks (in the case of *Buffy*) and the WB (in the case of *Angel*). They have not been shown on Fox's broadcast network, but the off-network syndicated episodes of *Buffy* have run on Fox's cable network, F/X. In 2006 UPN and the WB merged to form the CW network.
12. Originally, *Blake's 7* and *Doctor Who* were peak-time weekend viewing on BBC1. *Doctor Who* was revived in 2005 with new episodes shown in peak time on BBC1 to critical acclaim and high ratings.
13. Broadcasters' Audience Research Board ratings are published weekly as the BARB Weekly Report. Ratings data included in this article come from the period of January 1998 to November 2000.
14. Sam Rowden, email interview with Annette Hill, 5 September 2000.
15. Annette Maye, email interview with Annette Hill, 5 September 2000.
16. Ibid.

17. Jenkins, *Textual Poachers*, and "'Do You Enjoy Making the Rest of Us Feel Stupid?'"
18. Quoted in *Cult Times*, November 1999, 5.
19. Gallup Survey for Pace Micro Technology, "Pace Report 2001."
20. Jenkins, *Textual Poachers*, and "'Do You Enjoy Making the Rest of Us Feel Stupid?'"
21. Quoted in a letter to the fan Haley Elliott, "Me Moaning about BBC Again," BBC Online *Buffy*/Cult TV message board, 19 August 2000, BBC.co.uk/buffy.
22. Sally Taylor, "Re *Angel* Cock-up," BBC online *Buffy*/Cult TV message board, 20 August 2000, www.BBC.co.uk/buffy.
23. Jenkins, *Textual Poachers*, 279.
24. Christopher Andrews, "Angel Cut on C4," 19 September 2000, www.slay-uk.com. This website was no longer operating at the time of publication.
25. "Slay-UK," 29 October 2000, www.slay-uk.com.
26. "The Angel Massacre," 29 October 2000, www.BuffyUK.org.
27. *Right to Reply*, 11 October 2000, Channel 4.
28. Independent Television Commission, *Programme Code* (London: Independent Television Commission, 2001), 4.
29. "All Join in for Scheduling Fun," www.BuffyUK.org, 29 October 2000.
30. Channel 4.com, quoted on www.BuffyUK.org.
31. As of November 2000, 48,000 units of episodes 1–12 of season 4 of *Buffy* had been sold; 44,000 units of episodes 1–12 of season 1 of *Angel* had been sold. Also, 193,000 units of season 2 and 159,000 units of season 3, both of *Buffy*, had been sold. Figures courtesy of Chart Information Network, phone interview with the author, 2 November 2000.
32. Chris Leversuch, 9 December 2000, www.buffyslayer.net. This website was no longer operating at the time of publication.
33. Jenkins, *Textual Poachers*, 278.
34. Ibid., 179.
35. "Age of Fans," The Stakehouse, BBC Forum, 8 March 2000, www.BuffyUK.org.
36. There are a sprinkling of American and European *Buffy* fans who chat online at these sites, but the majority of the fans are British.
37. "New," 17 August 2000, BBC online *Buffy*/Cult TV message board, www.BBC.co.uk/buffy.

4

Amelie Hastie

THE EPISTEMOLOGICAL STAKES OF *BUFFY THE VAMPIRE SLAYER*:

TELEVISION CRITICISM AND MARKETING DEMANDS

As a series that clearly engages with feminist and other cultural issues currently in play, *Buffy the Vampire Slayer* understandably has attracted the attention of popular and academic critics alike. In this essay, I am concerned with the economic and epistemological stakes of the convergence between the show's narrative production and our own scholarly attention to it. I am especially interested in how popular texts such as *Buffy* help to drive a "market demand" in scholarly production, and how this series, as an ongoing text in continual transformation despite the show's cancellation, challenges academic criticism in particular ways. As part of its ongoing narratives, *Buffy* produces a way of knowing—for both its fictional characters and its viewers. It is a series that is invested in knowledge and in history, and as such it provokes this same drive for knowledge in its viewers. At the same time, this drive for historical knowledge—particularly in academic criticism about the show—seems shaped by the very temporality of television itself, based as it is on an ideology of "liveness." Of course this is the same temporality that defines the capitalist market—a need for the ever new, the present.

Learning from *Buffy*, then, I want to consider how television criticism sometimes functions as a mirror of the very medium it investigates, drawing as it does on a state of "liveness" and remaking itself according to market demands. In turn, I want also to consider how collections like this one have the potential to be (and the potential to avoid becoming) merchandising tie-ins themselves. While some of these links may be inevitable, how do we avoid producing academic criticism that is simply a reproduction of television textual production and structure? How do we avoid falling into television's own traps of ephemerality, obsolescence, and market demands? Moreover, how might *Buffy* help us answer these questions? How do the undeniable pleasures in viewing and writing about this series challenge us? Finally, what might an examination of *Buffy the Vampire Slayer* and its ancillary texts teach us about our own textual production? To try to answer these questions, I am going to place this collection and this series in a double context: in terms of other anthologies produced in television studies (and marketed to the "youth" audience of students) and in terms of the *Buffy* franchise itself. Following a consideration of other anthologies, I will thus look at a range of merchandising tie-ins that accompanied, and were sanctioned by, the series. By moving in this way, I will attempt to bridge—and even reverse—the market and epistemological economies that organize television production and scholarship.

TELEVISION AND TELEVISION CRITICISM IN THE PRESENT

To link these various texts and issues, I want to begin by delineating some concurrent temporal structures of television and television criticism. Indeed, an important point of debate in television studies has concerned the temporality of the medium itself: as a form characterized by an ideology of "liveness," television essentially always exists in present time. While "liveness" especially describes nonfiction formats, narrative television—like other formats and media, from writing to film—can be understood in this way as well.[1] Even when a viewer's relation might alter a perception of the temporal state of the narrative (as when one sees a television show for the second time) or when programming directly frames a series in terms of "history" (as on Nickelodeon's Nick-at-Nite), television remains in a virtually continuous present state. This temporal structure is consistent with the dictates of other market trends. That is, in order to generate interest in a product—from a new style in clothing to a television show—some measure of novelty is essential. In the case of television, this may mean that TV is also *im*measurable, as it is known in part through its very ephemerality. Mary Ann Doane describes this structure in her claim that "television thrives on its own forgettability."[2] Surely some degree of forgettability is basic not only to the temporal organization of television but also to the production of television texts. That is, in order to maintain novelty and thus exist in an ephemeral state, television demands that its viewers must, to some extent, "forget" past television series (or even episodes) in order to recognize what we watch in the present *as* present, as new.

The inevitable ephemeral nature of television is, perhaps, obvious. Certainly its structure of "forgettability" is evident in its very programming, within and across series. This is clearest in the mundane example of episodic series programming. The episodic series itself is organized around repetition of plot structure, characters' relationships, and so on. In conventional terms, most series present weekly a problem to be solved; these resolutions to problems are necessarily forgotten, so that the same problems—or variations of them—might resurface in subsequent weeks. The same logic is at work across other formats, such as news programming. Not only is the same kind of news produced day after day, but different news programs explicitly draw from one another in the production of news. These "synergistic" relations not only suggest a contradiction in the very term "news" but ultimately also depend on "forgetting" that one has seen the same story repeatedly across programs and networks. These forms themselves work against the production of historical knowledge at a structural level.

Furthermore, while ephemerality and obsolescence guide the structure of such television programs, these concepts organize television itself. That is, television is so vast—it includes so much programming—that it can never be fully archived. Much of television is lost as soon as we see it. This is particularly true of more typically "live" broadcasting: daily news shows and some sporting events, especially. But it is also true of fictional formats. Thus, for instance, while the Museums of Radio and Television are continually building their archives for public review, such institutions cannot store every moment of television ever produced; no matter how extensive new digital technologies are, those programs that have been lost will ever remain so.[3]

Much cable and syndicated programming attempts to guard against ephemerality and obsolescence. Once a network program enters syndication, its episodes may be viewed over and over again. And certain cable networks bill themselves as having an archivist, or historical, design. Hence Nick-at-Nite and its spin-off, TV Land, tap into and perform television nostalgia as they replay old television favorites. Yet such programming often ignores those very series—such as *Beulah* or *Hazel*—that offered, though often through the guise of stereotypes, an alternative to the white middle-class world otherwise typically associated with TV in the 1950s. In all of these ways—the artificial narrative of progress established by a cable channel such as TV Land, the camp sensibility, the segregated programming—certain channels seem to be concerned with some form of television history, but even they cannot and do not fully "store" all of television's history through their programming practices. The piecemeal storage and presentation of history that instead takes place on television works to affirm the ephemeral nature of television and its history. What effect, then, do this perpetual presence and its accompanying ephemerality have upon television criticism? If television itself lives in the present, in what temporal state does television criticism reside?

The answer to these questions lies, at least in part, in a consideration of television studies and marketing demands. Indeed, the field of television studies often displays an economic relation to television itself. In this way, the field even has a kind of "ancillary" relation to television texts—functioning, at times, as merchandising tie-ins, though this may often be a fantasy on the part of academics and university presses. If such an economic relation is made complete, it is at least partially done so through the shared temporal relations between television production and criticism. This is perhaps most evident in the loss of and the changes to collections of essays, especially those designed for teaching. For instance, both *Television: The Critical View*, edited by Horace Newcomb, and *Channels of Discourse*, edited by Robert C. Allen, have been through substantial revisions, seemingly based greatly on a need to "update" television examples therein. This form of updating itself necessitates a loss.

Issues of "change" are iterated as precisely the reason behind many of the revisions made to the various editions of *Television: The Critical View*. Hence, in the short preface to the sixth edition (which precedes a longer, new chapter by Newcomb that puts the collection into context), the editor begins by claiming that "the meaning of . . . 'television' continues to shift and change. What once seemed so familiar, so solid, regularized, routinized, so 'common' and commonly shared, has in many ways disappeared."[4] Here Newcomb explicitly notes that criticism must match the change in television's own programming. While this is true of any discipline, what is particularly striking in changes such as those among Newcomb's various editions of his anthology is not simply the *change* that takes place, but that it necessarily occurs alongside a *disappearance*. Because the volume continually holds thirty-two to thirty-four essays in the fourth through sixth editions, many essays must be cut in order to make room for new ones. This fact might seem obvious, yet there still exist interesting ramifications for television studies in this process.[5] Just because a book goes out of print does not mean that it has "disappeared" from history, but a shift in editions has a slightly different operative function for scholarship. While the essays of the prior editions still exist in book form—in the library, on our bookshelves—the shifts in subsequent editions mark them *in time*. Even while the act of reading them might always be, like television viewing, "live," they now belong to the past.

These shifts between volumes underscore and design a particular temporality of television scholarship. And the specific alterations with regard to television criticism and programming suggest a vision of the importance of particular ways of thinking about the medium. From these changes, and those to Allen's *Channels of Discourse*, emerges a way of seeing how television scholarship both meets and contradicts the operations and trends of television itself. As Allen writes in *Channels of Discourse, Reassembled*:

> We have also updated the examples we use to illustrate critical points in each chapter. There is no way a book on television can be "current." The television schedule in place at the time we write is certain to be different by the time this edition is published, and it will be different still at the time you read this. For this reason, choosing examples from programs likely to be familiar to the reader is a tricky business. Some examples are drawn from the "current" prime-time schedule; others are from programs in their second lives in U.S. syndication or in worldwide release; still others are from programs, last seen on U.S. network television decades ago, that have found third, fourth, or subsequent "lives" through new delivery systems— cable, satellite, or videocassette.[6]

In part, what Allen is describing is the desire for accessibility. By attempting to be "current," the anthology seeks those programs that are accessible as teaching tools, as well as those that are accessible—or familiar—to the students reading the work. This goal of accessibility is fairly self-evident. My concern here regards how this form of textual production—the updating of these anthologies—puts such television scholarship in a temporal and historical framework. Indeed, I would suggest that Allen's remarks are fundamental both to television studies as a whole and to this particular project on *Buffy the Vampire Slayer*. The admission that a book on television cannot be "current" and the preoccupation with examples that are themselves "current" (either new to the television schedule or in present syndication) are clearly in response to TV's ontology of "liveness" as well as its structure of obsolescence. By Allen's and Newcomb's indirect acknowledgment, the timing of television scholarship is always one step behind television itself. In this way, built into television criticism is also a sense (and a fear) of obsolescence. The timing, or temporality, of television criticism—or at least of certain trends inherent to television study— is simultaneously "present" and "past."[7]

The desire to be "current" clearly has its foundations in the audience, whether it be the audience of television or television criticism. This is illustrated by Robert Allen's use of "you" in the remarks above. Allen seems to refer to a reader without a pronounced sense of (television) history; in this case, Allen writes to a reader who is, like a television viewer, constructed or interpellated out of a text whose basis is "liveness" and presence. In that the study of television potentially shares television's ontology of "liveness," in cases like Allen's it is always, in a sense, a study of the present made for a "present" audience. An anthology—such as one like Newcomb's that focuses on television in general or one like this collection that focuses on a single series—therefore reinscribes an audience of criticism based on an audience of television. Lacking a sense of history, or at least an access to past television programs, this "new" audience is presumably also young—if not in the literal sense of age, then at least in an interpellated sense. We might thus recognize the intended audience of these sorts of collections as a youth-oriented one—not unlike that constructed by Nick-at-Nite's programming or the WB network. This concern for the new— on the part of the editors of particular collections, as well as on the part of television producers and viewers—will always also produce a paradox of sorts. That is, this sort of novelty also presumes, or anticipates, a future datedness.

Issues of currency (temporal as well as economic) are particularly relevant for this current volume on *Buffy the Vampire Slayer*, as the series itself raises questions about textual borders—and their potential mutation over time. First, the issues of both "temporality" and history are significant for a project that concerns a contemporary television series. That is, as we began to write our contributions, *Buffy* was still in production. As we revised these same essays, *Buffy* was still on the air, and we reworked our essays in order to take textual changes into account, especially considering the series' general propensity for mutation (at a literal level), its switch to another broadcast network, and its syndication in its sixth year. And as we revised yet again, the series had ended its regular run but was available in syndication. Second, the original timing of the anthology invites questions concerning a television series' textual borders as well as what constitutes an appropriate piece of text to consider in a scholarly work on television—from individual episodes to single series to multimedia forms to television as a commercial and formal phenomenon to the very makeup of an audience. Since "television" itself is such a vast enterprise, scholars necessarily redefine constantly its textual borders in order to manage both research and analysis. But there exist also potential pitfalls in defining "television" and television study through particular, relatively isolated texts, such as a series or pieces of series.

For instance, this kind of criticism—especially that regarding contemporary texts in production—has the potential to follow the same line as television: as it concerns the present, it may become obsolete over time. In this way television criticism might fall into television's own traps of ephemerality, the targeting of youth, and even consumerism. Indeed, when scholars write about a series in process or syndication that very act allows television itself to drive the decisions they make in defining textual borders; that is, it is impossible to write about a series or the range of spin-offs (and other textual expansions the series promises) in their entirety. Presumably, the arguments we make about any series in process will have to change with the series. Certainly, this fact suggests that criticism—like television—is necessarily mutable. But it also points to the question of what defines scholarly "research" about television. Is partial viewing of a particular show—for reasons of necessity, access, or timing—adequate to a study? Does the desire, then, to publish work on a show in progress—presumably to meet the demands of television viewers as well as critical production—constitute a scholarly pitfall, or does it simply suggest the enabling characteristics of television and new media scholarship? I would posit that it potentially makes both cases. We are at a disadvantage if we limit (rather than broaden) the parameters of a television text, and I think we are also at a disadvantage if we blindly follow the logic of television in our own research. But doing so with open eyes is also a necessity in order to make any sort of coherent argument, and it might allow us to see enabling similarities between television and television scholarship. Finally, in the case of *Buffy*, this position is also linked to the concerns of the series itself, as it seems that the impulse to publish critical work on the show while it was in process was akin to its own ongoing narratives: the impending apocalypse and one young woman's attempt to stave it off.

"I HAVE KNOWLEDGE": *BUFFY*'S HISTORY LESSONS

Obviously, *Buffy the Vampire Slayer* exists in a consumer economy. This is evident not only in the show's appearance on broadcast television, surrounded by commercial advertising (including Sarah Michelle Gellar's own ads for Maybelline products), but also by its marketing of companion texts and objects. The entire *Buffy* franchise is a subdivision of the massive Fox franchise, of the series's broadcast network (first WB and then UPN), and of television as a whole. Undeniably, the epistemological economy (that is, an economy based on a system of understanding, a way of knowing) that I am describing here is tied to this consumerist economy. But the economy based on knowledge is also responsible for the driving of the consumerist economy in many ways, especially as this myriad of texts produces and reiterates what we "know" about *Buffy*. While the range of merchandising associated with a show like *Buffy* interests me, my argument is especially based on those "products" that might be broadly defined as "narratives" or having a narrative base: novelizations of episodes, original novels based on the series, episode compilation books, other print tie-ins such as the *Buffy the Vampire Slayer Pop Quiz*, and a board game. These products are, of course, fundamentally different from the fan-produced alternative materials explored by scholars such as Henry Jenkins and Constance Penley.[8] As the cover of *Pop Quiz* illustrates (fig. 1), a work such as this is a seemingly transparent promotional tool for the series; as an industrially sanctioned product, its goal is to be reiterative rather than alternative.

Mimi White considers another form of textual proliferation and expansion

through the capitalist, consumer world of self- or inter-referential television in her essay "Crossing Wavelengths: The Diegetic and Referential Imaginary of American Commercial Television." In this work, White sketches the ways in which self-promotional advertising, cross-series appearances and "pollination," and other forms of "program inter-referentiality" all work to create a "textual effect of an increasingly hermetic, self-encompassing world of television."[9] Together, for instance, diegetic mixing across shows exemplifies how "the world of television's individual fictions is brought together as parts of a larger, continuous imaginary world."[10] In their self-referential style, the ancillary texts of *Buffy the Vampire Slayer* promote the series (and, in some ways, television itself). In this case, the world these texts create together is not the "larger, continuous imaginary world of television" (though at times the series operates to produce this state), but instead a "larger, continuous imaginary world" of *Buffy*. Together these works create a self-enclosed world of *Buffy* (and *Buffy*'s fans) based on the interdependence between knowledge and consumerism. In so doing, their function as commodities becomes less transparent; at least they demand an investigation of what exactly they are promoting for consumption. As I am arguing here, they regulate a desire for and a production of knowledge.

The series itself—its setting and its plotlines—is first and foremost responsible for the production of this epistemological economy. Indeed, in what other television show has a library been so central to so much activity? Its centrality in the first three seasons, and Giles's vocation as a librarian, produced the perfect setting both for the show's training in "research" and for debates about the accumulation and dispersal of knowledge. While the library was destroyed at the end of the third season and the characters moved on to life after high school, "research" remained central to *Buffy*'s plots and its very definition. And even when "research" is often a sort of shorthand (so that the actual work of research may be represented less frequently), the necessity of proper study is frequently underscored in the show. Indeed, one of the primary ways in which Buffy's gang is distinguished from the government-run, demon-controlling "Initiative" of the fourth season is through the former's turn to history in order to understand what they are fighting. While there are extraordinary research tools at the disposal of the Initiative and while we frequently see scientists study the captured demons, the activities of this group—especially the foot soldiers such as Riley—are primarily represented through hunting and fighting. This is in great contrast to Buffy's cohort, whose job is essentially to uncover and then provide information so that Buffy can better destroy the "forces of darkness." In fact, when Buffy temporarily joins the Initiative herself, she distinguishes herself from the other soldiers not only by her dress and her gender but especially by her desire to know. Riley's comrade Forest appears to speak for the group when he comments: "She's a pain. She always wants to know why this, why that." As she becomes the slayer who knows too much, Buffy also becomes the target of the brains behind the operation, Maggie Walsh. After Walsh attempts to have Buffy killed, Buffy and Giles suspect that the slayer was "becoming too inquisitive" for her own good.

Research is not only essential to uncovering facts about various demons, but it is also particularly imperative for an understanding of several main characters. While the library functions as a backdrop for the gathering of knowledge, the inclusion of characters who are upward of two hundred years old gives ample opportunity for the production and dissemination of history. Angel's and Spike's embodiments of history, in particular, are the focus of several episodes and ongoing arcs of the series. "Amends" (season 3) is structured to present viewers—as well as characters—with a historical consciousness. It begins with a moment in "history," one when Angelus kills an old friend. Through dreams shared by Angel and Buffy and through the presence of the "First Evil," the episode continues to integrate the series' own past and other moments in Angelus's history with the present day. As Angel pleads to Giles, "I've been having dreams about the past. It's like I'm living in it again—it's so vivid. I need to know. I need to know why I'm here." After Buffy, too, begs Giles for help to understand what is going on with Angel, Xander asks, "Where do we start?" Answers Giles, "We start, unsurprisingly, with research." At this the whole gang begins a research session, represented by a montage of overhead shots of them at work while the night wears on. This focus on historical research—as in later episodes, such as a two-part crossover with *Angel* in the fifth season—makes explicit the show's repeated concern with this theme. In turn, it produces a viewer with an investment in historical knowledge—even if it is often of a self-enclosed world.

The research trope is a common one in the various books produced as companions to the series. But perhaps more interesting is the insistent investment in knowledge about the "real" and fictionalized history of the series that is also inscribed in these various ancillary texts. While the *Pop Quiz* might be the most obvious example of the ways in which these works market knowledge, the other texts—from *The Watcher's Guide* and *The Sunnydale High Yearbook* to the array of novels and novelizations based on the series—all illustrate the same epistemological stakes. Each, for instance, recounts the plots of particular episodes, encouraging readers and viewers to revel in their knowledge of the show. Such recounting is clearest in the suggestively titled *Watcher's Guide* (volumes 1–3), as these volumes literally summarize all of the episodes from the run of the series and outline all major characters and the monsters they face. A play on Giles's vocation and the fan's avocation, the title suggests that the act of "watching" *Buffy the Vampire Slayer* is somewhat unlike that of watching other television shows. Thus, while this volume is not unique in the way it depends upon a reader's prior knowledge of the show (or creates the knowledge for novices), it is unique in the way in which it conflates viewing and "watching."

Specifically associating the act of viewing the show with Giles's occupation of "watching" Buffy on the show draws inherent relations between viewing, watching, researching, and knowing. Samuel Weber comments on the definition of "watching" television; focusing on the parallels between television and "liveness," he notes: "To 'watch' something that itself cannot simply be seen, because it is not composed primarily of *images*, is to *be on the alert*, to watch *out* for something that is precisely not perceptible or graspable as an image or a representation. To 'watch' is to look for something that is not immediately apparent. It implies an effort, a tension and a separation."[11] While Weber here does not take into account the seeming contradiction of the fact that those who "watch" television are actually called "viewers" (which might detract from the active stance a "watcher" has), the definitions of "watch" that he offers are especially pertinent in a discussion of *Buffy* texts. That is, the accompanying materials to the series refocus our attention on what it means to "watch" *Buffy*: watching is effectively learning, or coming to know. Like Giles, we are "on the alert" when we watch the show.

This effect is greatly a cumulative one, in part because of its serial form; we are trained in epistemological viewing practices, and we gain a sense of the show's history over time. A series that builds its own self-described mythology inevitably encourages such an accumulation of knowledge on the part of viewers; this knowledge is both of the show and of pop culture more broadly. Hence we are also "on the alert" for the pop culture references the show giddily makes; these references, in turn, become a substantial part of the "history" of the show in texts such as *The Sunnydale High Yearbook* and *The Watcher's Guide*. Thus the knowledge one gains from viewing is in turn reiterated, or rerun, in these latter works via summaries of and stills from various episodes, just as it was expanded via additional publicity materials when the show was on. As noted, this knowledge is not just obviously self-referential: while it functions to produce a self-enclosed world, it also branches out to other aspects of popular culture and history.

Watching is also a key trope in some of the "original" *Buffy* novels, especially when it is articulated in tandem with the investment in "historical knowledge" prevalent in these works.[12] The dual consumer and epistemological economies are particularly enunciated through the temporal structure of the respective works. While novelizations, of course, essentially reiterate certain episodes (in a much more direct and linear way than do the above works), the "original" novels based on the series neither wholly replay past episodes nor wholly offer new material. These novels are clearly preoccupied with issues of history and knowledge, but they are also limited in their narrative production. Trapped in the moment of the series' own production, they cannot expand or transform the world of *Buffy the Vampire Slayer* in the ways in which fan fiction does. Rather, the characters are all essentially relegated to those roles they play on the series; though the characters might be put in particular situations or places not documented in the series, the novels offer no new information or back story about the program's main figures. In the end, the "new" adventures of the novels did not produce marked changes to the ongoing plot of the series.[13] In this way, the novels essentially exist in a "series" rather than in the "serial" format generally followed by the television program—though there is also an attempt to serialize plots across the novels as well.

This format is partly evident in the ways that the novels, too, replay various episodes of the television show, even as they attempt to offer new material. This combination of new and old material comes largely in the form of lengthy "historical" subplots about "guest" characters (normally the evil force Buffy must destroy). Even while these subplots are already based on particular episodes or tropes of the television show, the histories they offer are quite extensive, and they usually intensify the evil doings or characters on which the novels are based. This intensification, in fact, seems to spring from the fact that these "new" characters have been around in history for a much longer time. The adult novel *The Evil That Men Do*, for instance, essentially retells the primary arc of the second season: Spike's and Drusilla's attempt to take over the world.[14] In this novel, Julian and Helen, the main evildoers, are, like Spike and Drusilla, characterized as British goth hipster vampires who were acquainted with Angel in his evil days. More importantly, Helen is characterized as mentally unstable: she is even more disturbed than Drusilla, with a seemingly greater passion for Angel and a special penchant for killing slayers. Like Drusilla, she has also been "ill" of some ambiguous malady that has left her weak, and this story marks her return to the well, if not the living. The representation of Helen is illustrative of the excessive form of variation common to these novels: every aspect of this work that draws on the television plots is more intense, more evil. Besides the extreme case of Helen's lunacy, these main characters are also much older than Spike and Drusilla; they have been around since Caesar's time, and a back story based on this history inevitably becomes a lengthy part of the book's plot. While this history could essentially exist as an independent story line, it is interspersed not only with a major plot taking place in the present but also with various references to past episodes of the series.

Certain histories—real and imagined—recur across these texts. In both the young adult novel *Night of the Living Rerun* and the adult book *Prime Evil*, for instance, readers receive history lessons, to greater and lesser degrees, about seventeenth-century Salem.[15] Moreover, *Night of the Living Rerun*, as the title attests, integrates this lesson with a play on television structure. Basically, the story is that Buffy, Giles, and Xander begin channeling figures from the seventeenth century: a slayer, her watcher, and a "witch." They see the characters in their dreams, but they also act out certain events in their waking lives. At the same time, a group of four people (television and print tabloid reporters, and two "psychics") channel the "enemies" of this gang—namely, figures who persecuted witches in Salem. This entire scheme is orchestrated by the Master, who is attempting to redo the original outcome of events in order to rise to Earth and, presumably, bring about total evil and chaos. In this novel, "dreaming" about this history is equated with viewing television; this association, in turn, points to the overinvestment or identification on the part of viewers who end up "living" in the world of television, as they are embodied by the characters they are "watching." Thus, the characters whom we usually view on television—especially Buffy and Xander—end up becoming "viewers" themselves, as they watch the historical back story inscribed in their dreams.[16]

What, then, do we make of the inevitable relationship that follows the one sketched here? That is, if Xander, Buffy, and Giles are all characters inscribed as "viewers" who then become the characters they watch, what does that mean for viewers and readers of *Buffy* texts? On the one hand, as these sorts of narratives usually do, the relationship appears to suggest the dangers of overidentification with subjects on the screen. But it also points to the process of viewing as itself a lived, or "live," process. Viewing is thus a process in which one comes to *know*—to know the character one watches (and becomes) and to know history. Importantly, in the novels, as on the television series, this epistemological process is explicitly formed through a relation to television itself.

Indeed, the parallel histories that run through all of these novels open up a number of questions about televisual structure and textual definition. Within all of the works, as with texts such as *The Watcher's Guide* and the television show itself, four types of history are narrated: the "history" of the series *Buffy the Vampire Slayer*; the fictional histories of the various characters; "real" histories (for example, well-known events such as the Salem witch trials); and histories of popular culture more broadly. This continuous attempt at historicism is fairly remarkable, especially considering television's own ephemeral structure and scholarly approaches, which either mimic this structure or work against it. Through their association with one another, each of these histories essentially becomes an equivalent of the others. One effect of this association is that the "history" of *Buffy* becomes "real" in a couple of senses. First, it exists in the same framework with the other histories—fictional or factual—narrated in the novels. By making references to the past episodes of the series, the novels make themselves more "authentic"; at least they are sewn into the intertext of the series as whole. The novels extend—even if they do not transform—the narrative life of the television series. Second, this "authenticity" is itself based on the knowledge of the viewer. That is, the texts reiterate and produce a kind of knowledge; they are part of the epistemological, as well as the consumer, economy of *Buffy the Vampire Slayer*. Finally, through the "history" of popular culture also sketched in the novels, the *Buffy* texts become connected to broader popular knowledge, making the show itself—and its attendant products—an important part of popular culture. In all of these ways, the reader and viewer of these novels is essentially constructed by the text through a particular act of interpellation. The ideal reader and viewer is one who has and takes pleasure in knowledge.

ACADEMIC MERCHANDISING

This production of a knowing fan and an investment in knowledge—by both the series and its ancillary texts—links *Buffy the Vampire Slayer* to the work of the critic in a couple of different ways. For instance, one might argue that the television text innately produces its own criticism in that the ideological temporality of television texts, as live and therefore "present," often produces a model for the temporality of criticism. Moreover, as critics are also necessarily viewers, their paths of critique—consciously or unconsciously—often follow the narrative focus of the shows they view. *Buffy*'s attendant interests in feminism and femininity, finally, directly invite feminist consumption and critique.[17] One can only imagine that this same room for pleasure and critique is the foundation for the massive proliferation of academic work on *Buffy the Vampire Slayer*: this volume joins at least two other anthologies, several single-author studies, and an online journal entirely devoted to *Buffy*.[18] Surely, the production and reproduction of knowledge in all of the *Buffy* texts is directly related to academic occupations and preoccupations. As we have seen, *Buffy*, like other "cult" shows, is often explicitly about investigation and knowledge. The *Buffy* anthologies are part of a growing trend in television criticism: the production of anthologies devoted to particular television series. Many of these concern cult shows that are about investigation in some form: *Full of Secrets: Critical Approaches to Twin Peaks*, *"Deny All Knowledge": Reading The X-Files*, and *Enterprise Zones: Critical Positions on Star Trek*.[19] Part of the reason that these series have become cult shows surely rests on the fact that they are all invested in knowledge; with their narrative tropes and their often open-ended nature, they invite fans to participate in this world of knowledge and to construct further "knowledge" about these worlds.

This textual interest in investigation appears to invite scholarly investigation into these works. Thus, the academic investment in such shows indicates a couple of interesting, and related, points. First, the cult show is understood as such because of the deep, even obsessive loyalty and knowledge of its viewers and fans. Academics, though they may not identify with the typical "avid fan," participate in at least a parallel form of viewing and gathering of knowledge. Second, this scholarly attention suggests the academic interest in investigating investigation itself. It is basically self-evident to note that any academic work is predicated on expertise or knowledge, but noting this fact seems especially important when tracking parallels between televisual and scholarly texts. While characters in cult shows such as *Buffy* witness strange events in their diegetic worlds and want to get to the bottom of them, academic critics recognize something "strange" going on in and around these series. Typically, scholars look into how these "strange doings" narrated on television reveal something about the culture that produces and receives them—reading against or across the grain. In the case of *Buffy*, a form of "identification" does take place: scholars of television might identify not only with the characters' quest for knowledge, but also with the various characters' special abilities that allow them, time and again, to save the world—even if, for some scholars, that means from television itself.

Other more recent anthologies focus on "quality" programming, particularly popular series broadcast on the premium cable network HBO: anthologies have already been published on *Six Feet Under*, *The Sopranos*, and *Sex in the City*; a volume on *Deadwood* is forthcoming. (Relatively scant academic attention has been paid to those HBO series more focused on issues of race, such as *Oz* and *The Wire*.) These works, including the previously mentioned academic books on *Buffy*, seem to be fairly transparent examples of an attempt to capitalize on a show's popularity, but they also seem to be drawn to "quality" shows as a way of suggesting a hierarchical understanding of television.[20] Importantly, however, these are also largely works produced by scholars who do not regularly work in television and media studies; hence they imply a lack of understanding of television as a medium that is *generally* appropriate as an object of academic scholarship. This implication therefore also follows a kind of logic produced by certain elements of television culture as well (a slogan for HBO, after all, is "It's not TV. It's HBO"). In this way, then, these examples of academic works do not attempt—by their nature, that is—to read "against" the grain of television production.

Given the inclination to produce multiple essays on the same series and to market such anthologies often while the series is still on the air, we must ask what kind of television criticism is being produced, particularly when scholars and scholarly works are implicated in the same logic as the medium that they are investigating. Considering the intimate links between the projects of a television series (and its attendant texts) and that of scholarly work begs the question of what roles in time, in the production of knowledge, and in the market these scholarly writings take on. In the present case, this collection is very different from the various volumes of *Television: The Critical View*, but its temporality is potentially also the same. Focused on a contemporary text— whose moment of production was inevitably limited—this volume will forever be marked in time, though its publication after the initial end of the series suggests that it joins *Buffy*'s own interest in history. Therefore, it need not merely be replaced by more books on more current television series—though, of course, it probably will—for doing so would further force this critical text, and others, to follow the patterns set out by the medium it examines. Still, the fact that it is necessarily a work of the present in some form points to the ephemerality of criticism, born from the medium that invites (and even produces) it.

Like its synchronous temporality with television, critical texts such as this one are also born from the particularities of the medium and the texts themselves: after all, television is first and foremost a consumerist medium, often with a proliferation of ancillary texts. In a sense, a collection such as this one takes up the position of the ancillary text, or merchandise: the tie-in.

The publisher I. B. Tauris describes its volume, *Reading the Vampire Slayer: The Unofficial Critical Companion to "Buffy" and "Angel,"* as follows: "This is a book of critical appreciations which examines a variety of the complex ways in which *Buffy* and its spin-off series *Angel* have won the hearts of their target audiences and the minds of intellectual commentators."[21] The hopeful aim, then, for these various kinds of anthologies is that they will remain somehow apart from that market, yet will also address the attempt to capitalize on the market (the Tauris anthology, like the sanctioned *Watcher's Guides*, includes an episode guide to the series). To be just another ancillary text would make scholarly studies complicit in a primarily consumerist economy rather than an epistemological one, even if the latter is precisely the economy that texts such as *Buffy* themselves exist in and produce. However, the very timing of the production of such anthologies bespeaks a desire also to become attached to the *Buffy* franchise—even if as an "unofficial" tie-in—in order to sell copies.

Is it possible—or entirely desirable—to avoid having the work of scholars become just another tie-in, a reiteration or only a slight transmutation of the original text? One answer to this question might be to work outside purely close readings of the text in order to recognize the intertextuality of television and various texts attendant to it. Television studies demands some examination of works in a larger cultural framework, one that also always takes into account the contexts of their production. But even attempts to see television intertextually are themselves a rehearsal of television's innate organization and of the organization of *Buffy the Vampire Slayer* in particular. Thus, might the presence of this anthology—as well as the others like it—indicate the inherent overlap between consumerist and epistemological economies present both in television itself and in television criticism? In many ways a certain duplication of *Buffy the Vampire Slayer*, its textual structure, and the knowledge that it circulates is indeed impossible to avoid. Moreover, given that the academic's position itself is often aligned with the fan's position—in that academics are often also "fans" and in that fan knowledge itself is a broad arena for academic study—the "critical understanding" of something like *Buffy* is also not far removed from the fan's understanding. Finally, a complete remove—from either the fan or the text—may not even be that desirable. However, some remove from the temporal structure of the tie-in and of some forms of television might be possible.

The production and consumption of knowledge on the part of the *Buffy* texts are surely tied to the issues of temporality I outlined earlier. But is it possible to draw from one aspect of these works (their investment in knowledge) and avoid the other (the temporal traps that potentially foreclose the field of knowledge)? In the case of the novels as well as the other tie-ins, such as *The Watcher's Guide* and the *Yearbook*, narratives are reiterated and rerun. This textual reproduction, coupled with its variation, produces a particular kind of temporality related to television's own time. These texts together exist in a cyclical pattern. Trapped by repetition, they seem to exist in both a "historical" state and an ever-present one. Yet, because this cycle is also a trap of sorts, their structure suggests an underscoring of the present over the past or the future. This is a strange temporal logic, in a way, but it is also a prevalent one. Indeed, with their coterminous patterns of reiteration and renewal, the temporality of these texts is that of the market itself. However, considering their narratives' concerns with history and the production of knowledge, we can see a simultaneous attempt on the part of these texts to engage this market with other issues. And because of this particular production, these works defy a simple ahistoricism (as does television itself).

Criticism, too, could defy this ahistoricism by getting outside of this cyclical trap. Or, at least we might consider what patterns of reiteration—in the series and in critical work—are productive and, in turn, what patterns of criticism we might renew rather than rerun. One pattern of reiteration that occurs in the series includes feminist media studies. The creators of the show explicitly acknowledge their debt to their study of feminist film theory, for instance.[22] And many of the themes of the show—from the sheer grrrl power of Buffy to the discourse about male/female and lesbian relationships—appear also to follow feminist models. To write about the series from a feminist perspective might, then, seem a further reiteration of feminist theory, of what we already know. But the feminist influences on the show more importantly direct academics to a potentially different mode of analysis. While feminist analysis has generally been designed around "reading against the grain," in the case of *Buffy* this form of interpretation is not the only possible kind. *Buffy*, in fact, could be set within a "tradition" of prime-time representations of feminism that often invites other forms of interpretation: of revelation, perhaps, of analysis in relation to nonfeminist (or anti-feminist) models, or of historical examinations.

Throughout feminist analyses of feminism on television, scholars have continued to argue for an opening, rather than a foreclosure, of meaning.[23] This call is itself part of the serial logic of feminist criticism. In this way, the form and methodologies of feminist scholarship are inherently related to the medium of television, for it is one that produces an endless—if sometimes ephemeral or reiterative—proliferation of texts. This production might be then met by a proliferation of theoretical possibilities as well.

Critical readings of *Buffy* similarly invite new modes of analysis that must remain critical but that must also acknowledge the debt for our analysis to the very texts that we study. This also means that a reading of *Buffy*, while potentially both critical and celebratory of certain tropes on the show, can avoid existing as a mere tie-in, especially as those sanctioned tie-ins—from *The Watcher's Guide* to a novel like *Prime Evil*—necessarily reiterate and vary rather than fully transform the textual content and structure of the television series. In this way, criticism does not have to exist in the same self-enclosed world of either the *Buffy* texts or television more broadly. In the context of *Buffy*'s own logic, this might mean that criticism can see alternative "dimensions" to the world of *Buffy* as not inherently threatening; rather, scholars might see this kind of simultaneity as an enabling place for critical work to exist. But this also means that readings of *Buffy* inevitably follow some line of the show and of its ancillary texts, for the series itself (unlike many of the tie-ins associated with it) allows for open-ended possibilities. Moreover, scholars might also be drawn to this show for its own interest in history—which potentially works against television's otherwise obsessive relation to the "present."

Through this intertextual examination of the television series, its ancillary texts, and television criticism, I have tried to show how these works not only stretch the boundary of the definition of the "television text" but also how they potentially invite an analysis of scholarly practices alongside them. For these practices produce further intertextual dimensions, again in a dual economy of consumerism and knowledge. In this way, it is impossible to "save" ourselves or our own readers from television (if that was ever a desire in the first place), as we are often complicit in its own logic—and it is often complicit in ours.[24]

NOTES

1. Feuer, "The Concept of Live Television," 14. Feuer describes nonfictional formats, but given the slipperiness of the term "live," its relation to the continuous "flow" of television, and the general act of the narrative process—which essentially always occurs in the "process"—"liveness" becomes a term that can apply to fictional formats, as well as nonfictional ones.
2. Doane, "Information, Crisis, Catastrophe," 226.
3. Television has, however, been archived in VHS and DVD formats. Yet even these works go out of print or stock—certainly the VHS copies of *Buffy* are already largely obsolete, and new versions of the DVDs replace earlier ones.
4. Newcomb, *Television*, xi.
5. In fact, the changes in television criticism are mapped in a new essay in Newcomb's sixth edition by Charlotte Brunsdon ("What Is the 'Television' in Television Studies?").
6. Allen, *Channels of Discourse, Reassembled*, 26.
7. As do particular types of television programming, a strong vein in television criticism guards against the ephemerality of the medium and of its study. Hence, recent collections focus explicitly on the representation of history on television and a construction of television history in scholarship. This is particularly true of such anthologies as Haralovich and Rabinovitz, *Television, History, and American Culture*; and Spigel and Curtin, *The Revolution Wasn't Television*. It is also true of collections such as Torres, *Living Color*, that examine a particular issue in its historical and current dimensions, and of those anthologies that seek to collect significant contributions to the field, such as Brunsdon, D'Acci, and Spigel, *Feminist Television Criticism*. These latter works, like Brunsdon's individual volume, *The Feminist, the Housewife, and the Soap Opera*, seek to historicize the field of criticism, while they also necessarily "historicize" the medium itself.
8. Jenkins, *Textual Poachers*; and Penley, *NASA/TREK*.
9. White, "Crossing Wavelengths," 52.
10. Ibid., 56.
11. Samuel Weber, *Mass Mediauras*, 118–19.
12. These novels have continued to be produced long after the show was cancelled.
13. Caroline Kallas, an executive at Fox, oversees all licensing rights for the series, from novels to episode guides to "generic" products. As she notes, the novels must be consistent with the series: they mustn't "interfere" with the plots of the television series, and they must generally adhere to the original and then ongoing vision of the show as set forth by Joss Whedon, its creator. Telephone interview with Kallas, 22 June 2001. However, the creator and the writers of the show do not have control over licensing rights, including the novelizations.

14. Holder, *The Evil That Men Do*.

15. Cover, *Night of the Living Rerun*; and Gallagher, *Prime Evil*.

16. This sort of overidentification with a "character" is a recurring theme in "cult" television shows and in *Buffy* itself. This character is analogous to the overinvested fan—one who seemingly wants to become a part of the fictional world he or she views. *Buffy* has certainly toyed with identity reversals and bodily inhabitation. The episode that most clearly works through fan relations is "Superstar," in which the ever-marginal character Jonathan produces an alternative world in which he, and not Buffy, is the slayer extraordinaire.

17. For one such insightful critique, see Fudge, "The Buffy Effect."

18. These publications include the following anthologies: Wilcox and Lavery, *Fighting the Forces*; Kaveney, *Reading the Vampire Slayer*; and South, *"Buffy the Vampire Slayer" and Philosophy*.

19. Lavery, *Full of Secrets*; Lavery, Hague, and Cartwright, *Deny All Knowledge*; and Harrison et al., *Enterprise Zones*. David Lavery has also co-edited, with Rhonda Wilcox, an anthology on *Buffy* as cited in note 18. This sort of scholarly production by one central figure itself raises questions of franchises and textual proliferation, much like these series themselves.

20. David Lavery has also edited two anthologies on *The Sopranos*, one on *Seinfeld*, and, at this writing, he has anthologies forthcoming on *Deadwood* and *Lost* (the latter is co-edited with Lynnette Porter). Open Court Publishing has a series of anthologies dedicated to film and television texts "and philosophy"; this series includes a book on *Buffy* (South, *"Buffy the Vampire Slayer" and Philosophy*, as noted above), as well as *The Sopranos*, *The Simpsons*, and *Seinfeld*.

21. This copy appeared in the I. B. Tauris Visual Culture listing of new books for 2001, p. 11. See also Kaveney, *Reading the Vampire Slayer*.

22. Marti Noxon, the show's co-executive producer, made this point when she spoke at the University of California, Santa Cruz in February 2000.

23. For works explicitly concerned with the representation of feminism on television and the role of the feminist viewer, see in particular Mayne, *"L.A. Law* and Prime-Time Feminism"; Feuer, "Feminism on Lifetime"; the *Camera Obscura* special Lifetime issue as a whole (33–34); and Brunsdon, *The Feminist, the Housewife, and the Soap Opera*.

24. My great thanks go to Lisa Parks and Elana Levine for their insightful suggestions for improvement. Many thanks also go to Lisa Nakamura, David Crane, Sirida Srisombati, and especially Lynne Joyrich for useful discussions concerning this work, to Caroline Kallas for information concerning *Buffy* merchandising, and to Marti Noxon for her inspiration.

5

Cynthia Fuchs

"DID ANYONE EVER EXPLAIN TO YOU WHAT 'SECRET IDENTITY'

MEANS?": RACE AND DISPLACEMENT IN *BUFFY* AND *DARK ANGEL*

Whiteness is everywhere in U.S. culture, but it is very hard to see.
GEORGE LIPSITZ, *THE POSSESSIVE INVESTMENT IN WHITENESS*

Representation is the means by which race establishes social power—hence the metaphor of a dividing "line" between black and white identities; yet it is through representation that we are able to envision challenges to the color line's authority.
GAYLE WALD, *CROSSING THE COLOR LINE*

I would say that, absolutely, race was an integral part of our casting process. We were looking for an actress who was perhaps of mixed race so we could say, "Look, this character is supposed to represent the best in all of us; the best of the human race." We didn't want to fall into the chauvinistic mistake, that I think science fiction films have made in the past, where the superior race happens to have a certain Nordic quality as opposed to the alternative, which I don't think has ever really been explored.
JAMES CAMERON, EXECUTIVE PRODUCER OF *DARK ANGEL*

"We are alone." When Buffy Summers meets the First Slayer, she hears a few things she would rather not, including the preceding assessment of a slayer's existential lot in life. This scene comes at the end of "Restless," the fourth season finale of *Buffy the Vampire Slayer*. Whereas the nightmares of other members of the Scooby gang have been somewhat mundane—Willow is unprepared for a school play and Xander is left out of some gang activity—Buffy's takes place in a spectacularly antediluvian desert, an apt setting to demonstrate her most acute fear, which is, no surprise, being alone. She demands the return of her friends. "No friends!" growls the First Slayer, "Just the kill." This is too much for Buffy; she fights back.

As the two slayers kick and chop and roll around in the sand dunes, it becomes clear that the First Slayer, while the original source of Buffy's powers and sense of purpose, is also wholly unlike her. The First Slayer is somehow "African"—she wears animal skins, tribal paint, and wild hair, while Buffy has imagined herself, in her dream, wearing a stylish pink ensemble (see fig. 1). Though the First Slayer's primal instincts and ferocity represent a threat to Buffy in the desert, when the two cross time and space, out of the nightmare and into Buffy's middle-class suburban reality (specifically, her mother's bedroom), the First Slayer's menace essentially evaporates. Straddling the prone Buffy, the First Slayer stabs at her frantically with her stake and misses repeatedly. Buffy is thus inspired to her customary sarcasm: "You're *not* the source of me," she snipes. "Also, in terms of hair care, you really wanna say, 'What kind of impression am I making in the workplace?'" And with that, the First Slayer is vanquished.

The comedy of this summary ejection is complicated some minutes later, when Buffy hears the First Slayer's voice, warning, "You think you know what's to come, what you are. You haven't even begun." This is the series' standard approach to Buffy's dilemmas, to reveal the always imminent hazard with which she lives ("You haven't even begun") while privileging her resilient and capable youthfulness. Still, Buffy's triumph here privileges her contemporary sensibility over the First Slayer's rudimentary rawness. This sensibility is famously emotional, ironic, fantastic, and clever, as well as violent and traumatic, serving as a metaphor for the "universal" trials and traumas of youth, "universal" in a white, straight, middle-class, suburban sort of way. In this context, it is worth underlining that the First Slayer is black.

This rendering of race, like almost every other category of experience and identification in *Buffy the Vampire Slayer*, is at least partly metaphorical. When Buffy rejects the First Slayer as her source, denying her aloneness, as well as her dour brutality and inelegant rage (Buffy's own rage at this point in the series is, well, cuter), she is also rejecting her own "otherness." The image of the

Fig. 1. The First Slayer confronts Buffy, "Restless," 23 May 2000.

First Slayer is troubling in various ways: at the same time that she represents the African roots of Buffy's Euro-American present, she also can be read as an ignorant (not to say racist) image of a primitive black character being bested by a white girl's "modern" know-how and training.

Significantly, the First Slayer is unable to speak; Buffy hears her "thoughts" during the dream sequence, spoken by Tara, who is conveniently inserted into the background of the action for this purpose. But this particular "lack" is exceedingly complicated, as it not only initiates a layered communication and community among Buffy, the First Slayer, and Tara, but also establishes a subtle continuity of purpose, experience, and desire, a continuity contingent on their shared youth. Charles Acland has argued that the ostensible and over-determined "deviance" of youth allows it to function as an identity category in distinct contrast to adulthood, which is constructed as the norm. This troubled opposition between youth and adult enables an ongoing process of struggle for dominance through which social and political systems sustain themselves.[1] Because Buffy is a spectacularly representative youth, her encounter with the First Slayer exemplifies and exacerbates such crisis. Buffy's perpetual sense of displacement, her sense that she belongs to another "race," apart from her world (which is populated by humans, demons, and vampires, communities into which she never quite fits), is made concrete for her in the First Slayer.

The First Slayer is distinctly other; she does not easily fit the category of white youth with which Buffy and her friends identify and she thus reminds Buffy of her own uneasy place.

This chapter considers such displacement as it characterizes youth and race in *Buffy the Vampire Slayer* and *Dark Angel*, a science-fiction-action-teen-melodrama series that aired on Fox from 2000 to 2002. Both series present youth and race as metaphorically related identities, especially as race refers to human and nonhuman and youth refers to a deviant other. Both programs denote the complications and intersections of these categories through the protagonists' "secret identities."

Whereas Buffy is a slayer posing as a high-school student, a college student, and, in the later seasons on UPN, a "normal" suburban head-of-the-household, nineteen-year-old Max Guevara (Jessica Alba) is a genetically enhanced warrior (a "transgenic") posing as a bike messenger for Jam Pony X-Press, a gig that allows her an access pass to most of the city's militarized sectors. More obviously (literally) than Buffy, Max is a member of an "other" race; she is one of twelve fabricated, bar-coded, and brainwashed soldiers, the X-5s, also called "my kids" by the man who designed them, Donald Lydecker. Max and her siblings escaped from Manticore (a facility in Gillette, Wyoming, where genetically enhanced soldiers are made in *Dark Angel*'s near-future, science-fiction world) some ten years before the series' present, 2019. Max helpfully and repeatedly recalls this past in nightmarish flashbacks featuring a nine-year-old, crew-cut Max (Geneva Locke), who performs training drills, schemes with her fellow baby soldiers, and, following their escape, repeatedly struggles to elude dogs, ATVs (armed transport vehicles), and uniformed, heavily armed men, across an icy-blue-lit, decidedly creepy American West. In her current life, Max must avoid detection by Manticore, whose agents continue to pursue her, an expensive project gone rogue.

"Death is your gift."

THE FIRST SLAYER TO BUFFY, "THE GIFT"

As the *New York Times* observed of Buffy in 1997, she is a post–*Patty Duke Show*, post–*Beverly Hills, 90210* phenomenon. According to Thomas Hine, Buffy is an attempt to represent the experience of teen-agers' lives today. She is part of an unprotected generation, one that must live with its elders' insecurities as well as its own. She rubs shoulders with monsters, and like many of her age-mates, she is sometimes suspected of being a monster herself. She's powerful, responsible, scary to know—and personally at risk.[2]

Her own "monstrosity" is, of course, Buffy's most excellent gift and dreadful secret, her youth made at once reassuringly recognizable and dramatically disturbing. She might moonlight as a Maybelline model, as a beauty-queen slasher victim in *I Know What You Did Last Summer* (1997), or as an incestuous vamp in *Cruel Intentions* (1999), but Buffy is, primarily and importantly, the kick-assingest girl on television. Her appearance in a weekly series made being a teenager metaphorically understandable, as a set of ongoing daily rituals, trials, desires, and aspirations. Buffy's "secret identity" as the slayer exacerbates such ordeals and dreams. When she first appears in Sunnydale, for example, in the first season's "Welcome to the Hellmouth," Buffy discovers that several residents—including Giles, who is her watcher, and a few vampires—have anticipated her coming. Having been expelled from a number of high schools already (for being aggressive and incendiary), she is looking to "start over," to live a "normal" life. But no, she discovers that she has been chosen to beat off demons; moreover, that "having a secret identity in this town is a job of work."

Part of this work is defining who she is in relation to that secret identity, as "other" and as "regular" human. The saga enacted on *Buffy the Vampire Slayer* has everything to do with her desire to fit in, at high school, at home, at college, in the world. That the series is set in a place where "fitting in" is so crucial (the suburbs, or more specifically, the Hellmouth) allows the story line to run a sweetly ironic course. Throughout the series, Buffy is driven by her sense of singularity and isolation, conveyed by her status as the chosen one, the slayer. The fact that there is, theoretically, only one slayer at a time amplifies this sense. (The series occasionally fudged this point, aligning Buffy temporarily with fellow slayers Kendra and then Faith, who were brought in because of a confusion in the universal order when Buffy was dead—though, as she points out, she "was only gone a minute.")

While Buffy initially resists her calling, Max's conflict comes from the opposite direction: her superior skills. Her strength, speed, agility, telescopic and night vision, hypersensitive hearing, mental abilities, and catlike reflexes are engineered, and she uses them to take vengeance against the engineers who wanted to use her as a weapon. As Fox's official website had it, "She's a revved-up girl trying to make a run-down world a better place." Max and Buffy inhabit narratives that don't worry about "explanations." They are tough chicks, driven by equal parts aggression and frustration, empathy and moral rectitude. In "What's My Line? Part 2," Buffy's break with slayer tradition (according to which she is not allowed to tell *anyone* who she is) provokes by-the-book Kendra to voice her frustration, asking Buffy, "Did anyone ever explain to you what 'secret identity' means?" Buffy's response is typically sardonic—"Nope, must be in the handbook, right after the chapter on personality removal"—emphasizing her refusal to accept those rules she sees as restrictive. Kendra, speaking in her exaggerated patois (to underline her extremely noticeable difference from everyone in Sunnydale), insists, "But de Slayer must work in secret, for security." Buffy, of course, does not quite see it this way, believing that her friends provide as much security as they pose risks.

"Pete's not like other guys, is he, Debbie?"

BUFFY TO CLASSMATE WITH A DEMON BOYFRIEND, "BEAUTY AND THE BEASTS"

The series repeatedly shows that Buffy's dedication to the gang is a function of her whiteness (her suburbanness, straightness, and so forth). Significantly in this context, *Buffy the Vampire Slayer* depicts the whiteness of Buffy and her friends with a forthrightness that is rare on series TV, or in the broader culture. Ruth Frankenberg writes that "whiteness makes itself invisible precisely by asserting its normalcy, its transparency, in contrast to the marketing of others on which its transparency depends."[3] Indeed, Buffy's whiteness is anything but transparent. The series consistently investigates whiteness as a cultural construction and presumption, by parody, by metaphor, and, occasionally, as with the First Slayer, by contrast. In the fifth season episode "Fool for Love," for instance, Spike, a formerly vicious vampire now suffering from a chip in his head that prevents him from killing humans, and suffering as well as from a dire attraction to Buffy, explains his complicated feelings in a series of flashbacks in which he kills two earlier slayers, a Chinese slayer during the Boxer

Rebellion in 1900, and Nikki the Afro-ed slayer, whose neck he breaks during a fierce battle on a New York City subway, circa 1977 (see figs. 2a and b). These glimpses of past slayers of color reinforce the idea that Buffy's (and Faith's) whiteness, normalized in the 'burbs and in the hackneyed iconography of youth culture, is actually unusual in the long history of the slayer biz.

While Buffy is surely "white" in almost every sense of the term, the very overstatement of that whiteness also highlights and draws attention to it (her name *is* Buffy and she does live in a place called Sunnydale, after all). Indeed, part of *Buffy the Vampire Slayer*'s genius lies in its ironic undermining of the very status quo it appears to epitomize. In defying the conventional parameters of whiteness, Buffy also resists an idealized and traditional adulthood by way of her violence, immaturity (in her mother's eyes, her sneaking out at night is just childish), and seeming deviance (even if it is in the service of saving the planet from the Hellmouth's perpetual spewing forth of demon-spawn). The series' ongoing joke hinges on the ways that adolescence, as a collective cross-cultural "stage," simultaneously demands and prohibits such fitting in. Kids know all too well that conformity is more of an agonizing and perpetually shape-shifting process than an achievable end. Even during the sixth season, when Buffy, newly resurrected from the dead, confronts traditionally "adult" tasks, such as managing money and monitoring her little sister Dawn's education and social life, she remains—stubbornly and perhaps hopefully—lost, partly affected by her unsettling time as a corpse, but also by her ongoing resistance to "growing up," or becoming like everyone else.

Aside from Buffy herself, the series manifests whiteness in her peers' ironically perky affects and in the everyday assumptions that guide life in suburban Sunnydale—that Buffy must patrol graveyards and back alleys at night, that demonic invasions are inevitable, that parents are not even close to being sources of support or comfort (rather, they tend to be clueless or odious). Whereas malevolent adult authority figures such as Principal Snyder suffer just desserts, parents other than Buffy's late mom, Joyce, rarely make appearances, and when they do, like Tara's, they are unpleasant and essentially run off the show. Buffy and her friends face frequent questions concerning their "race," metaphorized as their humanness. Whereas the problems for vampires such as Spike and Angel who hang out with humans are obvious (the avoiding daylight thing, the need for blood), other problems arise for characters

Figs. 2a and b. A Chinese slayer and an African American slayer, "Fool for Love,"
14 November 2000.

Fig. 3. Xander is split into two "races" — Scruffy and Suave — as Buffy tries to understand the difference, "The Replacement," 10 October 2000.

who cross race or species borders, including the werewolf Oz, the former vengeance demon Anya, and the witches Willow and Tara. Xander, ostensibly the straightest, whitest boy on the show, may have the most bewildering race-identity history of all: he has been split into two characters, "Scruffy-Xander" and "Suave-Xander" ("The Replacement"; see fig. 3); transformed into Dracula's bug-eating lackey ("Buffy vs. Dracula"), and mutated into a hyena-boy ("The Pack"). As Anya's fiancé, Xander dealt with her lengthy nonhuman history (and accumulated habits) on a daily basis.

The series also wrestles with the problem of race—human, youth, and race-race—in the menace accommodated by the gang's excessively suburban surroundings. Each comfy domestic space, classroom, or youth hangout (for example, the Bronze) is potentially what Carol Clover has termed the slasher film's "Terrible Place."[4] Moreover, as in many of these slasher films, from *A Nightmare on Elm Street* to *Scream*, the nighttime brings greater visibility to the terrors of adolescence—sexual activity, emotional yearning, acts of violence, and, perhaps worst of all, betrayal by well-meaning as well as self-serving adults. These terrors take particularly embodied forms: vampires lurk in the cemeteries and alleys, demons pop up just about anywhere, and the once quiet

Willow becomes, in the sixth season, a full-fledged witch, increasingly and unhappily addicted to a dark side.

"How do you get to be renowned? I mean, like, do you have to be 'nowned' first?"
BUFFY, "THE FRESHMAN"

Buffy regularly walks on the dark side, of course, which is demonstrated most emphatically in her long-term relationship with Angel and, beginning in the sixth season, in her just-can't-help-herself liaison with Spike. Their impulsive, often violent sexual trysts have literally caused floors and ceilings to collapse ("When did the building fall down?" she asks Spike the morning after their night of wild sex and fighting, in "Wrecked"). For all the excitement she feels, Buffy resists her inclination toward this dark side, angry that, post-resurrection, her attraction is manifested in such a crude and youthful recklessness. Spike pushes her, not a little irritated at himself for his cross-species craving, saying, "I knew the only thing better than killing a slayer would be f——. . ." With this, Buffy has to recognize her own desire, but she accuses him first: "Is that what this is about? Doing a slayer?" Spike's insight is devastating: "Well, I wouldn't throw stones, pet. You seem to be quite the groupie yourself . . . vampires get you hot."

Here Spike makes fun of Buffy's otherness as a slayer by comparing it to her will to humanness, her desire to be normal, "straight," or prototypically "white"—nevertheless, she lusts across race, or more specifically, across species. Spike's own difference, of course, is also raced, in that he is a vampire who has developed a romantic desire for human (or nearly human) flesh. Buffy's difference is parallel to his and also more complicated. Her near humanness makes her unlike her school chums and also unlike her adversaries, as even the demons and vampires in the series tend to be white, or effectively white looking, with some exceptions, including the second season's "Inca Mummy Girl," Ampata, and the fourth season's Chumash vengeance spirit, Hus, who terrorized the gang on Thanksgiving in "Pangs." More often than it introduces characters of color, however, the series tends to displace raced identity and anxieties about race onto species-related anxieties, which are typically performed as various romances. These include Willow's first romance, with Oz (which was rather cuddly, despite his monthly conversions), and the somewhat nervier one between the human Xander and the demon Anya. While these relationships involve characters that look very white, they also explore the compromises needed in order to cross cultural borders. Not incidentally, the gendered shapes of these compromises also represent attitudes of youth culture: Oz left Willow in order to be with "one of his own" (but really so that the series could set up Willow's new queer relationship with Tara), while Xander tried to teach Anya how to be properly, passably human.

Anya is probably the series' "youngest" character, and the bulk of her role comprises her learning to become a responsible (read: adult) human. Her eagerness and clumsiness are typically played for comedy, and her efforts to "pass" alternately parallel or reframe Buffy's own. Like the newly resurrected Buffy of the sixth season, Anya must reorient herself, learn to appreciate or at least perform human rituals and expectations, and control her own, less human urges. Because Anya is so adorably blonde and naïve (not to mention sexually voracious and frank, about which Xander is simultaneously embarrassed and thrilled), Buffy's more disturbing inclinations, as well as the troubles and stakes of her own passing, are thrown into relief. Passing as normal (read: human), Buffy reveals the constraints and constructedness of the categories into which she is trying to pass, as well as those she is trying to elude ("monstrous," "dead").[5] Tracking her continual movements in and out of these categories, the series raises multiple questions, asked as well by *Dark Angel*: What does it mean to be human, young, visibly raced? What does it mean for cultural hierarchies when girls become expert killers, slayers, or genetically designed soldiers? What changes, for whom, when girls take care of themselves, not only brilliantly, but with pleasure? And what is at stake, for whom, in representing girls who understand themselves in relation to hostile cultural environments?

"Listening to you two, it's like reading original text. Talking about yourself in third person. The whole suga-boo dealio. I totally get where it comes from now."
MAX, TO ORIGINAL CINDY AND HER GIRLFRIEND, DIAMOND, "SHORTIES IN LOVE"

The interrogations of race and youth in *Buffy the Vampire Slayer* and *Dark Angel* are premised on their protagonists' abilities to transgress, to move in and out of such culturally constructed categories, which in turn open up those categories for viewers. Much like Buffy, Max struggles to maintain a balance between her superheroic responsibilities and her regular girl routine: she has a complicated social life, a stressful day job, and a superheroic sense of responsibility. The primary difference between the two characters is that Max's domain is archetypically urban while Buffy's is archly suburban. Buffy is caught between her conflicting desires, to wear pop-girl halter tops and to destroy all demons, but Max is torn between wanting to live an anonymous, uneventful life, not pursued by Manticore agents, and wanting to find her family and identity. Her search for her fellow soldiers takes up much of her emotional energy and the series' plotlines—she has discovered several of her siblings, as well as members of other transgenic generations.

The flashbacks at Manticore that color Max's current experience create something of an instant and overlapping character development. Her crisis is thus continual. Tormented as a child, she fights back as a very stylish adolescent—dressed in a sleek black leather jacket, tight black jeans, and black motorcycle boots—with a compelling sense of self-righteousness that Buffy sometimes lacks. Then again, Buffy's duties as a slayer are mostly laid out for her: she does not kill humans, and when she kills demons and vampires they usually evaporate into dust. Max, in contrast, often sees herself in and as her opponents. While Buffy came up in a more or less stable single-parent home, Max came from an expansively abusive environment, and so her sense of allegiance, admirable and sympathetic as it is, has more to do with careful crafting of character than conventional motivation.

In fact, Max is designed with a built-in drug addiction (to tryptophan, which stabilizes her brain's jumpy serotonin levels), which means that she comes equipped with a typical youth and street problem (essentially she is a junkie, and she looks like one when she is low on the drug) that carries with it none of the usual moral condemnation. Trying to make sense of her old addiction, her new designer virus, and her deadly super-soldier skills while also maintaining friendships with her human friends, the not-quite-human Max has little patience for legalities or proprieties. Unlike the generally straight Buffy, Max thinks nothing of breaking rules to get what she wants, because she understands such rules as inherently corrupt, designed to maintain power for those who make them.

Max's only visible "parent"—the figure against whom she directs her rage—

is the genetic scientist Lydecker (later known as Deck, since his Spike-like turn at the beginning of the second season to help her work against the increasingly insidious Manticore). When, for example, Max wants her job as a bike messenger back after being absent for months (at the beginning of the second season, in "Bag 'Em"), she flashes her nerdy employer, the ignominiously named Normal. The scene begins as Normal refuses even to hear her explanation: "Your name is mud, missy-miss. I've heard some lame excuses for missing work, but faking your own death for a three-month sabbatical is a new low." Missy-miss protests that she didn't exactly "fake" being dead, only had a heart transplant. Normal demands proof, and he is suitably aghast when she shows him the big nasty scar on her chest (see figs. 4a and b). Sexy-girl body display this is not.

Max and her coworkers Original Cindy, Herbal Thought, and Sketchy regularly disrespect their employer and their jobs, treating low-paying "kids'" jobs (as opposed to career options) as inconveniences rather than seeing them as appropriate stakes. Such conditioned (and for the most part, acceptable) contempt for adults and the structures they signify or trust in sets the kids apart in *Dark Angel*. In contrast to mainstream films' representations of "youth," here "the kidz are aiight," as one *Dark Angel* episode title has it. Henry Giroux writes that in films featuring youth violence, white kids are "isolated and estranged . . . and can offer no indictment of American society not only because they embrace a disturbing nihilism, but because they appear marginal, shiftless, and far removed from Dan Quayle's notion of American Family Values."[6] By the same token, Giroux continues, films pathologize black youths as a group, such that "black powerlessness becomes synonymous with criminality."[7] Quite the contrary case appears in *Dark Angel*, where violence by youth works to restore a social order decimated by adult abuses and oppressions.

Most adults are trying to kill or recuperate Max back into Manticore, as she is a costly and valuable product, so that hiding from them (usually visualized as hiding her barcode from them) is a standard plot point. Soon after his introduction, Joshua, Max's transgenic "relative," leads Max to the scientist he calls "Father," the generally malicious and aptly named Ames White, who developed Joshua's dog-boy DNA formula and then abandoned his experiments. This old-school villain has no compunctions about destroying his own creations, seeing only a large picture that has to do with world domination. That *Dark Angel* sets this guy against the radically multi-raced Max and Joshua exacerbates and refines its politics and cultural critique.

Figs. 4a and b. Max flashes Normal, showing her scar, "Bag 'Em," 5 October 2001.

"If you see me going to the dark side, do me a favor: smack me really hard right in the face."

MAX TO ORIGINAL CINDY, "MEOW"

Max's capacity to think beyond these immediate circumstances, to envision a better world, is one of her signature traits. At the end of most episodes, she retreats to the top of the Seattle Space Needle, her favorite spot for contemplation, where her isolation is, of course, profoundly underlined. Max's contemplations set her apart from her friends, but they also give viewers access to the way she is processing her emotions, investments, and beliefs. In her examination of youth culture and femininity, Angela McRobbie asserts that girls stake out an investment in society in their formation of a youth culture and that, in doing so, "there is a greater degree of fluidity about what femininity means and how exactly it is anchored in social reality."[8] Such anchoring in *Dark Angel* is most clearly pictured in Max's sessions at the Space Needle. At the end of the second season's premiere, "Designate This," Max looks out on the city and sighs: "Funny how from up here, it looks like nothing's changed. Only everything's changed . . . The whole time I was at Manticore, all I wanted was my strange little life back. Never figured it could get any stranger." Such self-awareness, framed as a witty appreciation of strangeness as well as crisis, saves *Dark Angel* from an occasional inclination toward melodrama in the style of *Dawson's Creek*. But Max doesn't fret so much as she ponders: "I don't get why people call it a depression," she says of her world's dire economic and political state. "People are broke but they're not all that depressed."

Feeling isolated and "strange," Max works to be (or at least appear) "normal," resisting and resenting aspects of her design that mark her as other. For instance, she has feline DNA in her enhanced makeup, which sets her in heat every few months. In "Meow," her roommate, Original Cindy, describes the condition this way: "So, basically, because of this feline DNA that you got in you, every few months you run around acting like an average male?" Max nods, "Somehow, guys can pull it off. I just turn into this freak show." That masculine behavior makes her a "freak show" speaks to adolescent anxieties about proper behaviors, but Max will never be Buffy, who, for all her virtuoso violence, restrains herself in sex, at least until Spike; her heavy breathing with Angel was always romantic and her sessions with Riley were famously stilted, but her outbreaks of passion with Spike are explicitly brutal.

Where Buffy's business with Spike was a terrific new direction, Max had been sexually predatory and aggressive from the start. Her desires are youthfully adventurous, pushing across categories: for Max, whose makers had planned to breed her with a fellow X-5, Alec, looking for love (or even sex) with a non-X-5 is an express act of rebellion. The series' primary romance recalls Buffy's longtime turmoil over Angel: Max is simultaneously distracted and sustained by her love interest and fellow underground activist, the cyber-journalist Logan Cale. In fact, in the premier of *Dark Angel*'s second season, this relationship becomes abruptly like that of Buffy and Angel, when Max learns that she is infected with a genetically targeted retrovirus that is transmitted through bodily contact and was designed to kill Logan. Max thus becomes fatal for her boyfriend, much as Buffy's sexual liaison with Angel turned him back into a bad, soulless vampire. The girls are not only highly trained and lethal fighters, then, but also literal embodiments of the "noxious" threat of young female sexuality and sexual desire.

As disparate as their sex stories are, the most significant difference between Buffy and Max is manifestly racial. Whereas Buffy is a super-white pop-girl, however ironically, Max is straight-up hip-hop, wary, politicized, and tough. Max's dystopia, while hardly unusual (drawing from *Blade Runner* and the *Terminator* movies, among other sources), is definitively unstable. In her Seattle, the apocalypse is defined as post-"Pulse," an electromagnetic shock-wave unleashed by nuclear terrorists in 2009, which zapped the United States into a "third world" nation, poverty-stricken and plagued by disease and violence. She thus inhabits a city that is always on the verge of collapse, where chaos is ordinary and morality is relative. Max's society, in other words, hardly seems worth upholding, except that it is the only one she has.

Her questions and reservations concerning conformity (and family ties) are both more and less vexed than Buffy's, because her world allows for more overt racial multiplicity. In herself, her body, Max represents and functions along a continuum of race; appropriately, her world is categorically hip-hop in style and politics. The look of post-apocalyptic Seattle's streets recalls those depicted in contemporary "'hood" movies. Chuck D co-wrote the series' theme song, the radical underground group is known as the S-1Ws (the name of Public Enemy's affiliated step group), and the kids' speech and dress approximate a tricked out version of today's hip-hop 'tude and gear. Max moves easily in this ostensibly hostile, literally dark environment (brown-outs are

Fig. 5. Max and Original Cindy's hip-hop style, "Bag 'Em," 5 October 2001.

standard occurrences, as power is both precious and unpredictable), at home on the street and amid stereotypical urban diversity.

Not only does she use hip-hop slang (as do her peers at Jam Pony, regularly aggravating their boss, Normal), but she also wears low-rider jeans, midriff tops, and leather jackets, only rarely wearing dresses or skirts (in episodes where she is "undercover") (see fig. 5). Though feeling displaced while living among humans, Max also understands her skills, her otherness, and her relation to those who do not know her (and very few do). She hides her mission and her abnormality beneath regular-seeming teen apathy and anger, appearing pissed off at work and drinking beer at a local hangout after hours. This familiar youth activity is about as far as Max will go: she is programmed to be hyper-vigilant.

"Christ. Damn thing talks."

COP, ASTONISHED AT JOSHUA, "TWO"

Max faces dilemmas of definition daily. She lives between species and races, and not only in her own body, which is infected with feline DNA. Motivated by a sense of her own deviance from the norm, her "monstrosity" and isolation, Max seeks connections, urgently. According to James Cameron, the co-creator of the series, "Max's real goal is to find a sense of family, of belonging."[9] This may be so, but the show is also blunt—and not at all idealistic—concerning the dysfunctions of traditional (read: white, middle-class) family structures. Max's initial strategy toward this end is to track down her transgenic relations—those of her own generation and of previous and subsequent generations, including the second season's addition, Joshua, whose canine DNA gives him a dog-like face and behaviors; in an episode called "Two," he woofs and sniffs, and he quickly develops an undying loyalty to Max (this apparently *despite* her own feline DNA). In turn, she looks after him, bringing him food and keeping him hidden away in a secret place, because, as he recites after an unauthorized outing (during which a dog has bitten him!), "I know. People are afraid of what they don't understand. I know." Max looks stern: "Never forget it."

Otherness, Max knows, can be construed in calamitous ways. And since Joshua, so distinctive in appearance, cannot maintain a "secret identity," he must stay literally out of sight: he was "developed" years before Max, escaped from Manticore before Max and the X-5s, then hid in tunnels beneath the facility. Even as Max pursues her identity in and as community, she is aware of the risks posed by her, and Joshua's, difference out in public.

In the episode called "Two" in the second season, Joshua's younger brother Isaac (whom Max released from the Manticore tunnels) is killing people in the street. Joshua explains to Max that this behavior is a result of abuse at Manticore. When the cops come after Joshua, Max defends him and is unexpectedly jumped by Isaac, whom Joshua then has to kill to save her. When she discusses the events with Logan, she tries to parse her part in them: "I shouldn't have let them out, Logan. I should've known something like this was gonna happen." When Logan reassures her that she "did the right thing, the only thing," she won't buy it. "Tell that to the families of those cops who died." In this way and others, *Dark Angel* repeatedly complicates the sides it appears to establish, indicting *all* sides for their sins. In a world as relative as this one (and much like our own), survival depends on an ability to shape-shift emotionally, culturally, and politically, to imagine a reality beyond your body and desires, to cross over, again and again. *Dark Angel* comments on the process of such cultural and identificatory movements, their significance and their stakes. Max's apparently tireless pursuit of her peculiar past, while she is trying to build a future with her makeshift family (Logan and Original Cindy), means that she is always trying to define herself as part of something, a race, a community, a politics.

"Who knows. Maybe we can beat this thing. I guess we need to see where the road takes us."

MAX, "BAG 'EM"

Both Max and Buffy have made key, even radical, forays into otherness by dying. Buffy dies at the end of the fifth season; upon her return at the start of the sixth season, she is fraught with emotional distress as she resists fitting back in with the gang (and, as mentioned above, finds self-flagellating solace in sex with Spike). Max dies (differently, of course) at the end of the first season, when she is recaptured by Manticore, then shot and apparently killed by the next generational version of herself (an X-7 played by that same silent and completely riveting girl who plays Max in flashbacks, Geneva Locke). "Designate This" has Max salvaged at the last minute by the Manticore doctors, when her X-5 brother Zack shoots himself—rather spectacularly, in the head— so they can transplant his genetically enhanced heart into her damaged chest. Max's reappearance in the second season, after her stay at Manticore, changes everything: she cannot touch Logan and yet they continue to pursue their projects, tracking down transgenics and fighting the good fight. So all is different, and nothing is different.

It is hard readjusting to life after death. Buffy and Max must recomprehend themselves in their bodies (Buffy's with a perpetual sense of loss, and Max's with Zack's heart) and in relation to the humans and nonhumans around them. In "Wrecked," Buffy describes her liaison with Spike in language that she imagines will put him off: "The only thing that's different is that I'm disgusted with myself. That's the power of your charms. Last night was the most perverse, degrading experience of my life." Alarmed by his knowing smirk, she continues, "That might be how you get off, but it's not my style." No, he observes, "It's your calling." This is precisely the danger and vulnerability of

Buffy's secret, whether she accepts it as her "identity" or not—she is "called" to be other, to transgress, to cross categories. And she can't help herself.

NOTES

The third epigraph to this chapter is quoted from Carrillo, "To the Max," 24.

1. Acland, *Youth, Murder, Spectacle*, 41.
2. Thomas Hine, "TV's Teen-agers: An Insecure, World-Weary Lot," *New York Times*, 26 October 1997, sec. 2, p. 1.
3. Frankenberg, "Introduction," 6.
4. Clover argues that the "Terrible Place" is a womb-like space in which the killer's potential female victim is trapped. Clover, *Men, Women and Chainsaws*.
5. As Elaine K. Ginsberg observes, "Both the process and discourse of passing interrogate the ontology of identity categories and their construction." Ginsberg, "Introduction," 4.
6. Giroux, *Fugitive Cultures*, 89.
7. Ibid., 90.
8. McRobbie, *Postmodernism and Popular Culture*, 156–57.
9. Carrillo, "To the Max," 26.

Allison McCracken

AT STAKE: ANGEL'S BODY, FANTASY MASCULINITY, AND

QUEER DESIRE IN TEEN TELEVISION

If you can contain a utopian vision of how you see anything, including gender, but [audiences] are not positive that they want that to exist, [fantasy] is a way to get what they feel out.

JOSS WHEDON, BRAVO'S *TV REVOLUTION*, 2004

Hello salty goodness! Pick up the phone. Dial 911. That boy is going to need some serious oxygen when I'm finished with him.

CORDELIA, ON HER FIRST SIGHT OF ANGEL

In a revealing episode in the third season of *Buffy*, a demon grants Cordelia's wish to change history and erase the effects of Buffy's move to Sunnydale. In this alternative timeline, Xander and Willow are now vampires and Buffy's vampire-with-a-soul boyfriend, Angel, is caged and chained as their "puppy." As a reward for her loyal service, the Master Vampire allows Willow to "play with the puppy," in other words, to torture him. In one scene, Willow sits astride Angel's chest, opens his shirt to display the scars from their previous play dates, and happily begins throwing lit matches on his chest, as an obviously aroused Xander (who gave her the matches) looks on (fig. 1). "That's right, Puppy," she says with much glee, "Willow's gonna make you bark." Angel begins screaming in agony as the scene fades to black.

Despite the fact that it is set in an alternate universe, "The Wish" is hardly an anomaly in the *Buffy*verse, which wholeheartedly revels in the spectacle of female sexual aggression, male masochism, and homoeroticism. Indeed, "The Wish" is a pivotal episode for the way in which it exposes Angel's primary function in the series as an object for teen girls' erotic and sadistic fantasies. The episode also foreshadows the eventual manifestation of the characters' dormant and underdeveloped queer aspects—namely, Willow's lesbianism and Angel's repositioning as a homoerotic object in his own spin-off series, *Angel* (WB, 1999–2004). Tellingly, Angel sets both of these transitions in motion, underlining his role as the originator and catalyst of queer desire in the *Buffy*verse. Vampire Willow, coded as bisexual, returns later in the third season and comes on to Good Willow, who is at once repulsed and fascinated by her. "That's me as a vampire? . . . I think I'm kinda gay." While most of her friends assure her that she has nothing in common with her vampire twin, Angel alone politely suggests that Willow might indeed share some of Vampire Willow's tendencies. The episode also sets up a homoerotic connection between Vampire Xander and Angel, foreshadowing Angel's regular positioning as an object of male sexual desire in his spin-off series. As "The Wish" makes clear, the joys of torturing Angel are linked to non-normative sexual practices, both male and female. But instead of "demonizing" such practices in the conventional sense, *Buffy* and *Angel* open up a fantasy space in which they are acceptable, pleasurable, and empowering for girls and queer viewers.

While much attention has been paid to the way in which *Buffy the Vampire Slayer* charts new territory in representations of young women and girls, one of the program's more remarkable accomplishments is its construction of a new kind of masculinity through the character of Angel. As a vampire fighting on the side of good, Angel is at once the show's most powerful male and its most deviant.[1] Yet his deviance, his vampirism, is here put in the service of an explicitly feminist text. Although the show certainly capitalizes on his black-leather-jacket allure, Angel is not a traditional bad boy vamp. In fact, any potentially threatening hypermasculinity is replaced by a male body that is not merely an object of female desire, but is continually and aggressively acted upon by teenage girls within the text: Angel is beaten, stabbed, burned, staked, and shot with arrows. What sets Angel apart is *not* simply the fact that his body is the show's primary eye candy, but more importantly, that it is the

Fig. 1. Vampire Willow plays with her boy-toy, Angel, as Vampire Xander eagerly looks on, "The Wish," 8 December 1998.

primary site of pain and trauma: Angel suffers, Angel bleeds, Angel screams so Buffy does not have to. Through Angel, a seemingly normative white male body is recoded as queer, not only through Angel's vampirism but more importantly through his function as a masochistic object of teen girls' erotic pleasure.

As a feminist text, *Buffy*'s privileging of female desire goes beyond that previously associated with traditional "feminine" television forms such as the soap opera and melodrama. Through generic hybridity and gender reversals, *Buffy* combines female desire with feminist agency, offering audiences a heroine with a much more active and potentially subversive relationship to the male body. Moreover, the program's serial structure permits girls' desires to shift and complicate over time, promoting the idea of sexual desire not as a fixed identity or goal-oriented pursuit (ending in a "solid" relationship), but as a queer continuum of erotic possibilities, opportunities, and challenges.

The word "queer" most appropriately describes the kinds of transgressive fantasy spaces *Buffy* opens up, since the term encompasses a variety of non-normative sexual activities, from homoeroticism (both male and female) to sadomasochism. But "queer" also acknowledges, as other descriptors cannot, the way in which *Buffy*'s feminist focus works to queerly recode a relationship between a pretty blonde and a hunky male that could otherwise be read as "straight." Sexual norms are always set atremble in situations where a female is on top, and *Buffy*'s feminism enables queer readings in a way that distinguishes the program from other instances of queerness on television. Generally, television's polysemic texts seek to appeal to broad audiences and invariably replicate traditional socio-sexual hierarchies; most queer activity is either momentary and merely provocative (as in a same-sex kiss during sweeps ratings periods, or a deviant procedural villain) or a single, usually marginalized aspect of the text (the perennial gay or slutty supporting character). In contrast, because *Buffy* was conceived with the specific purpose of targeting an underserved audience of girls, it centralizes and naturalizes non-normative gender positioning and roles (Buffy *is* the chosen one, no question) and thus makes queer dynamics part of the internal logic of the narrative itself.[2] What makes *Buffy* a unique example of queer TV is that the series not only acknowledges but actually *privileges* a broad spectrum of queer desires that are typically marginalized in prime-time television.

REVAMPING MASCULINITY: ANGEL'S IMPRESSIONABLE BODY

Angel's body is a playground for sadomasochistic fantasies: endlessly penetrable, its simultaneously hard and soft features invite viewers to linger over the erotic possibilities of the passive male. *Buffy*'s presentation of Angel's body depends on two hallmarks of the show's structure: its generic hybridity and revisionism, particularly in relation to the horror genre, and its reversals and recodings of conventional constructions of gender. As its title suggests, *Buffy*'s initial gender reversals are most obvious in its reimagining of the horror or slasher film, particularly the figure of the "Final Girl." The Girl is the only character who remains alive at the end of the slasher film by successfully destroying the monster, but only after she has suffered extreme trauma.[3] Joss Whedon, the creator of *Buffy*, is well versed in the conventions of Hollywood's gender politics and consciously revised the horror film for young female audiences by constructing a Final Girl who is defined as a superhero from the outset and whose pain, fear, and suffering are largely displaced onto a male figure, Angel.[4] In this reframing of gender, Buffy is the active, desiring character at the center of the text; she controls the gaze, and she is the agent of change propelling the narrative forward. Angel actually reinforces her strength by taking on, to an excessive degree, two roles most associated with women: the spectacularized, eroticized body and the traumatized body.[5] Angel's character not only departs from the gendered conventions of the classical Hollywood narrative model (to which most television series also subscribe), but redefines them by presenting the masculine body as not only or merely visual spectacle but as the object of continual, unrecuperated assault by young women within the narrative. Angel's real challenge to patriarchy and heteronormativity lies in the fact that his body is a fantasy space *within the text* as well as outside of it, a body to be literally inscribed with girl, queer, and gay desires.

Of all the characters' bodies in *Buffy*, Angel's body is the most displayed and eroticized. He reverses the usual spectacularization of the female body by functioning early on as Buffy's *homme fatal*, a mysterious stranger she first describes as "gorgeous," and whose body becomes the object of her gaze and that of others.[6] Angel's bare chest is displayed prominently and often in the series as both an aesthetic and an erotic object, but more importantly, the women of *Buffy* are not similarly represented as sexual objects. While Buffy's body is notably on display in terms of her trendy clothing, the camera does not fetishize her or linger on her body or that of the other female characters the way it does with Angel. A lengthy sequence at the beginning of "Band Candy," for example, portrays a half-naked Angel doing Tai Chi while Buffy secretly watches, aroused (fig. 2). Such framing was deliberately intended for the pleasure of the series' young female fans: producers admitted to fans online that they conceived this shot as eye candy, even scoring the scene to match "Angel's rippling shirtlessness."[7]

In the second season of *Buffy*, the relationship between Buffy and Angel forms the program's primary story arc and carries the weight of the narrative. This relationship, and viewer investment in it, is predicated on the naturalization of their reversed gender positioning. Although the narrative continually hints of the potential risks to Buffy if she gets sexually involved with him, Angel largely functions in the conventional female supporting (and suffering) role. Buffy acts and interacts, and he aids and is acted upon. While she has a "day job" as a high school student, occupying public (day) as well as private (night) space, he lives only for her, existing solely in private (night) space. While she actively pursues relationships with friends and boyfriends, he

Fig. 2. "I didn't know you could do that": Angel does Tai Chi, with Buffy covertly watching, "Band Candy," 10 November 1998.

is pursued solely as an object of erotic interest by Darla, his fellow vampire, and Cordelia, Buffy's high school rival. Angel's occupation of the traditional female role of the action/adventure genre climaxes in "What's My Line?," a two-part episode in which Angel is captured by the vampires Spike and Drusilla, and Buffy must rescue him. Like the male action hero whose wife and children have been threatened by outsiders, Buffy's resolve to defeat Spike is intensified by the threat to Angel: "I've had it. Spike is going down. You can attack me, you can send assassins after me, that's fine. But nobody messes with my boyfriend!" Buffy successfully rescues Angel, and the camera lingers on the spectacle of Buffy cradling the wounded, bleeding, shirtless Angel in her arms (fig. 3).

The display of Angel's wounded body is also essential to *Buffy*'s narrative redefinition of the male role. In the first season's episode "Angel," Angel defends Buffy and is wounded, and Buffy takes him home to dress his wound (which, of course, requires the removal of his shirt). But the eroticism of Angel's body here is not simply in the sight of him; *Buffy* also frequently emphasizes the softness and vulnerability of his body. The large bird tattoo on his back, which Buffy remarks upon in this scene, represents another way in which

Fig. 3. Buffy cradles the wounded Angel, "What's My Line? Part 2," 24 November 1997.

the program reappropriates "bad boy" masculine iconography to serve a feminist agenda: by pairing the tattoo with the wound, the dominant cultural connotation of body armor is here reconfigured to serve as an early and enticing indication that Angel's body is one on which impressions can be made.

The impressionable male body was a popular construct in the culturally liberal 1990s; the classically sculpted yet soft body was prevalent in advertising and television as an appeal to trendy urban dwellers, specifically gay men, straight metrosexuals, and women.[8] While these greater industrial and cultural changes helped enable *Buffy*'s presentation of Angel's body, *Buffy*'s text still significantly differs from these mainstream images in that the soft body as eye candy is not here an end in itself. Rather, the nudity and softness are just foreplay, a prerequisite for the more rewarding and transgressive assaults. The real erotic content of the show is most obvious in scenes in which Angel's body is repeatedly penetrated and traumatized, causing him to scream and writhe in agony. The paradoxical permeability and resilience of Angel's body separates him from the other shirtless hunks of the 1990s and signals *Buffy*'s reappropriation of another popular genre figure, the vampire.

Through Angel, *Buffy* reimagines the vampire of gothic horror, constructing him as a vampire *with a conscience*, a soul, thus retaining the romantic and erotically stimulating aspects of his character and body without the misogyny, homophobia, and sexual threat with which the vampire is most often portrayed. The choice of the vampire is particularly fitting, since the vampire's difference from "normal" men has often been portrayed as part of his attraction for women. The vampire seduces women so easily, it is usually implied, because he is able to satisfy their sexual appetites far better than the average man. Not surprisingly, vampires have also been favorites of queer audiences and scholars, who feel an affinity with their sexual deviance, especially the way in which the dominant culture portrays their desires as threatening and forbidden.[9] In traditional vampire tales, the woman or man who succumbs to the vampire either dies or becomes one of the loathsome undead. In *Buffy*'s version, however, it is the vampire who succumbs. Repeatedly.

Most importantly, *Buffy*'s vampire retains those aspects of the monster's body so common to gothic horror. As feminist critics have noted, bodily permeability is often characterized as monstrous because it evokes the female body, which has long been characterized culturally as impure and without boundaries, its oozing fluids making it grotesque in comparison to the closed, sleek, masculine classical body.[10] In contrast, male permeability is not monstrous or repulsive in *Buffy*, but is instead a positive characteristic, narratively necessary and unequivocally desirable to the women of the *Buffy*verse; *Buffy* repositions the female heroine as active, productive, and impenetrable in relation to a male body that is passive, non-procreative, and highly penetrable. Indeed, the text emphasizes Angel's body's impotence (because he will not feed) and its diffuseness—even his name suggests the fantastic permeability of his body, its lack of solidity. And because he does not eat, only fluids go in or out of him. Angel's body is thus a fantasy construct, a classical body but also a Christ-like, feminine one that is open, vulnerable, and subject to bleeding.[11] But unlike Christ, Angel is not just a figure to be adored with nun-like rapture—rather, *Buffy*'s narrative encourages girl viewers to act upon his body.

The permeability of Angel's body is accompanied by its resilience, another characteristic of the vampire that is here especially designed for girl erotics. Because Angel is immortal and will not die in a single narrative climax, his beauty and body can survive repeated torture and thus be enjoyed multiple times. Angel recovers quickly from wounds, often within the span of a few minutes, and generally by the end of the episode. Once he recovers, his body returns to its pristine state ("Over two hundred years of living, and so little external damage," remarks one admiring tormentor). Television's "feminine" serial nature also ensures the continuation, repetition, and variation of such pleasures, providing an alternative erotic space that can be cultivated and enjoyed for many years. Angel's trip to hell at the end of the second season necessitates, for example, an unusually long recovery period in which he is shirtless and enchained for several episodes; the serial narrative allows for audiences to become accustomed to and/or savor the new foregrounding of bondage elements in the relationship between Buffy and Angel.

Perhaps the best part of Angel's torture and bondage is that it is guilt free because, within the narrative's larger context, he deserves it. As a result of a gypsy's curse in 1900, Angel's soul was restored, so his suffering is presented as cosmic payback for his 150 years as a bloodsucking vampire who terrorized and murdered women. In other words, he now bears the burden of centuries of patriarchy. Angel continually feels the pain of what he has done and believes he deserves, on some level, any punishment he gets. The masochistic elements of his character are defined early on in the first season when, in order to kiss Buffy, he endures having the cross around her neck burn into his skin, leaving a bloody impression ("Angel").[12] Christian themes are reworked again: Angel is a Christ-like martyr figure, but his sacrifices are in the service of women, whom he has sinned against, rather than the holy male trinity.

The program's conflation of female sexual pursuit with violence and Angel's guilt neatly comes together in scenes of Angel being tortured by women, usually current, spurned, or would-be lovers. One of the program's first extended torture scenes comes in the second season at the hand of the mad female vampire Drusilla, Angel's former vampire lover ("What's My Line? Part 2"). The sadomasochistic content of this scene is obvious: Angel is tied, half-nude, to a bedpost while Dru hovers above him dripping holy water onto his chest (fig. 4). The water burns him each time, and he reacts by throwing his head back and screaming in orgasmic agony. Dru's sadism is made particularly guilt free and gratifying because it is an act of revenge—Angel made Dru a vampire and killed her whole family in the process. The suggestion of incest payback is explicitly made; as Dru's sire, Angel is both her former lover and the "father" of her vampire state. She is thus punishing him for taking away her innocence: "You've been a very bad daddy," she tells him.

Fig. 4. "You've been a very bad daddy": Drusilla tortures a bound Angel with holy water, "What's My Line? Part 2," 24 November 1997.

In such scenes, *Buffy*'s narrative historically justifies (even revels in) Angel's suffering, providing a stark contrast to the more familiar presentation of the masochistic white male in popular culture, which emphasizes his suffering while erasing his historic and continued social dominance.[13] Film versions of this narrative, for example, often feature the extensive torture and even rape of their male protagonists, but ultimately such films serve a masculinist narrative in which the hero reasserts and affirms his manhood through vengeance or triumphant escape (for example, the *Rambo* and *Lethal Weapon* series and *The Shawshank Redemption*), or by soliciting sympathy for his white male victimization, thus drawing attention away from more pressing social inequalities such as class difference, sexism, or racism (for example, *Mystic River*, *The Prince of Tides*, and *Falling Down*).

In the *Buffy*verse, however, the wounded, masochistic man is the ideal man, the man for all seasons. *Buffy* does not need to recuperate scenes of Angel's torture because these moments are significantly presented as desirable and fun. Thus, for *Buffy*'s viewers, the series's strategy of queering the masculine role makes possible an opening up rather than a closing down of alternative sexual roles and practices that are denied by much of mainstream culture.[14] Moreover, *Buffy*'s seriality allowed producers to nurture and develop their reconceptualization of the masculine role over many years, naturalizing their fantasy man and slowly unveiling the erotic possibilities his penetration offered their impressionable young viewers.

THE STAKES OF QUEER DESIRE

While *Buffy*'s conflation of sexual desire and penetration is hardly new to the vampire genre, these elements have rarely been put in the service of teenage girl erotics in ways that open up queer avenues of exploration. For *Buffy* is simultaneously about the expression and complexity of adolescent female desire and the pleasure of acting upon other bodies, particularly through "staking." *Buffy* gives girls permission both to fantasize and to enact non-normative sexual activity, especially variations on penetrating both male and female subjects. However, if *Buffy* remained merely on the level of utopian sexuality, it would lack resonance with viewers, who know that such achievements do not come without tremendous risks and costs. Indeed, much of the show's emotional power comes from its frequent acknowledgment of the fleeting and fragile nature of illicit desires. Like any effective serial, it both gives and takes away, offering tantalizing transgressions of gender and sexuality that are both haunted and fueled by the threat of reversal. Thus the intensity of Buffy's attachment to Angel, her adolescent fears and longings, become even more urgent because they also represent extratextual anxieties about the difficulties of sustaining *Buffy*'s new queer erotics in a straight (TV) world.

In the *Buffy*verse, girls are both narrative and sexual "tops." Buffy, Willow, Cordelia, Faith, and Anya are the program's active romantic pursuers, and they savor the control they have over their sexual and social interactions with their love objects. The first scene of the series reveals this romantic reversal, as the vampire Darla penetrates (through biting and drinking the blood of) a boy she has lured on a date. Similarly, the show's conflation of the woman as slayer and romantic aggressor is articulated clearly by Cordelia, who remarks to Buffy during her pursuit of Angel, "You may be hot stuff when it comes to demonology or whatever, but when it comes to dating, I'm the slayer" ("Halloween"). Cordelia continually refers to boys as vulnerable objects to be finessed by her; while the text often punishes her for her bitchiness, her dating confidence is a source of envy within the text and pleasure and empowerment by viewers.

When the series eventually portrays actual sex, girls are almost always on top (and when they are not, there is literal hell to pay, as we shall see). Remarkably, girls on *Buffy* decide if, when, and how they will be penetrated by boys: Faith instructs Xander in sexual techniques ("The Zeppo"), while Anya approaches him for sex repeatedly in her characteristically pragmatic fashion (in one notable instance, through crude hand gestures). When more passion is involved, the girls always initiate, and such scenarios typically involve the boys being beaten soundly beforehand. Willow shoots and subdues the werewolf Oz, for example, before any kissing between them takes place ("Phases"). In one of the most intense moments of the series, Buffy pounds Angel repeatedly in the face until he agrees to "feed off her" to save his life (he would just as soon die). Buffy's romantic and erotic action is rewarded when Angel gives her an orgasm that remains the true climax of the third season ("Graduation Day, Part 2"). In an equally shocking scene from the sixth season, Buffy beats her vampire-lover Spike (Angel's replacement) silly before triumphantly mounting and riding him to her prolonged climax. Even as the intensity of their passion causes the house to fall down around them, Buffy remains on top of Spike throughout, continuing to grind away as they literally fall through the floor ("Smashed").

While these scenes are heterosexual, they are not heteronormative. Instead, they offer girls an opportunity to be sexual aggressors without the penalty of being considered "bad" or "scary" girls, even if some of the decisions they make do not always work out so well. These acts, however, also serve as a gateway to other forms of non-normative sexual activity, specifically lesbian sex. The lesbian writer Dorothy Allison has written fondly of how the science fiction and fantasy novels that consumed her as a girl spurred her erotic imagination by providing similar examples of female aggression.[15] What is unusual about *Buffy* is that the producers actually turn lesbian subtext into text on camera, as Willow identifies herself as "gay" in the second half of the series and enjoys two long-term lesbian relationships. *Buffy* thus risked losing viewers in order to show the variety of erotic possibilities open to girls, eventually "slashing itself" to make explicit the sexual alternatives the text offers.[16] The value and significance of such alternatives, however, were indicated much earlier in the text by the relationship between Angel and Buffy, when, midway through the program's second season, the pleasures of the text's reversed gender positioning are suddenly, shockingly, taken away.

In *Buffy*, the emergence of normative masculinity is presented as monstrous and tragic. In the episodes "Surprise" and "Innocence," Angel and Buffy make love. Because he has attained perfect happiness, Angel loses his soul and reverts to his evil vampire state. In the horror film genre, the often gender deviant monster threatens normalcy; in *Buffy*, it is the pleasures and comforts of *difference* that now become threatened by normalcy. By making Angel a real "monster" in narrative terms and by restoring the conventions of action and horror—making Angel active and Buffy reactive, Angel the stalker and Buffy the stalked—*Buffy*'s text is transformed from one of idealized female empowerment and romance to one of profound grief and loss. The gravity achieved in the second season (remarked upon by several critics) is due to the way in which the loss of Angel's permeable body and the restoration of gender hierarchies this signifies expose and accentuate the value of *Buffy*'s generic transgressions. When Angel "turns," his vulnerability and the pleasures of his soft body disappear, and the viewer no longer has access to them. Although ostensibly still a vampire, his body becomes coded along more conventional masculine lines: hard, violent, defensive, and impenetrable.

This transformation is worth examining in some detail. Whedon has called these two episodes "the mission statement" of the show, and they focus on the events leading up to and directly following Buffy's and Angel's first sexual intercourse. In "Surprise," Buffy and Angel cannot keep their hands off each other; they face a crisis together, and the episode movingly climaxes with Angel giving Buffy a claddagh ring and declaring his love for her. As soon as they have sex, however (with Angel on top—an act significantly portrayed in flashback after his change), everything changes. His act of sexual penetration reverses the gender dynamics of the program, and he becomes as physically threatening as he was non-threatening before. In a single episode, "Innocence," he viciously bites and drains the blood of a prostitute (in the style of Jack the Ripper), nearly strangles Willow, kills a gypsy wise man, and kicks and punches Buffy, at one point slamming her up against the wall. The literal rise of Angel as a bad alpha male is accompanied, narratively, by the physical incapacity of the female characters: Drusilla falls to the floor in agony and ecstasy as he is transformed, while Buffy curls up into a fetal position on her bed and weeps.

The transformation of Angel's body is made explicit in "Innocence"'s most pivotal scene. Buffy, not knowing Angel has transformed, goes to his room, and he pretends that their sexual encounter meant nothing to him. The emotional power of this exchange resonated with fans and critics because the fantasy space Angel had represented suddenly disappears, replaced by a literal and painfully all-too-human morning-after reality. Angel reverts to being a "typical" guy who tells a girl he loves her to get her into bed, then betrays her by emotionally withdrawing and dumping her. The scene doubly reinforces the horror of such a moment, for as Angel torments Buffy with words, he puts on his clothes, constructing a barrier not only between him and Buffy but between him and the viewer, one that emphasizes both the character's and the viewer's loss of access to his body. This point is again made at the end of the episode, where Buffy confronts Angel, fights with him, and finds she does not have the heart to stake him: "You can't do it. You can't kill me," he taunts. His body can no longer be penetrated by her or by anyone. Instead, he has to be fought like a boy, and she kicks him in the crotch.

For the rest of the second season, Angel remains a violent killer, every girl's nightmare. He continues to exemplify characteristics associated with dominant masculinity: he smokes, calls women "baby," manhandles Dru, and stalks Buffy and her friends. In "Passion," a particularly traumatic episode, Angel snaps the neck of the recurring character Jenny Calendar—a more belittling act than feeding on her. He then becomes the voyeur to Buffy's pain (another normative reversal of *Buffy*'s gender practices) by standing outside her house and watching as she and Willow sob over the news of Miss Calendar's death. When he is briefly inhabited by a female ghost, Angel vigorously scrubs off the taint of having been "violated"; now adhering to rules for masculine behavior, he prizes his hard body.

While the second season climaxes fittingly with the restoration of Angel's soul and of the program's original dynamics, the price is high. Because of Bad Angel's actions, his death is now required to save the world. The final act of the season is Buffy's penetration of Angel with a sword, an act she performs almost immediately after he has returned to his original vulnerable state (fig. 5). Buffy's heartbreaking sacrifice conforms to the program's heroic narrative, but the fleeting presence of the old Angel in this scene reminds viewers of both the rewards and the risks of loving beyond social boundaries.

This cycle of intense transgressive passion and heartbreaking loss is repeated

Fig. 5. "I told him that I loved him . . . and I kissed him . . . and I killed him":
Buffy stabs Angel, sending him to hell, "Becoming, Part 2," 19 May 1998.

when Angel permanently leaves the program at the end of the third season, which again signals a loss of queer erotics. Angel's absence is all the more acute for fans because the opportunities for queer activity his body has made possible are strikingly obvious by the limitations of his replacement, soldier-boy Riley. Buffy has to be careful with Riley's all-too-human body, which is too fragile to sustain Angel-style intrusions. Although he gamely removed his shirt more than once, Riley could not satisfy fans who expected and desired more from *Buffy* than male body spectacle. Fans despised Riley until, tellingly, he became broody and depressed and started letting female vamps bite him and drink his blood. He departed the series in the middle of the fifth season, with comparatively little sense of loss.

Since *Buffy*'s queer relationships were those championed by fans and most easily accommodated by its feminist narrative, it is not surprising that Riley was quickly replaced as Buffy's beau by the vampire Spike (a fan favorite), who fit Angel's queer blueprint beautifully and proceeded to take on Angel's previous functions as a lover and an aid to Buffy and a suffering and erotic object for Buffy. Spike endures extended and highly intrusive torture sessions in the last two seasons of *Buffy*, in once instance to become en-souled like Angel and thus worthy of Buffy's love. If anything, his masochism is even more pronounced; Marti Noxon, *Buffy*'s producer, noted that "the whole notion that, because Buffy can beat him up like nobody else, he's madly in love with her, just sort of fit Spike's character. He needs this kind of abuse from a woman."[17] So popular did Spike become with *Buffy*'s fans that industry executives considered him essential to the fifth season renewal of *Angel* after *Buffy*'s demise, where he offered yet another potential homoerotic pairing in what had become, by then, quite a testosterone-laden affair.

GAY IS THE NEW BLACK:
ANGEL'S "WEST HOLLYWOOD LIFESTYLE"

Unlike its committed feminist mother text, *Angel* does not have a specific ideological framework; the gender politics of the program constantly changed over its five years on the WB network (producers almost yearly referred to the program as finally "coming into its own"). But as a spin-off, the show initially maintained narrative, industrial, and audience ties with *Buffy*, which greatly influenced the generic development and erotics of the new show. *Angel*'s first two seasons, which I will focus on here, most closely replicate *Buffy*'s appreciation of Angel's queer body and its deployment of the penetrable male body to critique normative masculinity and explore the instabilities of contemporary gender categories. Like *Buffy*, *Angel*'s flexible approach to gender and genre nurtures and accommodates a number of queer characters and situations. In *Angel*'s West Hollywood world, however, penetrating girls are supporting characters; instead, the centrality of Angel's queer body jacks up the homoerotic content of the program, giving Angel's relationships with men a sexual tension that distinguishes the series from *Buffy*. Producers' deliberate gay coding was wildly popular among fans, who actively promoted slash readings of the text, resulting in the increased awareness and popularity of slash generally and the proliferation of such practices by television producers.

When *Angel* debuted on the WB network in the fall of 1999, it connected to *Buffy* on many fronts: the programs followed each other on the same Tuesday evening, and they shared many staff members, including several writer-producers. *Angel* was textually tied to *Buffy* through crossover characters and plots that depended on audience viewership of both programs (indeed, the climax of *Angel*'s second season assumes the viewers' knowledge of Buffy's death the hour before). *Buffy*'s fans and the critical community wanted to continue to take pleasure in those aspects of Angel they had previously enjoyed, specifically those moments that drew on the spectacle of Angel's body and his suffering. The producers of *Angel* were unusually responsive to fan feedback and quickly shifted those moments from the margins to the center by the middle of the first season. As a result of the connection between *Buffy* and *Angel*, *Angel* veered from its original conception as an action/anthology series ("less of a Soap Opera than *Buffy*," Whedon had suggested) to a serial format emphasizing Angel's angst-ridden personal history and increasingly focused on Angel's body as an aesthetic, erotic, masochistic and—in *Angel*'s most innovative move—comic spectacle.[18]

In these first two seasons, *Angel*, like *Buffy*, transcends and deconstructs contemporary boundaries between normative and deviant bodies. Instead of ignoring Angel's complexity, the producers revel in it, presenting his body through multiple narrative frames that simultaneously revere and mock it, traumatize and tease it, queer it and straighten it out again. This flexibility allows for a wide range of viewing positions in relation to Angel's body, although three seem to dominate: normative (valorized as heroic), critical (mocking the normative) and gay/queer (homoerotic object and/or penetrable plaything). While these positions are not uncommon, especially in the television programs that followed and imitated *Angel*, *Angel*'s text *is* unusual in that the critical and queer positions remain equally valid and narratively interdependent—they are not used to buttress normative masculinity but to provide valid, often preferable, alternatives to it.

In its original anthology concept and debut, however, *Angel*'s narrative and Angel's persona differed from *Buffy*'s text in important ways.[19] Just by being the hero (instead of Buffy), Angel becomes the most powerful active agent in the text, and in these first episodes his body takes on many of the characteristics of a typical action hero or superhero without the feminist twist: a rational, natural leader who effectively uses brute force and ingenuity to quell his enemies by the end of each episode. He seems to have even more physical strength and agility than he did on *Buffy*, jumping from multi-story buildings without injury. His quick recovery here suggests masculine indestructibility rather than boy-toy availability because it is not specifically used to feed the desires of young female sadists, who are largely replaced by a succession of young blond women whom Angel rescues.

Yet even in these initial episodes, the heroic body is complicated by the influence of the series' own brand of film noir and its continuing narrative of

redemption. Whedon has identified the recovering alcoholic as *Angel*'s dominant metaphor, and *Angel*'s urban setting, the main character's status as a de-
tective and enforcer (working outside the law), and the use of flashbacks to account for his personal demons and reveal his character's troubled past all attest
to noir's influence. This generic choice is significant because noir, like melodrama and horror, traffics in characters who are traumatized and for whom
normative relationships and domestic bliss are unattainable.[20]

What makes *Angel*'s noir unusual is that, like *Buffy*, the show changes some
of the rules of the noir genre by suggesting that damaged masculinity and the
noir world are *preferable* to possible alternatives. This is not (yet) a text about
anxious masculinity or one that mourns the demise of dominant white masculinity. Rather, *Angel*'s text celebrates the character's (and his body's) continued
trauma because it is essential to preserving his humanity, specifically his ability
to empathize with others. His body continues to be the object of sadistic attention, and he continues to feel deserving of it. Given the chance to become
invincible in an early episode ("In the Dark"), Angel relinquishes the opportunity because it will put him out of touch with people who are suffering and
who need his help.

Moreover, *Angel*'s noir world is shown to be preferable to traditional domesticity. The program queers normative social relationships by having Angel
repeatedly identify his work partners Cordelia and Wesley as his chosen family,
and the bond between this group is the emotional center of the show. In *Angel*
as in *Buffy*, it is the straight humans, especially straight men, who are revealed
to be perverts or demons and must be policed. Cordelia, for example, is impregnated with demon spawn by her one-night-stand in the first season ("Expecting," a replay in many ways of *Buffy*'s "Innocence"). Demons are equally
in need of help in Angel's world; his status as a nonhuman gives him more license to embrace deviance, and *Angel* "humanizes" many of its demon characters (even making them regular players, like the demon half-breed Doyle of the
first season). For example, the episode "I've Got You Under My Skin" presents
a queer twist on *The Exorcist*: in a case of apparent possession, a demon begs
Angel to pull him out of a sociopathic child, who turns out to be the real monster. As in *Buffy*, dominant masculinity is particularly hard hit in *Angel*, which
features a parade of bad fathers, abusive boyfriends, and, its central villains,
evil corporate lawyers.

In contrast, gay masculinity and homoerotic attraction are not pathologized; indeed, *Angel* exposes and celebrates the queer subtext of the noir genre. Although a typical urban noir labyrinth in many ways, Los Angeles is shown to be a refuge for "deviants" like Angel, whose character's roots in the gay aesthetics of the 1990s are made explicit in scenes in which he is the object of gay desire or assumed to be gay. "You are a beautiful, beautiful man," says a gay agent to *Angel* in the premiere episode. "Thank you," Angel replies straightforwardly. When female characters think he is gay, Angel is equally unperturbed. Significantly, the program blurs the line between gay and straight desire by suggesting Angel's attractiveness to his male co-worker Doyle, who is otherwise marked as straight. Doyle describes Angel's "long coat flowing behind him in that mysterious and attractive way," and Cordelia prompts Doyle to admit, "Maybe I am a little attracted."

In addition to making men more active admirers of Angel's body, *Angel* also connects him with the codes of West Hollywood's gay subculture by continually foregrounding Angel's gym muscles, meticulous grooming, impeccable wardrobe, and refined tastes (for a straight audience, Angel was "metrosexual" before the term was coined). Where *Buffy* only hinted at the importance of clothes to Angel, Angel makes clear that his jock body is actually housing a dandy, a persona he shares with contemporary West Hollywood gay men.[21] Angel collects art and antiques, draws, reads, continues to do Tai Chi, and is highly self-conscious about his appearance. While other characters appreciate the effect of Angel's perfectly cut T-shirts and sweaters and carefully styled hair, they also affectionately chide him for his vanity, especially Cordelia, who refuses to indulge in Angel's would-be idea of himself as the epitome of masculine "cool."

Angel's heroic body is also kept in check by putting him in situations where his body is spectacularly humiliated, where he suffers not just the expected slings and arrows a hero must endure but, much more troubling to masculine norms, the threat of public dancing and singing Barry Manilow tunes. The most significant of these scenes is the beginning of the episode "She," midway in the first season. During a party, Angel is asked to dance. The camera goes inside Angel's head for a few moments as he thinks about himself dancing, a hilarious blend of overwrought rhythmic movements, while all the party guests gape at him appalled (fig. 6). He refuses the invitation, although the episode's closing credits feature extended clips of Angel's bad dancing inter-

Fig. 6. Angel's spastic dancing, "She," 8 February 2000.

cut with his partner Wesley's equally awkward efforts, linking the two men as nerdy comic spectacle.

This scene reifies Angel's straight masculinity (he is such a man that he cannot dance) only to mock him for it. The noir and action codes of the series are here replaced with those of the musical, a genre in which Angel's body cannot be heroically active; instead of being the leader comfortably in charge, he is visibly uncomfortable and inhibited. The scene was not simply a fleeting moment of subversive commentary, quickly forgotten; instead, it was celebrated by both fans and producers, who recognized it as a key moment in the development of Angel's character and a new direction for the series as a whole. The "Angel Dancing Scene," as it came to be referred to by online fans of *Buffy* and *Angel*, became the most popular moment in the show that season. *Angel*'s fans recognized this scene as part of their concept of Angel; they reveled in Angel's discomfort and made continual reference to his "cute," "adorable," and "geeky" dancing (not exactly the words usually used to refer to a superhero). *Angel*'s producers also widely publicized the scene; instead of action scenes being used to promote the program on talk shows, David Boreanaz's guest spots featured the dancing scene.

The dancing scene works because it both draws from and builds upon

Fig. 7. Angel reluctantly sings Barry Manilow's "Mandy," even while he admits to the Host, "I kinda think it's pretty," "Judgment," 26 September 2000.

Angel's character on *Buffy*, in which his body's masculine display is not over-bearing or triumphant, but is always tied to the character's suffering and self-abasement. *Angel* adds new generic frameworks for the torment of its title character by including musical and comedy dimensions; Angel's body is thus tested by dance music and social interaction as much as it is by hot pokers and bad memories. The formula set up in the dancing scene decisively shapes the second season, the tone of which is established in its remarkably queer opening scene: a green demon, a literal "lounge lizard," picks up a microphone and sings an accomplished a cappella version of "I Will Survive." This character, known as the Host, runs a karaoke bar/demon sanctuary, where he does readings for guests who "bare their souls" by singing. The Host becomes Angel's mentor and guide through the rest of the season after this initial episode, in which Angel is forced to again make a spectacle of himself by singing a very bad rendition of Barry Manilow's "Mandy" so that the Host can "read" him (fig. 7). Angel's singing, like his dancing, was repeated in the show's credits and shopped around the talk shows; it was a huge hit with the fans as well; their pleasure in Angel's torment is most obvious in one fan's gushes: "Angel singing? It's sooo awful and wonderful at the same time!"[22]

Musical moments of Angel's humiliation continue throughout the season, framed specifically by the queer demon bar and its flaming green Host, who is heavily marked as gay.[23] In doing so, *Angel*'s producers cleverly appropriate a "straight" musical practice, the karaoke bar, and queer it, turning it into a "sanctuary" for demons called "Caritas" (which Angel translates incorrectly as Latin for "mercy"—it is actually "charity"), where queer characters (chiefly demons) thrive while normative masculine pretensions are exposed and critiqued (weapons are not allowed). The Host's critiques of Angel's moments of arrogance and narcissism are always validated by the text, and he also continually foregrounds Angel's body, commenting on Angel's clothes and mood in terms of both desire ("Smart *and* cute") and envy ("How fabulous would I look in that coat?"), and invents pet names for him ("Angelcakes").

Queer boys aren't Angel's only critics, however. Angel's traditional tormentors, sadistic girls, return full-force in the second season. Where queerness functioned primarily as an element of reception in the first season (homoeroticism especially), in the second season it became a key structuring agent in the narrative due to the continuing presence in the second season of Sunnydale *femme fatale* vampires Darla and Drusilla, who replaced the guest-star damsels. Darla and Drusilla mark both the continued strong female presence in the program and its full embrace of serial melodrama. Darla instigates a narrative arc in which her temptation and torment of Angel almost drive him to the dark side (signaled by his sudden smoking and obsessive working out). While the results are not always progressive (particularly regarding racial difference)[24] or as conceptually clear-cut as *Buffy*'s feminist approach, *Angel*'s second season is its queerest and its closest to *Buffy*'s gender politics. Angel is presented as a highly flawed hero throughout most of the second season: he makes arrogant mistakes, grieves, alienates himself from his crew, is staked and impaled by female and male characters, and allows Darla and Dru to kill a roomful of people. Frequent flashbacks to Angel's "bad-boy" past are central, underlining Angel's past misdeeds (the better to torture him with), and further emphasizing the dangers of dominant masculinity.

Not coincidentally, the return of strong women to Angel sparked renewed attention to Angel's naked body. While the writers for *Angel*'s first season thought they needed clever excuses to peel off his clothing (like sudden showers), the second season makes Angel's passive nudity integral to the narrative. Angel is both shirtless and prone for much of the first half of the second season as Darla visits him in his bed and in dreams, seducing him. She is the

Fig. 8. "I could eat you up": Darla seduces a drugged Angel, "First Impressions," 10 October 2000.

aggressor in these scenes, running ice over his pectoral muscles and sitting on top of him; "I could eat you up," she says triumphantly as he lies sleeping under her (fig. 8). In later scenes during the season, she becomes more sadistic, at one point running a stake through Angel. Even when he inevitably sleeps with her in an aggressive sex scene (but thankfully does not lose his soul), she frames the encounter in terms of her triumph over him: "You gave yourself over so completely. I felt you surrender."

The melodramatic move in *Angel*'s second season puts more emphasis on the relationships between characters, and this in addition to the greater queer content of the show gives all of Angel's relationships with men an even greater homoerotic charge. Suggestive scenes, sexually ambiguous characters, and open-ended dialogue encourage homoerotic readings of almost every relationship in the show: Angel and his partners Wesley and Gunn; Wes and Gunn with each other; Angel and his main rival, Lindsey; Darla and Drusilla. Indeed, the now well-known thread "Homoeroticism, Yeah!" ("HoYay!" for short) on the televisionwithoutpity.com website was begun by fans of *Angel* in order to address the plethora of "slash" available for program viewers.[25] The renewed focus on Angel's manly but frequently nude and penetrable body creates a great deal of sexual tension between him and the men on the show who desire or envy him (basically, all of them). For example, when Lindsey comes on to Darla, she suggests, "It's not me you want to screw, it's him, Angel," and he does not contradict her. Indeed, the producers often back up such readings online, and the text provides quite a lot of evidence that this is indeed the case, since Angel and Lindsey frequently engage in passionate teasing, gratuitous hair-pulling, and sadistically tinged beatings and strangulations. The playfulness, ambiguity, and gender-inclusive pleasures of such scenes, however, seriously diminish in the last three seasons of the show, as Angel begins to take on more normative "adult" responsibilities: he becomes a father.

"HO NO!": THE MIXED LEGACY OF *BUFFY*'S BLUEPRINT

The values and uniqueness of *Buffy*'s queer spaces are most obvious, sadly, in how rare they remain in the television landscape. Despite *Buffy*'s undeniable influence promoting queer politics and erotics, none of the programs that have followed it have managed to sustain its critique of normative masculinity or produce a comparable alternative fantasy masculinity. Without *Buffy*'s feminist framework to anchor its gender politics, even *Angel* eventually shifted from its gender-fluid, girl-friendly queer aesthetic to a masculinist, patriarchal one readable, more narrowly, as straight or gay-coded. The more *Angel*'s producers asserted that the program was "coming into its own," the more it abandoned *Buffy*'s feminist frames and vampire rules (and, notably, *Buffy*'s female writing staff). The year *Buffy* moved to the UPN network, Angel discovered that he was somehow able to reproduce and he sired a son from a one-night stand with the vampire Darla, who nobly staked herself in order to give their son Connor life ("The one good thing we've ever done together") during the episode "Lullaby."

This scene encapsulates the way later episodes of *Angel* "right" many of the gender reversals *Buffy* had initiated. The program develops a strong nostalgia and longing for a "real family" as a naturalized nuclear family. Because Angel is a more normative patriarch, his body, now fatherly and therefore erotically off limits (unlike Dru's vampire "daddy"), goes back under wraps. And when he is tortured—which is much less often in these later seasons—he often remains fully clothed and impenetrable (much to the dismay of online fans).[26] While the superhero remains in fraught relationships with both his son and his partners, the visible physical and emotional suffering that Angel has endured passes instead to the supporting characters: the leaner, brainier, and more conventionally vulnerable partner, Wesley, and the "muscle" of the program, the African American Gunn.[27] *Angel*'s female characters fare even worse: all either die or become hot-looking demons that toss around the men with abandon but have little subjectivity. In short, the women become boy fantasies. Penetrating girls become penetrated girls. Cordelia's trajectory here is particularly disheartening; the lone regular female transplant from *Buffy* pays for her desire to redeem her bitchy ways by being deceived, impregnated, demonized, put in a coma, and then killed, after a mystical comeback in which she acts as a supportive guide for "her man," Angel. "Feminine" men also take a hit, as Caritas is destroyed and the Host becomes instead a supportive "aunt" character with much less authority (although at least he is allowed to live).

While fans still get pleasure from conventional homoerotic "slash" readings of the now almost solely male characters, such readings noticeably diminish from those of earlier seasons. *Angel*'s producers remained aware of fans' interest in the homoeroticism of the show, but its presentation changed from the early seasons to the later ones: it became driven more by producers than by fans, more by dialogue than by characters, and ultimately, I would argue, it became pandering and cynical. Gay references abound in later episodes of *Angel*, but they are not developed, nor do they act as critiques. In fact, such references more often function in the later episodes of *Angel* as the type of ambiguously homoerotic and/or phobic jokes found in more conventional action texts, the kind used to deflect, rather than develop, homoerotic relationships.[28] The combination of serial melodramatic fantasy, homoerotic references, marginalized women, and the abandonment of feminist and queer politics results in a text that is more normatively masculine, even hypermasculine, but at the same time still readable as gay and containing elements appealing to gay viewers.

Sadly, it is this later version of *Angel*, not the *Buffy* version, that has been most influential in the television universe. The "boy soaps" that blanket the television landscape as of this writing (for example, *Smallville*, *The OC*, *Everwood*, *Jack and Bobby*, and *Supernatural*) emphasize normative familial bonds (especially fraternity and paternity) over community, foreground "slash-friendly" homoerotic elements, and relegate female characters to conventional supportive and ornamental roles; the expression of female adolescent sexual desire of any brand is remarkably absent or presented entirely, for girls, as a relationship stepping stone.[29] Of these, the fellow WB series *Smallville* seems most directly inspired by *Angel*'s eventual generic model, revolving around a male superhero whose relationships with other men are central to a serial text in a way that is both openly acknowledged by producers as readably gay and eagerly consumed by fans as homoerotic. *Smallville*, however, also demonstrates the limitations of slash in a televisual environment in which it is often paired with reactionary gender politics (and one in which *Buffy*'s portrayal of actual lesbian and queer relationships makes it much less transgressive than it had once seemed). Not surprisingly, *Buffy*'s permeable, femme-friendly male is absent in these new boy soaps; the indestructibility of *Smallville*'s Clark Kent, whose "man of steel" notably cannot be penetrated even by a doctor's needle, contrasts sharply with Angel's permeable masculinity.

Buffy's influence is more noticeable in aspects of the few female-centered programs on television that followed it, such as *Veronica Mars*, *Alias*, *Dead Like Me*, *Wonderfalls*, *Tru Calling*, and *Joan of Arcadia*. While these programs all offer smart female leads and often incorporate female fantasy elements, none employs the consistently feminist frame, fantasy masculinity, or queer inclusiveness that *Buffy*'s viewers enjoyed. And sadly, the precarious network status and short runs of most of them suggest the challenges involved, textually and industrially, in sustaining programming that is merely female-centered, let alone queer-friendly.[30]

Given such challenges, the presence of *Buffy*'s new queer erotics on commercial television was and remains all the more remarkable. Angel's body inaugurated a new type of television male, one who served largely to undermine and critique masculine dominance and normalcy—on *Buffy*, through a feminist reversal of television gender and genre traditions, and in *Angel*'s early years, through a continual troubling of the same. While both texts allow for moments of mourning for his vampire character's lack of humanity, it is clear that making Angel a "real boy" is ultimately undesirable. The disappearance of such pliable models of masculinity in television since only highlights the significance and originality of *Buffy*'s gender transgressions, the way in which carefully crafted television can indeed provide viewers with alternative sexual and gender positionings—and in doing so charge their erotic imaginations and change their lives.[31]

NOTES

1. Angel's whiteness is central to his being perceived as erotic in a normative sense. While I am arguing that Angel's body in *Buffy* and *Angel* serves feminist, critical, and queer ends, it can do so only because it also appears to embody white masculine aesthetics (as Buffy does for femininity), even if Angel is supposedly also a vampire (and therefore ripe for queering).

2. Joss Whedon, the creator of *Buffy*, has often acknowledged the way in which he explicitly developed Buffy to be a heroine for girls because of the lack of young female heroines in

movies and television, particularly in typically male genres such as action, fantasy, and horror. *Buffy* was one of several television texts in the 1990s that began finally to target girls and young women by making teenage girls and their particular concerns central to their texts, most famously in the ABC series *My So-Called Life* (1994–95). For a discussion of the industrial development of such programs, see Mary Celeste Kearney's essay in this volume, and Murray, "Saving Our So-Called Lives."

3. Clover, *Men, Women and Chainsaws*, 17.

4. Whedon has spoken of his desire to rework the conventions of the horror genre according to a feminist framework in many interviews, among them, his commentary and interviews in the introduction to *Buffy*'s first season (VHS and DVD) and Bravo's *TV Revolution* (which was directed by Marijane Miller and Elise Pearlstein, 2004).

5. While *Buffy*'s version of the erotic *and* continually penetrable male is an original creation, Hollywood cinema has a long history of representing male bodies as both erotic and homoerotic spectacle, especially in genre films such as horror, film noir, musicals, action, and melodrama. These genres seek to appeal to viewers through shocking depictions of sexual deviance (horror and noir), spectacles of male dancers in tight costumes (musicals), heroic activity and corporeal tests (action), and arousing depictions of male beauty, nakedness, and vulnerability (melodrama), all of which *Buffy* draws from in creating Angel. See Cohan, *Masked Men*; Dyer, *A Matter of Images*; Studlar, *This Mad Masquerade*; Tasker, *Spectacular Bodies*; Jeffords, *Hard Bodies*; Weigman, *American Anatomies*; and Cohan and Harke, *Screening the Male*.

6. Angel's status as a mystery object of desire is reinforced through star discourse on the actor, David Boreanaz, that emphasizes his being "discovered" in the style of Lana Turner while walking his dog. In comparison, the star discourse on Sarah Michelle Gellar emphasizes her many years of experience and hard work in the industry before *Buffy*. See, for example, the official show companion, Golden and Holder, *Buffy the Vampire Slayer*.

7. Bronzebeta.com VIP Posting Board, 11 November 1998.

8. As Susan Bordo has argued, gay male aesthetics are at the root of these portraits (typified by Calvin Klein's underwear ads) of highly masculinized yet openly eroticized young men in attitudes of "male sexual supplication" that would have seemed unmanly to earlier generations. Bordo, *The Male Body*, 168–93. Versions of the more vulnerable but gym-primed male body on television in the 1990s include the flashes of male nudity on *NYPD Blue*, the bulked-up chest of lead actors in legal dramas such as that of *The Practice*'s Dylan McDermott, the boy-men of teen shows such as *90210*'s Luke Perry and Jason Priestly, the good fathers of domestic dramas such as that played by *thirtysomething*'s Ken Olin, and the soulful investigators of genre programs such as that played by *The X-Files*'s David Duchovny. While individual episodes of these programs may be considered feminist or queer, they are ·still operating within an overall framework in which the baring of male flesh is a largely hegemonic adaptation that still rarely allows for any consistently feminist or queer portrayals of male-female relationships. They do, however, allow for increased homoeroticism.

9. Case, "Tracking the Vampire," 10.

10. The monster in gothic horror is "a remarkably mobile, permeable, infinitely interpretable body." Halberstam, *Skin Shows*, 21. For discussions of the cultural construction of women's bodies, see Russo, *Female Grotesques*; and Douglas, *Purity and Danger*.

11. Angel's Irish Catholicism, emphasized in flashbacks on both *Buffy* and *Angel*, and his "sad young man" persona make the martyr imagery particularly resonant. This is also another

way in which Angel's character overlaps with gay aesthetics, since gay artists and writers have also usefully appropriated Christian images, such as that of Saint Sebastian. Dyer, *A Matter of Images*, 42. For more on Angel's Irishness, see Meaney, "Dead, White and Male."

12. In the seventh season, the vampire Spike repeats this gesture more emphatically by wrapping his arms around a cross ("Beneath You").

13. For a discussion of male masochism/suffering/recuperation in mainstream Hollywood films, see Smith, "Eastwood Bound," 87–88; and Robinson, *Marked Men*, 6.

14. Although such erotic possibilities are very likely new for many of *Buffy*'s young viewers, the embrace of an eroticized and tortured male star by a mass female audience has historical precedents within American visual culture. As Miriam Hansen's work on the female fan cult of Rudolph Valentino in the 1920s suggests, voyeuristic and sadistic viewing positions have not been limited to male viewers, although Valentino was not penetrated by women *within the text*. Hansen, *Babel and Babylon*.

15. "Alyx [the heroine] climbed on top of that boy and enjoyed herself. . . . This wasn't about coding or veiled references. It was flatly heterosexual but still seemed to offer tacit encouragement to female sexual desire and female sexual aggression. I thought it applied to lesbians as much as anybody." Allison, *Skin*, 98.

16. "Slash," as Henry Jenkins has defined it, "refers to the convention of employing a stroke or 'slash' to signify a same-sex relationship between two characters"; this homoerotic pairing of characters originated as a reception practice ("slash readings") and incorporates both physical and emotional aspects of the characters' relationship to each other. Jenkins, *Textual Poachers*, 186. For an in-depth analysis of queer texts that "slash themselves," see Wlodarz, "Maximum Insecurity."

17. Quoted in *TV Zone* 35, 20. Dominic May, "Judgment on *Angel*," *TV Zone* 135 (2000), 4.

18. Joss Whedon, quoted in Edward Gross, "Angel Gets His Wings," *TV Zone* 115 (1999), 19. In a BBC interview from the same year, David Boreanaz also emphasized the more "boy" friendly bent of the new show, targeting a broader audience than *Buffy* and incorporating action genre elements: "fast cars, lots of speed, lots of gadgets, humor, and beautiful women."

19. Other writers on *Angel* also cite film noir as the show's primary generic inspiration. See "Last Call" and "Number One with a Bullet."

20. Dyer, *A Matter of Images*, 61.

21. The video of *Angel*'s first two seasons, "My West Hollywood Lifestyle (Whatever)," by the online fan Luminosity, brilliantly details how easily *Angel*'s narrative and iconography can be read as that of a West Hollywood gay man.

22. "aliCe" at www.buffy.com, 26 September 2000.

23. The Host, whose fabulous singing abilities, colorful wardrobe, witty banter, and worship of black female singers (and Elton John) marks him as gay, is a figure of both power and benevolence. He also is clearly aligned with *Angel*'s audience on several occasions.

24. While the queer-friendliness of the second season and its stronger critique of Angel's superhero persona facilitate more progressive readings of the text, this is accomplished against the program's less successful attempts to incorporate an African American character (Charles Gunn) and a critique of racism. Having set up aggressive masculinity as pathological, *Angel*'s text does not distinguish between dominant white forms and oppressed black ones; Gunn is stereotypically presented as a dangerously out of control black body who

must be reigned in and domesticated by Angel's crew. While the program at times critiques its white characters' ignorance of racial issues, Gunn's "taming" and the uneasy juxtaposition of his world with Angel's does much to belie these attempts, and Gunn's character gets more confused and more troubling as the program develops.

25. As Henry Jenkins notes, slash has historically been practiced primarily by women. Though Internet sites would suggest its expansion to other groups, it is telling that slash readings diminish in later seasons of *Angel*, when emotional connections between men are not as pronounced, although gay jokes and innuendo continue to flourish. Jenkins, *Textual Poachers*, 191–93.

26. In the one exception to this pattern, "Smile Time," the now hardened Angel becomes a soft and vulnerable puppet, who gets his insides kicked out by his werewolf girlfriend, an episode frequently referred to by online fans as a "return to form" for the series (it also included musical elements). Sadly, however, such scenarios can no longer be enacted on Angel's actual body.

27. I want to thank Louisa Stein for discussing her analysis of Wesley with me.

28. Noted by Keely1116 on www.televisionwithoutpity.com, 8 June 2004.

29. For more on the limitations of the current boy soaps for female and queer viewers, see my article "Boy Soaps: Liberalism without Women."

30. The importance of feminist and queer-friendly writers, actors, and producers is essential to the creation of texts like *Buffy*. There are proportionally far fewer female and queer or lesbian writer-producers in television, especially in terms of program creation. Actors also must be willing to work on a female-centered program; for example, the actor who played Lindsey on *Angel* for its first two years agreed to return in the final year on the precondition that he "not have to get beat up by chicks anymore." Christian Kane, quoted on www .zap2it.com, 5 January 2004. Needless to say, fans were very disappointed with the new Lindsey.

31. These ideas were first presented as a Society for Cinema and Media Studies conference paper in the spring of 2001. For their helpful comments during the essay's development, I thank Margaret DeRosia, Paige Harding, Beth Kelly, Elana Levine, Lisa Parks, and, in particular, Joe Wlodarz, Lucas Hilderbrand, and Clark Farmer. For their continual warmth and insight, I thank as well the fans at Buffy.com, the Bronzebeta.com, and mightybigtv.com (now www.televisionwithoutpity.com). This essay is for my fellow Angel girls, Samantha Holland and Jennifer Gordon Jacobson.

7

Jason Middleton

BUFFY AS *FEMME FATALE:* THE CULT HEROINE AND

THE MALE SPECTATOR

M uch scholarship on *Buffy the Vampire Slayer* has drawn from theories of fandom as a progressive mode of using and transforming
popular cultural texts in ways that respond to the needs and desires of
socially marginalized groups.[1] This work has tended to suggest that
the show provides a valuable resource for young people, and girls
especially, to explore identities and identifications often perceived
as deviant or misfit within teenage culture. I am in full agreement
with these arguments, but in this essay I will explore a more politically reactionary form of spectatorship allowed by the show. Certain
formal elements of *Buffy* promote a voyeuristic and/or fetishistic male
gaze, although the show is strategically constructed to contain these
elements and keep them beneath its thematic surface. This form of
spectatorship links the show with a number of other filmic and televisual texts, fan magazines and comic books, and even video games,
all of which are centered around the figure of the action heroine.

　Television, and soap opera in particular, has provided a framework
for the exploration of alternative forms of viewer identification with
characters and involvement in narratives from those produced by the
codes of classical narrative cinema. *Buffy the Vampire Slayer* follows
many of the televisual conventions analyzed in feminist scholarship
in this area. Although there is a central protagonist, a given episode

usually features two or three different plotlines focused on various members of the show's ensemble cast. These plotlines are often continuous, spanning multiple episodes of the show. *Buffy* thus follows the televisual convention of providing multiple points of identification for the viewer, and it also involves the viewer in continuous stories that allow the characters to grow and change over time. The end of a given episode is generally only a temporary resolution that brings with it new problems to be addressed in subsequent episodes. The camerawork in *Buffy* often follows the soap opera convention of using a majority of close-ups and medium close-ups in a given scene. Frequently, we will get a single master shot—a long or full shot—of the characters in a scene, and then most of the remaining shots will be much tighter.[2] This style of shooting and editing reflects the show's strong emphasis on the characters' feelings and their relationships with one another, relationships that often face problems that must be worked out through intimate conversations.

These generic features of the show, however, are combined with conventions of action cinema and television as well. Each episode contains at least one extended fight sequence, in which Buffy (played by the stunt double Sophia Crawford in the long shots of such sequences) squares off with some nemesis. These scenes follow action conventions, including the frequent use of long shots to provide a good vantage point on the actors' acrobatics, rapid cutting, and the occasional punctuation of the action by a close-up shot/reverse shot between the two combatants wherein some pithy bit of dialogue is delivered.[3] Commentators have suggested that this generic combination accounts for the show's appeal to both male and female spectators. In this chapter, I focus on the specific ways in which the character of Buffy is constructed as an action heroine in an address to a heterosexual male spectator. *Buffy the Vampire Slayer* (the program), Buffy (the character), and Sarah Michelle Gellar (the actress who plays her) can be situated within a network of fan-oriented media that includes comic books, collectibles, and fan magazines such as *Femme Fatales*, *Scream Queens*, and *Draculina*. The common thread among these various media is the centrality of the sexualized action heroine of science fiction, fantasy, and horror who has a strong fan following. She is what I term the "cult heroine." These cult heroines, who grace the covers of magazines such as *Femme Fatales*, tend to be subject to multiple forms of representation across different media. The character is not anchored in any single closed narrative, nor in any single representational form. These characters may start out as comic book artists' illustrations, be subsequently embodied by one or more actresses in films and television, be memorialized in pin-up books, and be controlled by a player of a video game. Buffy—a concept encompassing different media incarnations and representations—occupies an ambivalent, somewhat troubled position within this network, in some ways accepted into it, in others not quite fitting in.

Most of the media this chapter examines employ a mode of address specifically oriented toward a heterosexual male viewer and/or reader. This mode of address includes images of women constructed according to the conventions of heterosexual male-oriented pornography, and writing that positions women as subjects of discussion rather than addressees of the prose. Additionally, the majority of the letters in fan magazines and comic books are written by boys and men, and the editors, writers, and artists of these comic books and magazines are with few exceptions male. The same is true of the majority of patrons and employees in most comic book shops, where the bulk of these materials are available.

In her book *Spectacular Bodies: Gender, Genre and the Action Cinema*, Yvonne Tasker argues that the emergence of women in central, active roles in film and television since the 1970s has been tempered in key ways. She points out that the sexualization of the male body in action films (a subject she analyzes in great depth throughout the book) is compensated for through an emphasis on the hero's activity. With the new action heroines of the 1970s through the present, the reverse is the case: in compensation for the male viewer's anxiety over the role of an active female protagonist who propels the narrative, this protagonist must consistently be sexualized, made an object of erotic spectacle. Thus, the glamorous heroines of *Charlie's Angels* functioned as much as fashion plates as private eyes. Tasker additionally points out that characters such as the *Angels* and *Wonder Woman*, protagonists such as Cathy Gale and Emma Peel in *The Avengers*, and cinematic heroines from *Barbarella* up through more recent incarnations such as *Red Sonja* were all derived in various ways from characters and imagery in comic books and pop art. These images, which borrow from certain stock pop-cultural icons such as the leather-clad dominatrix, suggest that such characters were constructed more for men's pleasure than for women's.[4]

Tasker's analysis indicates how cinema and television featuring action heroines has attempted to strike a balance between spectacle and narrative. In Laura Mulvey's classic analysis of visual pleasure in narrative cinema, the on-screen presence of sexualized female bodies provokes a tension between this spectacle and narrative progression. Narrative progression is restored, however, through the viewer's identification with the male protagonist.[5] In the cinema of the action heroine, a different form of tension emerges: the (male) viewer's voyeurism and identification are directed toward the same (female) character.

The form of male spectatorship implied by the fan magazines centered on the attempts by cult heroines to resolve this tension through a clear privileging of moments of sexual spectacle and a fetishization of the favored actresses' bodies over an interest in narrative elements and character development. Three of the most prominent of these publications, the magazines *Femme Fatales*, *Scream Queens*, and *Draculina*, are comprised mainly of photographic layouts of actresses from science fiction, fantasy, horror, and exploitation films and television. In the case of actresses in "B" films and exploitation film, the layouts are often nude or seminude. *Femme Fatales* is the only one of the three officially available for sale to persons under eighteen; it contains less explicit nudity and focuses more on science fiction and fantasy and on mainstream stars such as Heather Graham, Jennifer Love Hewitt, and Sarah Michelle Gellar. *Scream Queens* concentrates more on horror and exploitation and features stars such as Julie Strain and Linnea Quigley. *Draculina* is much like *Scream Queens* but with a particular focus on vampire narratives.[6]

In the fanzines studied by Henry Jenkins and other scholars of fan culture, fans create new narratives that explore their various forms of identification with the characters, or analyze the narratives and characters from television shows in forums such as Internet chat rooms. In magazines such as *Femme Fatales*, in contrast, analysis of narrative and character development is underplayed in relation to the photographic and textual fetishization of cult heroines. The writing in the magazines is secondary to the presentation of images, with the articles tending toward superficial profiles of the actresses or reviews of new video releases that feature the favored starlets.

This tenuous relationship between image and text, and the subordinate relationship of the latter to the former, is strongly in evidence in the several issues of *Femme Fatales* that focused on *Buffy the Vampire Slayer*. The August 1999 issue features three main articles on the show: a profile of Sarah Michelle

Gellar, a profile of Gellar's stunt double Sophia Crawford, and a (shorter) profile of the writer Marti Noxon. The articles on Gellar and Crawford are filled with pin-up style photos of the actresses, but the article on Noxon features only one small headshot of the writer (see fig. 1b). The other photos accompanying this article are of Gellar, and one in fact has nothing to do with the show written by Noxon. It is a still from Gellar's role as Kathryn Merteuil in Roger Kumble's 1999 film *Cruel Intentions*, accompanied by a caption quoting this provocative line of Kathryn's dialogue: "I'm the Marcia fucking Brady of the Upper East side. My advice is to sleep with as many people as possible" (fig. 1a).[7] The arbitrary and gratuitous placement of this image and caption is indicative of the primacy in these magazines of the titillating image over the accompanying article.

The pin-up, which freezes characters in easily fetishized still images, is an important element in the fan media surrounding cult heroines. The pin-up photograph effectively extracts the character from the temporality of narrative and thus allows for the isolation of scopophilic pleasure.[8] It is also often ambiguous as to whether the pin-up is constructed as a representation of the actress, the character this actress is most notable for portraying, or some gray area between the two. This ambiguity further effects the separation of this image from the narratives in which the character is situated. Pin-up books featuring both classical Hollywood and currently popular sex symbols are prominently on sale in many comic book shops and in the pages of fan magazines such as *Femme Fatales*, *Scream Queens*, and *Draculina*. The magazines themselves are comprised largely of photographs in the style of pin-ups and often contain a centerfold of a featured actress—a convention derived from *Playboy* magazine.

Comic books have begun to incorporate the pin-up into their format as well. The pin-up is sometimes featured in comics published by Top Cow Productions, a line that includes more explicit sexual and violent content than many other contemporary comics, and several titles such as *Witchblade*, *Aphrodite IX*, and *Fathom* that star highly sexualized lead female characters. The art throughout the main body of these comics tends to operate according to the logic of the pin-up. Comic book art has long since broken out of the confinement of sequential panels neatly laid out on a page, but in these Top Cow comics the rejection of sequential panels is employed largely to allow for the

Buffy, Vampire Slayer

MARTI NOXON, HEAD WRITER, ON SCARY EPISODES, ANGST, ADOLESCENCE AND ANGEL.

BY MITCH PERSONS

Sarah Gellar's CRUEL INTENTIONS. Dialogue: "I'm the Marcia fucking Brady of the Upper East side. My advice is to sleep with as many people as possible."

The usually reserved Joss Whedon, BUFFY's creator/co-executive producer and occasional director, positively gushes when our conversation broaches the series' co-producer and staff writer, Marti Noxon: "She can write the shit out of this show! She's good and she's efficient. She's got this show in her blood in such a way that it sometimes puts more experienced writers to shame. Before Marti came on board, David [Greenwalt], Rob Des Hotel, Dean Batali, Ty King and I were carrying the bulk of the workload. Now I know that if we get in a bind—and we do, more often than not!—I can always go to Marti and she can produce a good script in a very short amount of time. She is an absolute lifesaver."

Describing her function within Whedon's Mutant Enemy Productions, Noxon is a little more low-key: "I wrote six episodes last season. Part of the reason that I did so many is because we were trying to figure out who was working and who was not working. Some of our writers, like Ty King, live out of town; he lives in Seattle, and is more of a consultant writer. Also, last year, we had one man who didn't work out and he left right away. We also had a consulting producer whose own pilot sold but is the middle of all this, so he didn't stick around. He only wrote half an episode, then

took off. Rob and Dean had already been on the show for one season, and I think they were considering moving on. That left David, Joss, and myself. That's not very many people. When you come right down to the crux of the matter, I was really the only one besides Joss and David who was left.

"I was nervous, because BUFFY was actually my first staff job. My father, Nicholas Noxon, is the head of National Geographic, Documentary Division and I used to hang around him all the time when I was a kid, because I always knew that I wanted to do something in the film business. But I found out that I really didn't want to be a documentary person. I found it very frustrating, what with watching and waiting for animals to do things—I wanted to give them direction!

"I went to film school at UC Santa Cruz and when I graduated I worked in a bunch of different jobs in the industry, mostly as an assistant to a writer and then to a writer-producer and I just wrote a lot. I did spec scripts, both feature and television. I actually did have one produced, and that was for the show LIFE GOES ON. About three years ago I got signed by one of the bigger agencies for television and talent, and they passed my material to Joss at BUFFY. I met with Joss and David, and I thought it had gone miserably and I was never going to get the job. I couldn't tell if they liked me, but, much to

"I don't want to play the quintessential dumb blonde," says Gellar, who almost declined her role in I KNOW WHAT YOU DID LAST SUMMER ("I got that movie the same week that BUFFY [I] premiered."). S. Gellar on the BUFFY set with series creator Joss Whedon, who praises Noxon's aptitude: "If we get into a bind, she can produce a good script in a very short amount of time."

my delight, they did.

"I think one of the reasons they liked me was because I had a real taste for the macabre. When I was writing spec scripts, most of them were ghost stories or had some sort of supernatural element in them. One of the specs I wrote was for THE X-FILES. I love that show. I have always been obsessed with ghost stories, and it seemed that David and Joss were able to pick that up. That is why BUFFY was such a great fit for me.

"They could also sense that I've had a love of the dramatic genre, with episodic shows like PARTY OF FIVE and MY SO-CALLED LIFE. I expressed to them my opinion, that those kinds of series can overstay their welcome because the people are always so overwrought. Taking straight drama and mixing it with horror/comedy, as David and Joss did with BUFFY, was my all-time favorite kind of writing.

"One thing that viewers may have noticed about our second season, and now our third, is that the segments —though still stressing the tongue-in-cheek elements of horror—had taken on a more serious and episodic quality. When you take a look at BUFFY's first season, there were more stand-alone episodes—stories that dealt with different monsters, demons and so forth. You had the same recurring characters, but the show wasn't as dependent on those characters as they are now. Even so, we try to lighten things up if we feel that the story is getting a little too intense or too ponderous. Write a joke from Xander, an insult from Cordelia, or a twisted homily from Willow and the ten-

sion is dispersed. We're always very conscious of that, and even though the tone may now be darker—and the emotions of the characters deeper and more somber—there's still a whole lot to laugh about.

"For me, the emotional substance of BUFFY is very real. I don't think I'm alone in that assessment, either. People respond to it, even if they don't always know what's going on. This is particularly true for our younger audiences, the eight- to ten-year-olds. Sometimes that worries me. I expressed this to Joss one time in one of our breakdown meetings.

"I definitely considered Passion, with its grisly murder, an episode that was not for younger viewers. One of my favorite segments last year was Lie to Me, about the boy who wanted to become a vampire. That, too, was a little dark...a little too

Noxon, BUFFY's head writer: "One reason the producers liked me was I had a real taste for the macabre."

Figs. 1a and b. A still of Sarah Michelle Gellar and a quote from her character in *Cruel Intentions*, amid an article on and a still of Marti Noxon, the head writer of *Buffy*, *Femme Fatales*, August 1999.

12

13

scantily clad heroines' bodies to fill the pages. Top Cow Productions promotes many of its titles through advertising that represents a collage of images of its heroines accompanied by the slogan, "When was the last time you picked up a hot chick in the comic store?" This caption not only depends upon the assumption that the reader is a heterosexual male but also acknowledges the gendered space of the comic book store, in which the idea of "picking up a hot chick" is sufficiently absurd so as to be feasible only in the act of reaching for a comic book.

The *Buffy the Vampire Slayer* comic book, published by Dark Horse Comics, in some ways resembles the Top Cow comics, but in other ways it is distinctly different. Like the Top Cow comics, the *Buffy* comic does incorporate the pin-up, often featuring at least one image of the heroine in action or in some striking pose at the back of each issue. These pin-ups can represent a source of tension for some fans who want to demarcate the Buffy character from the sort of fetishization apparent in the Top Cow publications. In a letter published in issue 17 of the *Buffy* comic book, a male fan, Ben Naylor, takes the publishers to task for one of the pin-ups printed in the 1999 *Buffy* annual, describing it as a "sweaty-palmed, skimpy-clothed shot."[9] Naylor's use of the term "shot" to describe this illustration indicates that he perceives the pin-up to be constructed according to the logic of the photographic pin-up in soft-core pornographic magazines such as *Playboy*. The description of the image as "sweaty-palmed" further emphasizes his sense of the pin-up as being constructed for purely erotic, if not outright masturbatory, pleasure.

In a subsequent issue of the comic (23), another fan, whose name, Kaj Petersen, suggests she is (possibly) female, writes in to contest Naylor's argument about the pin-up. Petersen asserts, "If you actually look at the pin-up Buffy is wearing a baggy green shirt and capri pants. Not exactly what most people call skimpy. I don't believe you could find a picture in the entire comic series of *Buffy* where she isn't a 'strong, intelligent female character.'" The comic's editor, Scott Allie, replies to this letter with an indication of support for Petersen's interpretation of the image against Naylor's: "Thanks, Kaj. We've always tried to make her the exception to the rule of comic-book heroines."[10] The "rule" to which Allie refers here would seem to be the intense sexualization of the heroines of Top Cow comics, and Allie has made other remarks in the letters column of *Buffy* that suggest a certain disdain for these comics' fetishistic appeal. But to what extent do the creators of the *Buffy* comic book really attempt to make her an exception? And even if they do try, what is to keep some fans from taking such pleasures from the text anyway?

To begin to answer these questions, I want to "actually look" at the pin-ups featured in the *Buffy* annual. The pin-up section features six full-page images by different artists. Four of the six are constructed in a very similar fashion: Buffy is pictured in the foreground, while a menacing monster lurks behind her in the background. The fourth (fig. 2a), constructed more as a portrait than as an "action shot," represents Buffy in revealing, less action-oriented clothing (a skirt and tank top) than in the other three; in addition, she is gazing directly at the viewer, as opposed to looking slightly off the page. In contrast to the protestations of Petersen, I find it difficult not to see the eroticization of the character in these images. In addition to the basic premise of their presentation as pin-ups, the images emphasize the heroine's body in a much more pronounced manner than the panels in the main body of the comic book. In the contested image described by Naylor as "sweaty-palmed" (fig. 2b), Buffy stands with her back to the viewer; her legs are spread wide apart and positioned such that her backside is central to the frame. Her head is turned such that she looks over her shoulder in the viewer's direction, a common positioning of the female body in photographic pornography. The Master towers above her in the background, extending a menacing hand in Buffy's direction. The link between the representation of the female body as vulnerable and as eroticized has been demonstrated by much feminist analysis of images.[11] In these pin-ups, Buffy's positioning in relation to the threatening monsters that lurk behind her is another factor functioning to code the images as erotic.

The same sort of image construction is prevalent in publicity stills from the show selected to accompany the *Buffy* cover stories in the magazine *Femme Fatales*. In the article accompanying the October 1998 cover story, four of the six photographs depict a moment of frozen action between Buffy and a male demon: Buffy is pictured in the foreground with a male figure behind her. In two of these Buffy is being threatened or attacked by, respectively, Spike (see fig. 3a, left) and the Master (fig. 3a, right). In the third (fig. 3b, left), it is Angel who stands behind Buffy. Although in this image Angel and Buffy appear to be cooperating in some action, Angel's ambivalent position within the show as Buffy's boyfriend gone bad allows this image to function, like the others, to create a sense of vulnerability for Buffy and hence an erotic connotation.

Figs. 2a and b. Buffy as a pin-up,
Buffy the Vampire Slayer Annual '99,
Dark Horse Comics.

Figs. 3a and b. Buffy as threatened woman, "Buffy, Vampire Slayer," *Femme Fatales*, October 1998.

In the *Buffy* comic book, the eroticization of the character exists as a sort of undercurrent made available for the pleasure of male fans of cult heroines, while the book on the surface maintains the premise that Buffy is "the exception to the rule." Scott Allie's editorial comments sometimes indicate a certain winking acknowledgment of this dual mode of address. At the end of the letters section in the same issue of the comic in which Kaj Petersen's letter was published, Allie writes a brief plug for upcoming titles by Dark Horse Comics. He focuses on an issue of Dark Horse Presents, which will feature "a short tale of Buffy and male sexual aggression." This same issue, he promises, features "a very sweaty palmed cover by superstar Joe Chiodo."[12] Allie's appropriation of the terms from Naylor's letter protesting the Buffy pin-up suggests that his promotion of this cover is done in a wry manner, but this humorous disavowal does not change the very real sense in which the promise of sexual titillation is used to promote and sell the comic book.

Fan magazines such as *Femme Fatales* tend to support this idea that the show allows for different, and gendered, forms of spectatorial pleasure. In the October 1998 cover story on *Buffy*, Thomas Doherty suggests that the show is constructed so as to allow for "dual satisfactions."[13] On the one hand, he ar-

gues, the show provides empowerment and positive points of identification for teenage girls, "placing them at the center of the narrative as active agents who kick the butts of loutish, egotistic, overconfident and gross males." Doherty lists several other features of the show that he assumes constitute its appeal to teenage girls, but he posits a wholly different spectatorial position for the show's male viewers: "Tough, smart, and take charge, Buffy also prances about in short skirts and tight tank tops. As she jiggles through her aerobics regimen (in the high school library?), the Watcher is the only male around not watching."[14] Doherty thus posits a gendered split in *Buffy*'s spectatorship between identification for "girls" and voyeurism for "males."

Doherty is correct in identifying the ways in which costuming, particularly of the Buffy character, and other elements of mise-en-scène encourage this sort of voyeuristic spectatorship. I would argue, however, that the shooting and editing conventions in the show also work carefully to contain it and maintain a differentiation between the show's mode of spectatorial address and that of much narrative cinema and some male-oriented genres of television. This demarcation is clearly signaled as early as the first episode of the show, "Welcome to the Hellmouth," during a scene in which Buffy first meets Xander. Walking out of the principal's office, Buffy bumps into another girl, causing her to drop her books. As Buffy stoops to pick up her things, Xander, spotting an opportunity, rushes up to help her. We then get a brief series of medium close-up shot/reverse shots of the two characters as they exchange awkward introductions. They stand, and Buffy walks away from Xander and out of frame. The camera stays focused on Xander, still framed in a medium close-up, as he watches Buffy walking away. In a conventional teen film, we would here most certainly expect a point-of-view shot for Xander, showing Buffy's backside as she walks away. The short skirt and knee-high boots in which she is dressed would be appropriate for this kind of point-of-view shot, which would most likely be framed in medium close-up to emphasize the fetishization of its object, rather than maintaining the correct distance perspective from where Xander is standing. But instead we remain with the shot of Xander as he castigates himself for his blundering attempt at charming Buffy (fig. 4a) and then notices that Buffy has dropped something. We next cut to a medium long shot of Xander as he picks up the object (fig. 4b) and with some confusion calls out, "Oh, hey . . . hey! You forgot your . . . stake."

Only at this point do we cut to the expected point-of-view shot of Buffy walking down the hall, and the distance at this point, with Buffy framed in a long shot (fig. 4c), significantly cuts down on the fetishistic quality of the image. More importantly, the shot has a narrative justification in that it indicates that Buffy is out of earshot from Xander. The scene ends with a cut back to Xander in medium close-up, looking again with confusion at the stake. Thus, the scene is played out in a comic manner that presents the male character as awkward and ineffectual. It does not grant him a voyeuristic and mastering gaze toward the female character, which would provide for the sort of male spectator position often constructed in narrative cinema and in television shows that follow its conventions.

Nonetheless, Buffy's costuming and the point-of-view shot we do get of her walking down the hall suggest the *possibility* of a voyeuristic gaze. But the camerawork, editing, and narrative justification for the shot function to contain this gaze and render the sort of viewing position it implies a more *covert* one rather than one expressly legitimated by the show. This strategy of providing *covert* visual pleasures constructed according to conventionally cinematic modes of address to a male viewer has taken many forms within the show.

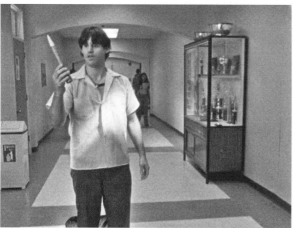

Figs. 4a, b, and c.
Eye direction, shot
scale, and editing keep
Buffy from being the
sexualized object of
Xander's gaze, "Welcome
to the Hellmouth,"
10 March 1997.

One notable example is "Who Are You?," a fourth season episode in which Faith switches bodies with Buffy. Faith has always served as the embodiment of Buffy's dark side, in that she possesses the same powers as Buffy but will not use them for good and lawful ends. Her appearance and costuming generically code her as both villainess and vixen (brunette to Buffy's blonde), and her self-presentation as highly sexual legitimates the displacement of a voyeuristic gaze away from Buffy and toward Faith instead.

In one scene, Faith (in Buffy's body) pays a visit to Buffy's straight-and-narrow boyfriend, Riley. Gellar's hair and costuming (tight black leather pants and a black tank top) in this scene are constructed so as to connote the overt sexuality by which Faith is characterized. Faith, playing the part of the dangerous seductress, propositions Riley to go to bed with her. Riley, although taken aback by his girlfriend's unusual behavior, admits that he "wouldn't say no." After Riley assents, we cut to a medium shot of Faith staring at him seductively, and she then moves to crawl onto the bed. As she crawls onto the bed, facing away from Riley, we cut to a medium close-up shot of her leather-clad backside (fig. 5a). This is ostensibly a point-of-view shot for Riley, although the low angle and close-up position from which it is framed do not exactly match his perspective—a common enough cinematic convention with this sort of shot. Here, the show momentarily positions the viewer's gaze in a highly fetishistic relation toward Buffy's body, a relation not usually invited.

But the show disavows this viewing position in a couple of key ways. First of all, we are to understand that it is Faith, not Buffy, who is positioning her body in this pose, which connotes its "to-be-looked-at-ness." Hence, the character of Buffy is disconnected from an image of her body that invokes a scopophilic viewing position. Second, the male character in the diegesis, Riley, with whom the viewer's gaze would seem momentarily aligned in the point-of-view shot of Faith's backside, disavows the scopophilic viewing position implied by the shot. Following the point-of-view shot, we cut to a medium shot from the side of Faith as she crawls onto the bed and provocatively asks, "So . . . how do you want me?" Riley, whose face is initially out of frame in this shot, sits down on the bed, and when we see his face (fig. 5b), his expression does not match up with the viewing position implied by the point-of-view shot. Rather than looking sexually predatory, he on the contrary appears confused and taken aback by Buffy's/Faith's behavior. Only after he has made it clear that

Figs. 5a and b. The camera looks at Buffy and Riley responds with confusion, "Who Are You?" 29 February 2000.

he doesn't want to "play" (but instead to make love in a more conventional manner), does he begin kissing her and we cut away to a different scene. Thus, a scopophilic position is here covertly allowed for the viewer, even as the show disavows this position by removing its heroine from the position of object of this gaze, and one of its male heroes from the position of subject of the gaze.

I would therefore argue that the form of fandom toward the show represented by magazines such as *Femme Fatales* could in one sense be understood according to the model of "textual poaching": the fans are deriving pleasures that are not thematically legitimated by the show, but which can nonetheless be derived from it. The difference here, however, is that it is the show that seems to legitimate more conventionally marginalized viewing positions, while the "poaching" is done from a more conventionally dominant (heterosexual male) position. But what sort of texts and characters attract this form of fandom? What are the common qualities among the figures from the genres of science fiction, fantasy, and horror that become cult heroines featured in magazines such as *Femme Fatales*?[15] Carol Clover's book on gender and horror film spectatorship, *Men, Women and Chainsaws*, provides a productive basis for beginning to answer this question.

Clover argues that the teenage male viewer of the horror film oscillates between identifying with the monster and with the "Final Girl" who kills the monster in the end. This oscillation, Clover demonstrates, is encouraged by the shot selection and editing in the films themselves. The films thereby provoke a destabilization of the male spectator's gendered subject position. The gendered identities of the monster and the Final Girl are destabilized as well. While the monster is superficially presented as male and the Final Girl as female, each possesses qualities that make ambiguous his or her position as "masculine" and "feminine," respectively. The *partial* adherence to a masculine subject position makes the Final Girl, in Clover's reading, a perfect stand-in for the adolescent male. Clover writes: "She is feminine enough to act out in a gratifying way, a way unapproved for adult males, the terrors and masochistic pleasures of the underlying fantasy, but not so feminine so as to disturb the structures of male competence and sexuality."[16]

At first glance Buffy would seem to embody Clover's character of the Final Girl, now given her own starring role in which she can repeatedly enact the Final Girl's part of tracking down and killing off the monster. There are certain key differences between Buffy and the Final Girl, however, which are indicative of the differences between the Final Girl and the cult heroine in general. Joss Whedon has made some often-quoted comments on how he initially conceived the character of Buffy for a film script. He explains that he had always been a huge fan of horror movies, but saw so many where "there was 'that blond girl' who would always get herself killed." According to Whedon, "I started feeling bad for her—I thought, y'know, it's time she had a chance to, y'know, take back the night." Hence, Whedon explains, the idea for *Buffy* stemmed from the simple imagined scenario of seeing "a beautiful blond girl" walk into an alley, be stalked by a monster, and trounce him.[17]

The way Whedon articulates *Buffy*'s narrative of origin seems to posit the idea of a girl fighting back in a horror film as a wholly original premise for his film and TV program. Of course, since he is a "huge fan" of horror films he must be aware of the central role of the Final Girl, and the fact that there is nothing new about a girl trouncing the monster. What does seem to be new, however, about Whedon's formulation is his desire to see the "beautiful blond girl . . . who always gets herself killed" trounce the monster. As Clover demonstrates, the Final Girl is differentiated from the other female characters in the horror film who "always get [themselves] killed" in several important ways, all of which serve to "masculinize" her. She is represented as less conventionally sexually attractive, favoring boyish, "practical" clothing; she is not sexually promiscuous; she possesses a detective-like curiosity; and she has an ambiguously gendered name such as Stretch, Will, Joey, or Max. *Unlike* these heroines, it is the other girls in the horror films, the "beautiful blond," sexually available ones, who get killed. Whedon thus seems to have wanted to combine the two versions of femininity in the horror film into a single figure: a "beautiful blond" cheerleader, whose name, Buffy, could not possibly be coded as more feminine, who gets to have sex with boys and still kill the monster.

It is the character Willow, really, who most closely fits into the character mold of the Final Girl. She is less conventionally attractive than Buffy, is adept with technology, has a strong investigative curiosity, and, in the early stages of the show at least, did not date. Even her name, containing the masculine "Will" by which her friends address her, is consistent with the construction of the Final Girl. Whedon's rewriting of gender conventions in the traditional horror film thus functions to remove the qualities from the central, Final Girl character that conventionally serve to "masculinize" her and pawn these qualities off on a secondary character. The central character, meanwhile, absorbs certain qualities of secondary characters in horror films—conventionally feminine sexual attractiveness and availability—and combines these qualities with the capacity for aggression and the ability to kill the monster.[18]

The development of a character such as Willow indicates how *Buffy the Vampire Slayer* is oriented more toward female spectators than the horror films Clover analyzes, which are directed mainly toward teenage boys. But Whedon's desire that gave rise to the program—to see a "beautiful blond" who can also kill the monster—is a desire upon which the fan magazines construct a mode of address to their readers. It is the combination of these qualities that gives rise to the construction of certain figures as cult heroines. A survey of the figures who grace the covers of *Femme Fatales* demonstrates this point: dangerous but beautiful female vampires such as Elvira or Vampirella (both embodied by different actresses at different points), Pamela Anderson as Barb Wire, Michelle Pfeiffer as Catwoman—all are sexualized, provocatively (un)dressed women who simultaneously wield guns or possess other deadly capabilities. While the Final Girl is "masculinized" in her appearance and neutered in her sexuality, cult heroines are characterized by *excessive* signifiers of femininity and sexuality. Their bodily proportions tend toward absurdly exaggerated versions of the "hourglass" figure and they wear revealing, fetishistic, and totally impractical clothing while engaging in improbable fights and action sequences. The comic book form is the ideal medium for the rendition of such fantastic excesses, and it is no surprise then that cult heroines tend to be rendered as comic book characters whether or not they originate as such.

Cinematic translations of cult heroine comic books do their best to maintain the integrity of these forms of excessive fantasy. In the film version of the comic book *Barb Wire* (a publication of Dark Horse Comics, the publisher of the *Buffy* comic book), Pamela Anderson, whose body, as a result of surgical reconstruction, matches the excessive proportions of comic book heroines, kills bad guys and blows up buildings while dressed in high-heeled boots and a revealing leather bodysuit. In addition to the campy, excessive way in which the heroine is represented, the film features many sequences that are constructed solely for visual pleasure in excess of narrative coherence.

The opening five minutes of the film feature the actress performing a highly sensational striptease, with little intercutting that would give us some clue as to how this performance will work into the narrative. We get a few shots of an appreciative crowd, but all these shots really do is align the viewer with the position of these men in the nightclub where the striptease is being performed. Finally, at the climactic moment of the routine, she removes her high-heeled shoe and hurls it at a man in the crowd, impaling him in the forehead and killing him. This sudden integration of the preceding spectacle into a narrative logic—she was only posing as a stripper in order to carry out this assassination—does little to contain the excessiveness of the drawn-out striptease sequence.

Another scene added to the "collector's edition" of the video copy of *Barb Wire* further demonstrates this privileging of sexual spectacle over narrative. The story has been wrapped up, the credits roll, and we then get a ten-minute reprise of the opening striptease scene, but with new footage added, and this time with no cutting to shots of the nightclub crowd or anything else. The inherent logic of the opening scene, which presents spectacle in excess of narrative, is here fully realized. The scene is extracted from the film and freed of the shots that allow for it to be subsequently integrated (uneasily) into a narrative logic. Cult heroines can thus be characterized by several different forms of representational excess. In films such as *Barb Wire*, their representation as visual spectacle is constantly in excess of the films' ostensible narratives. And, as we have seen, their representation exceeds any single medium. Popular characters tend to be simultaneously embodied in a variety of media, including films and television shows, comic books, and video games.

An additional and related quality of these characters is the way in which they often tend to exceed the boundaries of the "human." I have already noted the combination in the construction of the cult heroine of excessive signifiers of feminine sexuality with conventionally masculine action-hero powers. Her body is in effect rendered superhuman. Such excess uproots the characters from a stable gender position. The destabilization of the heroine's gendered identity is also affected through other characteristics that render her partially in- or post-human. Many of these characters' bodies are composed of elements of the alien, the supernatural, or the machinic. Sara Pezzini, the heroine of the Top Cow comic *Witchblade*, which was made into a television series for the TNT cable network, fights crime by means of a supernatural witch's claw that envelops her hand and gives her special powers. Vampirella (a comic book character who has been embodied by at least two different actresses in film versions) looks more or less human, but in fact she is both a vampire and an alien who possesses superhuman strength and transforms her body into a bat. Figures such as Lara Croft of *Tomb Raider* (a video game, a comic book, and a film starring Angelina Jolie) or Nikita of *La Femme Nikita* (a film, a television series, and a video game) are ostensibly human. But they have had their bodies reconstructed through rigorous training regimes that transformed them into efficient killing machines with abilities that could certainly be regarded as "inhuman."

Buffy's body is not rendered inhuman in any visible way, but her links to the world of the supernatural and her superhuman powers as a slayer set her apart from her friends and make her a liminal figure between the human and vampire characters in the show. Additionally, when cult heroines have sexual relations, they often take a de-naturalized form, wherein the heroine's body is penetrated by the supernatural, the alien, or the machinic—one need only think of the scene with Barbarella and Dr. Duran's music machine, for example. In the case of Buffy, her first sexual relations are also de-naturalized, as her boyfriend Angel turns back into the evil Angelus as a result. The body of the cult heroine is thus rendered unstable, unnatural, and permeable in different ways by elements of the in- or post-human.

Spectatorial pleasure in these texts is largely based on an appreciation of how well these spectacles of bodily mutation and transformation are rendered, a pleasure in the "special effect." Pleasure in special effects lies in the quality of the visual rendition of the fantastic in cinematic and televisual media. Cult heroines' identities are constructed through the rendition of excessive, spectacular bodies and bodily powers—special effects that produce viewer affects in excess of identification. Cult fan publications such as *Femme Fatales* are dedicated to the cultivation of such affects. This mode of fandom, while it extracts certain elements of texts for the pleasure of fans at the expense of others, cannot really be assimilated into Jenkins's model of textual poaching. It tends to be conducted from a majoritarian (heterosexual male) subject position, and it does not effect a significant transformation of the narrative elements and characters of a text. Rather, it involves an investment of libidinal energy in bodily and situational spectacles that exceed narrative and character.

Buffy the Vampire Slayer tends to be formally constructed so as to resist the more conventional cinematic mode of address to a heterosexual male viewer. Even as the shot selection and editing work to contain the possibility of scopophilic looking relations, however, elements of mise-en-scène, such as costuming, promote it, and the show covertly allows for it through devices such as Faith's possession of Buffy's body. As other chapters in this volume illustrate, academics and others have rightly demonstrated the show's rich narrative and strong characters, which lend themselves readily to productive and transformative reading practices among fans. I have attempted here to demonstrate the presence of a different form of fandom toward the program—expressed in fan magazines such as *Femme Fatales*—which latches onto the sort of covert pleasures allowed by the show and which seeks to construct Buffy as a cult heroine.

The uniting in the title character of conventional sexual attractiveness with superhuman powers that allow her to kill the monsters suggests Buffy's potential to be a cult heroine. However, Buffy is not characterized by the sort of excessive, caricatured femininity and superpowers that are integral to the construction of cult heroines such as Barb Wire. The attempt to assimilate Buffy to this role can provoke tension among some fans, as we saw in the letters page of the *Buffy* comic book. The discourse of Scott Allie, the editor of the *Buffy* comic book, indicates a split mode of address to his readers: even as he asserts that Buffy is the "exception to the rule" of comic book heroines, he at times promotes the comic through the promise of sexual titillation. I have argued that the show itself contains a split mode of address as well, allowing in covert ways for the possibility of a scopophilic relation toward its heroine even as it works thematically to contain this possibility. Fan magazines such as *Femme Fatales* in effect take this possibility and run with it, extracting the Buffy character from the show's narratives and situating her in a fan network that celebrates a fetishization of cult heroines. I think it is important to bear in mind amid celebrations of *Buffy* as a feminist and progressive text that Joss Whedon's original desire to see a "beautiful blond girl" who can also trounce the monster is a desire linked to those of an extensive network of fans and media that promotes a much more politically ambivalent form of spectatorship.

1. See, for example, the essay by Allison McCracken in this volume.

2. As Tania Modleski notes, so frequently are close-ups and medium close-ups of faces used in soap opera that it can be easy to forget the characters have bodies. This technique is markedly different from the fetishization of women's bodies prevalent in the cinema. Modleski, *Loving with a Vengeance*, 99.

3. This combination of generic elements from action and from soap operas is an example of Lynne Joyrich's argument that to resist the "overpresence" (for the spectator) that it has often implied, television has increasingly borrowed from cinematic conventions in many of its programs, including the injection of violent, "hypermasculine" elements into its narratives. Joyrich, "Critical and Textual Hypermasculinity."

4. Tasker, *Spectacular Bodies*, 18–21.

5. Mulvey, "Visual Pleasure and Narrative Cinema."

6. All three magazines are published independently. *Femme Fatales* is published in Baltimore and is available by subscription and in comic book stores. *Draculina* and *Scream Queens* are published in Illinois by Draculina Publishing, and they are available through the same channels.

7. Persons, "Buffy, Vampire Slayer," 12.

8. Laura Mulvey defines scopophilia as a (sexual and/or erotic) pleasure in looking at another person. Two main forms of scopophilia are relevant to Mulvey's analysis of spectatorship: voyeurism, which holds the object at a distance, subjecting a person to the seeming mastery of a gaze from an unseen viewer; and fetishism, which overvalorizes a part of the object (such as a particular body part or article of clothing), substituting this for the whole person. In Mulvey's analysis, the classical Hollywood cinema constructs a gendered form of spectatorship, in which female characters are conventionally presented as objects of voyeuristic or fetishistic spectacle. Mulvey, "Visual Pleasure and Narrative Cinema."

9. Watson, *Buffy the Vampire Slayer*, 17.

10. Golden, *Buffy the Vampire Slayer*, 23.

11. See, for example, Williamson, "A Piece of the Action." Yvonne Tasker also notes that the encoding of the female action heroine as vulnerable in "revenge-fantasy" films in particular plays an important part in her eroticization. Tasker, *Spectacular Bodies*, 21.

12. Chiodo is a comic book artist responsible for the rendition of several highly sexualized female characters. Golden, *Buffy the Vampire Slayer*, 23.

13. Doherty, "Buffy, Vampire Slayer," 8.

14. Ibid., 8–11. The articles on *Buffy* in *Femme Fatales* also make much of Sarah Michelle Gellar's naughtier personae outside of her role as Buffy; there is a particular focus on her part as Kathryn Merteuil in Roger Kumble's *Cruel Intentions* (1999).

15. I use the term "figures" here with reference to *Femme Fatales* 7, no. 10, which featured a cover story on "sci fi's all time fifty sexiest figures," with an illustration of Batgirl from the *Batman* TV series of the 1960s on the cover. The ambiguity of the term "figures" is highly suggestive: it includes both characters and the actresses who played them, with little real distinction between the two. It also connotes the "action figures," or toys, that often represent these characters and tend to be available for purchase in the same comic book stores in which magazines such as *Femme Fatales* are sold.

16. Clover, *Men, Women and Chainsaws*, 51.

17. These comments are taken from interviews with Joss Whedon on the compilation video-tape that includes episodes one through four of *Buffy the Vampire Slayer*.

18. The profile of Alyson Hannigan, who portrays Willow, in the October 1998 issue of *Femme Fatales* indicates that her character is less available for the sort of fetishistic representations applied to Gellar's character. Her profile is second-to-last among six profiles of "*Buffy* Babes." While the articles on actresses such as Charisma Carpenter (Cordelia) and Bianca Lawson (Kendra) feature provocative photos of them in skimpy clothing such as tank tops and miniskirts, the primary photo of Hannigan is a black-and-white head shot in which she wears a long-sleeved striped sweater. Hannigan's clothing, pose, and expression more resemble a high school yearbook photo than a *Playboy*-inspired pin-up.

8

Elana Levine

BUFFY AND THE "NEW GIRL ORDER":

DEFINING FEMINISM AND FEMININITY

Joss Whedon, the creator of *Buffy the Vampire Slayer*, has never hesitated to label his series a feminist show.[1] Journalists have often cited the program as a prototypical example of the "girl power" feminism of the 1990s.[2] Academics have eagerly dissected the feminist significance of the series.[3] Activists have called upon Buffy as a symbol of the contemporary feminist movement.[4] Yet the equation of *Buffy* and feminism has never been unanimous, nor has it been univocal in its understandings of feminism or of the show's relationship to it. Sarah Michelle Gellar has rejected the feminist label; "I hate the word," she has proclaimed.[5] The critic Rachel Fudge has argued that the series ultimately compromises Buffy's feminist potential.[6] Even Joss Whedon has hedged somewhat on his labeling of the series as feminist; "Yes, I have a feminist agenda, but it's not like I made a chart," he has explained.[7]

The debates around *Buffy*'s feminist authenticity are both specific to their historical moment and business as usual for television representations of the New Woman, a character type with some "feminist" or "liberated" traits who has been visible on American screens since at least the 1970s. Television's fictional New Women, from Mary Richards to Ally McBeal, have all been subject to debate. Are they emblems of a particular stage in our society's acceptance of female empowerment? Are they, in fact, feminist characters? If so, what *kind* of feminism do they represent? Does their femininity (that is, their caring and nurturing qualities, their conventionally attractive appearances) in some way negate their feminist potential? Do these ostensibly feminine characteristics make them more palatable to a mass television audience? The forms these questions take, and the vociferousness of the debate over their answers, have varied in different periods, but they have perpetually sought to define feminism and femininity in relation to each other and to the representation at hand. For example, in the 1970s, action-adventure series with female leads, such as *Charlie's Angels* and *Wonder Woman*, endowed their fictional New Women with conventionally masculine traits (for example, crime fighting) as a way to assert their adoption of a liberated lifestyle. However, these characters were also represented as excessively feminine, with their glamorous hair, revealing wardrobes, and propensity for using their feminine "wiles" to succeed in the workplace. In attempting to balance the characters' feminism and their femininity in these ways, these series participated in a major debate around women's roles at the time—a debate engaged in by a wide range of feminists and anti-feminists, and by the culture at large, over whether or not feminism required a rejection of traditional femininity.[8]

Buffy the Vampire Slayer is another installment in American television's history of the fictional New Woman that serves as a site of debate over feminism and its embodiment in individual women's lives. In many respects, it replays some of the same questions—and offers some of the same answers—as television's many series about the New Woman in the 1970s. Because *Buffy* is premised upon the seeming contradiction between Buffy's petite, pretty body and her conventionally feminine interests in boys, clothes, and cheerleading, and her conventionally masculine work as a physically powerful slayer of vampires, demons, and other hellish monsters, the program engages with some of the same terms for TV representations of the New Woman as have earlier series. Yet as we will see, the ways in which *Buffy* enters into debates over what it means to be a feminist and what it means to be feminine are different from earlier incarnations of the New Woman. *Buffy* has become part of the discussion around television and feminism in a specific historical context, one in which the meanings of feminism and femininity are in tension with earlier meanings.

The 1990s and early 2000s have been termed a period of "post-feminism," a period usually seen as having begun in the early 1980s and one that has included, as Judith Stacey has described, "the simultaneous incorporation, revision, and depoliticization of many of the central goals of second wave [or 1970s] feminism."[9] As Stacey's description indicates, the post-feminist period has not simply rejected the feminism of the 1970s. Instead, it is often characterized by a belief that the goals of the feminist movement of the 1970s have been accomplished and thus that there is no need to continue a fight that has already been won.[10] In a post-feminist culture, responsibility for change shifts from an organized social movement to individuals, as "political ideas and practices [are] transformed into a set of attitudes and personal lifestyle choices," a shift some see as antithetical to earlier feminisms' collective fights against the systemic injustices of patriarchy.[11]

Since at least the 1990s, however, certain post-feminist stances have been challenged by a new incarnation of feminism that still distinguishes itself from earlier generations, but that also embraces the feminist label and many of its long-standing principles. "Third-wave" feminism and post-feminism are both products of the gains achieved by the feminism of the 1970s. But third-wave feminism has been more selective in what it has rejected—or, more accurately, revised—from the earlier generation. While the post-feminist mindset sees the feminism of the 1970s as no longer necessary and the patriarchy against which feminism has fought as no longer a threat, third-wave feminism remains invested in collective feminist activism and in the fight against a still powerful patriarchy.

Buffy the Vampire Slayer has contributed to the debates over the meanings of feminism and femininity in a post-feminist and third-wave context as much as it has borrowed from them. *Buffy*'s engagement with these debates plays out in three key areas, each of which I will explore in this essay. The first is the way the series represents the New Woman's identity, and identity in general. In keeping with both post-feminist and third-wave feminist conceptions of social roles, *Buffy* downplays the New Woman's gender as the central facet of her identity in favor of a more multiply-positioned identity that sees gender as fundamentally intertwined with other axes of social experience. The second aspect of *Buffy*'s engagement with its post-feminist and third-wave contexts is the program's handling of femininity in terms of the New Woman's style and physical appearance—her (hetero)sexual attractiveness. Here, the series most explicitly continues the fictional New Woman tradition of balancing conventionally feminine traits with more conventionally masculine ones in order to achieve some sort of parity between the character's femininity and her feminism. Yet *Buffy* does not treat the New Woman's femininity in the same essentialist terms as have earlier TV representations. The third aspect I consider deals with the ways that *Buffy* counterposes individual empowerment and collective action, a key struggle between contemporary discourses of post-feminism and third-wave feminism. Ultimately rejecting post-feminist tendencies toward self-fulfillment over group cohesion, the series ends by taking a distinctive stand on feminist empowerment and the character of the New Woman. In all, I argue that although *Buffy* continues the television tradition of the feminine feminist in many ways, the series also participates in shaping the meanings of feminism and femininity in ways specific to its historical moment. In doing so, it intervenes in post-feminist and third-wave feminist debates to endorse a post-1970s form of feminism that adheres to many long-standing feminist principles.

POST-FEMINISM, THIRD-WAVE FEMINISM, AND TELEVISION

Feminist criticism of post-feminist discourse and its circulation on television has been substantial.[12] Less visible, however, has been a consideration of third-wave feminism as a potentially important context for television's participation in defining feminism and femininity through its character of the New Woman. Part of this scholarly reluctance to grapple with third-wave feminism has to do with the limited number of TV representations that *do* seem to resist post-feminist ideas. Another part is that third-wave feminism seems in many ways to replicate post-feminism's refusal of earlier feminist ideals. I argue, however, that third-wave feminism can be more usefully seen as being in *tension* with post-feminist ideas than in concert with them, although the two certainly have elements in common.[13]

The post-feminist perspective's refusal of the feminist label, as if a feminist position is outdated—even oppressive—in the contemporary environment, is ever present in media discourse, even that surrounding *Buffy*. Sarah Michelle Gellar's publicly declared distaste for the feminist title typifies this stance. "It makes you think of women that don't shave their legs," Gellar has said. "I hate the word."[14] Seeing the feminism of the 1970s as anti-femininity, as opposed to such conventional feminine rituals as leg shaving (and, by association, heterosexual attractiveness), Gellar embodies the post-feminist embrace of femininity as a purportedly progressive move beyond the no longer necessary strictures of feminism. Also characteristic of post-feminist attitudes, however, is an equivocating "but," or a statement that otherwise contradicts the seeming rejection of feminism. Alongside Gellar's embrace of femininity over feminism, she also has regularly made such statements as, "Do I consider myself a strong female individual? Uh-huh. Can I take care of myself? Yeah, sure," and "The wonderful thing about this trend [of powerful young women on television] is that young girls have something to look up to, that they can take care of themselves."[15] In such comments, her post-feminist positioning is all the more clear: being a "strong female individual" takes precedence over being a "feminist." Self-empowerment is a universally agreed-upon good; empowerment through collective resistance to oppression is outdated. Gellar's stance is an increasingly common one among women of her generation, but it is not the only attitude they take toward feminism and femininity.

Other women of Gellar's generation retain some of the same ambivalence about feminism that she expresses, but they do so without her ultimate rejection of the feminist label. For example, Trina Stevens, the twenty-three-year-old daughter of Nkenge Toure, a feminist and Black Panther in the 1970s, explains, "I guess I would call myself a feminist. I've never called myself one because I never knew what a feminist was. . . . If a feminist is a person who believes that women and men are equal, and that a woman can do what a man can do and should be paid for the same thing a man can do if she can do it, I believe in feminism."[16] Stevens's stance is more pro-feminist than Gellar's, but it is still clearly a product of her post-feminist times. Defining feminism in terms of workplace equality sidesteps questions about traditional femininity and its place within feminism; instead, it settles on a position that most women (and men) of the post-1970s agree upon.

Self-proclaimed third-wave feminists sympathize with a post-feminist stance that sees feminism and femininity as opposing pulls. At the same time, however, they seek to retain the feminist label and many of the principles it represents. Thus, these third-wave feminists explicitly recognize many of their peers' (and their own) ambivalence about feminism. Jennifer Baumgardner's and Amy Richards's dedication of their third-wave feminist tract, *Manifesta*—"To feminists everywhere—including those of our generation who say, 'I'm not a feminist, but . . .' and others who say, 'I *am* a feminist, but . . .'"—is an attempt to include Stevens, Gellar, and a host of other young women in its address.

Third wavers like Baumgardner and Richards have turned their generation's contradictory attitudes toward the feminism of the 1970s into a cornerstone of their movement. For example, Leslie Heywood and Jennifer Drake, in the introduction to their volume, *Third Wave Agenda*, state, "Because our lives have been shaped by struggle between various feminisms, as well as by cultural backlash against feminism and activism, we argue that contradiction . . . marks the desires and strategies of third wave feminists."[17] For Rebecca Walker, a third-wave activist and the daughter of the feminist Alice Walker, women of her generation need identities—and models of feminist activism—that are able to "accommodate ambiguity," that are able to contain the contradictions that today's women feel about feminism (and femininity) and about their identities generally.[18] This embrace of ambiguity and contradiction is evident in at least two of the three aspects of *Buffy*'s engagement with contemporary discourses of feminism and femininity that I discuss below.

BUFFY AND MULTIPLY-POSITIONED IDENTITY

Two of the key book-length collections of third-wave writing, Walker's *To Be Real* and Barbara Findlen's *Listen Up*, take as their subject the multiple, and often contradictory, identities of today's young women and of those women's experiences of feminism.[19] As Rebecca Walker explains in her introduction to her anthology, the feminist writers in her book "debunk the stereotype that there is one lifestyle or manifestation of feminist empowerment," thereby rebuking a common conception of feminism in the post-feminist generation.[20] The contributors to Walker's and Findlen's anthologies share personal stories of their multiply-positioned lives, exploring the intersections of gender, race, class, sexuality, and other aspects of their identities that keep them from being able to define themselves primarily along gender lines. This emphasis on the multiple axes of identity falls in line with a tradition of theory, criticism, and activism by women of color who have sought to challenge both their exclusion from some feminist organizations in the 1970s and the universalizing tendencies of some feminist thought of the 1970s.[21] While third-wave feminists are not the first to challenge an exclusive focus on gender in feminist thinking, they have found a way to deliver the message about feminism's openness to multiply-positioned identities to the post-feminist generation by linking social identity to personal experience.

In a range of ways, *Buffy the Vampire Slayer* shares third-wave feminism's emphasis on the contradiction and ambiguity that define the lives of many contemporary women (and men). As such, Buffy is simultaneously a fierce, fearless (feminist?) vampire slayer and an insecurity-ridden (conventionally feminine) young woman. But the series does not stop its exploration of ambiguity of identity with the long-standing television staple of the New Woman who is able to be both feminine and feminist. Instead, it extends its conceptions of femininity and feminism beyond gender-specific terms by considering the multiple identity positions occupied by nearly all of its characters. Thus, the character of Oz is both a ferocious werewolf and a soulful, teenage musician, and the character of Angel is both a bloodthirsty vampire and a heroic, loving protector of humanity. Even the monsters–of–the week often display these sorts of fractured identities. For instance, in "Living Conditions," Buffy's college roommate, Kathy Newman, is simultaneously Buffy's worst roommate nightmare (she blasts Cher's "Believe" repeatedly), a soul-sucking interdimensional demon, and a young woman trying to escape her father's control and follow her dream of going to college. The final season's villain, the all-powerful First Evil is the most multiply-identified of all, as the First manifests itself as any dead person, crossing boundaries of gender, race, age, and even humanness, alongside those of life and death.

To return to the character of the New Woman, we can see how the series participates in defining identity in ways beyond the feminism/femininity dichotomy that has so long shaped TV representations. One way the program does so is to make Buffy excessively self-aware of her multiply-positioned identities and constantly working to reconcile them. In the early seasons, she regularly struggles with her role as the slayer and her desire to be a "normal" teenage girl. In "Never Kill a Boy on the First Date," for instance, Giles questions her ability to be the slayer and to have a social life, to which she retorts, "This is the '90s, the 1990s in point of fact. And I can do both. Clark Kent has a job. I just want to go on a date." When she has to leave her date because of

174   ELANA LEVINE

her slaying duties, she asks him to think of her as two people—one who has to go, one who wants to stay with him. As the series proceeds, Buffy comes to recognize that she can take on or shed any of her identities at will, and she is sometimes frustrated by the lack of stability this offers her. For instance, in "Surprise," when Giles suggests that they meet up later in the day after he has had time to research a resurrected demon called the Judge, Buffy asks what she is to do until then. When Giles tells her to "go to class, do your homework, have supper," Buffy sighs, "Right. Be that Buffy," suggesting that the most seemingly normal and natural of her identities, that of a typical teenager, requires as much conscious selection, as much deliberate taking on, as any other.

Buffy's multiple identities become an even greater encumbrance for her later in the series, when she adds the responsibilities of caring first for her ailing mother and then for her sister once their mother dies. The fifth season finale emphasizes Buffy's multiple roles and the toll they have taken on her. The astonished near-victim of a vampire attack marvels after Buffy has rescued him, saying, "You're just a girl." Buffy's wistful reply, "That's what I keep saying," not only enforces the fact that this contradiction has been the premise of the entire series (she *keeps* saying it), but also that her ambiguous identity is a continual burden, even if she has carried it for five TV seasons. In fact, her weariness with this identity early on in the episode foreshadows her demise at its end.

As compellingly as *Buffy* deals with multiply-positioned identities in a metaphorical sense (through the "othered" races of demons, vampires, and so forth) and in the competing tensions in Buffy's life, the series generally fails to address the ways that most women and men experience these multiple axes of difference, particularly along the axes of race and class. People of color rarely appear on the show and, when they do, they are often silenced (for example, the deaths of Kendra and Trick) or exoticized (for example, the First Slayer).[22] In these ways, the program can be seen as falling into a postfeminist trap that is all too common. Because the most frequent expression of ambiguous and multiply-positioned identity is through the character of Buffy, the show can be read as presuming a white, middle-class hold on the problems and potential to be found in a multiply-positioned identity. Because Buffy is young, white, conventionally attractive, and heterosexual, she has the luxury of such identity quandaries as slayer or student, working woman or frivolous teenager. Multiply-positioned identity is no longer a site of multiple oppressions or multiple empowerments; instead, it is a matter of individual choice. This is similar to the ways the post-feminist mindset takes feminist arguments about the social injustice of women's competing social roles (mother, worker, activist) and argues that it is women's responsibility (as opposed to, say, society's) to manage these competing roles either through *choosing* one over others or through the balancing act of the superwoman. Not only does this post-feminist stance evacuate any critique of a patriarchal society (in which it is only women who are forced to make such choices) from its sympathetic view of women's multiple identities, it also fails to acknowledge that not all women have the luxury of making such choices. This way of thinking is post-feminist because it "defines feminism as no longer necessary because it already has successfully secured access to equality and choice for middle-class white professional and/or family women" while ignoring the *lack* of access to such privileges for others.[23] Women outside the white, middle class face different, and sometimes fewer, choices about their social roles, but the post-feminist stance is unable to acknowledge this. Nor is the series fully able to acknowledge this with the white, middle-class, heterosexual character of Buffy at its center. Indeed, even when Buffy's privilege seems jeopardized, such as when she finds herself in a financial bind after her mother's death and takes a job in the fast food industry to make ends meet, this condition lasts only a few episodes. With a surprise check from Giles and, eventually, a new job as the guidance counselor at Sunnydale High (acquired despite her status as a college drop-out), Buffy's economic woes cease. She comfortably returns to the position of privilege from which the post-feminist perspective derives.

BUFFY AND FEMININE STYLE

Buffy's compromised attention to multiply-positioned identities is only one way in which the series participates in defining feminism and femininity in its post-feminist and third-wave contexts. Another way *Buffy* engages these questions is in its handling of Buffy's feminine style. As we have seen, conventional feminine style is a major preoccupation of post-feminist thinking. Alongside women's supposed equality in the workplace in the aftermath of the 1970s is their supposed "freedom" to embrace traditional femininity now that the feminist battle has been won (think Ally McBeal's miniskirts). Third-wave feminism sees feminine style as central to young women's concerns, as well, although this perspective differs some from the broader post-feminist one. Third wavers have embraced a more contradictory notion of femininity—a simultaneously "girlie" and tough style that parodically plays with the culturally coded features of femininity and masculinity, as well as with the long-standing imagined distinction between feminism and femininity. As Melissa Klein writes in *Third Wave Agenda*, "We are interested in creating not models of androgeny so much as models of contradiction. We want not to get rid of the trappings of traditional femininity or sexuality so much as to pair them with demonstrations of strength or power."[24]

The trope of the girl has been appropriated in multiple ways in the 1990s and 2000s. Musicians and fans of punk music adopted the "grrrl" label to describe their angry brand of femininity. The mass media appropriated "girl power" to describe the pro-female, but not necessarily feminist, stance of groups such as the Spice Girls. Third wavers have turned to the notion of the "girlie" to represent an embrace, however ironic, of those aspects of girl culture most often denigrated in mainstream society—Barbie dolls, lipstick, dresses, anything pink. By celebrating that most often associated with girls, this perspective seeks to reclaim the value of girl culture. At the same time, however, the third-wave discourse of "girlie" style can be seen as rescuing femininity from the feminism of the 1970s and its stereotypical associations with hairy, angry lesbians. Thus, the third-wave emphasis on feminine style fits within a broader post-feminist mindset. Yet it also seeks to give that style a more overtly feminist mission than the post-feminist stance might ordinarily allow.

Debbie Stoller, the editor for the third-wave 'zine *BUST* has written, "It's as clear to us as it is to RuPaul that fashion is a costume, that femininity is a masquerade. . . ."[25] Such third-wave thinking refuses to link conventional feminine frills such as nail polish, high heels, and lipstick to some kind of "natural" femininity. Instead, it explicitly recognizes the element of "masquerade" in such feminine accoutrements, the very *un*-naturalness of their association with women. Culturally encoded objects like these, third wavers insist, mean what we decide they mean; they are no more markers of women's difference from or sameness to men than are neckties, combat boots, military uniforms, or any of the other trappings of power associated with men and appropriated by women.

This equalization of markers of femininity and markers of masculinity, of lipstick and of combat boots, is a common feature of the third wave's redefined notion of feminine style. *Buffy* is a frequently cited example of this trend. Much as with her multiply-positioned identities, Buffy's girlie characteristics are central to the contradictions that form the program's premise. Buffy is not just a teenage girl who regrets having to leave her date to slay vampires. She is a pretty, petite, blonde teenage girl named Buffy, a moniker that signifies feminine frivolity and an obsession with popularity, evoking the air-head, cheerleader-type "Valley Girls" who made life difficult for the more down-to-earth girls in cultural products of the 1980s such as the films of John Hughes. Although Buffy quickly proves herself to be a more serious, responsible, and tough person than her name suggests, her girlie style persists. In the early seasons in particular, Buffy regularly dresses in short skirts and dresses; she sports colorful hair accessories and mini-backpacks coordinated to match her outfits. She looks forward to her high school prom, eagerly discussing her "kick" pink dress with her best friend, Willow. And she doodles "Buffy & Angel 4-ever" on her high school notebook.

Buffy is perhaps most distinctly an emblem of third-wave girlie style in the ways these traditional markers of girlish femininity are combined with those more frequently associated with the masculine. Her no-nonsense fighting style is the most obvious of these contradictory qualities, but Buffy's style is more third-wave girlie than stereotypically girlish in other ways, too. Though her speech is sprinkled with girlish slang, her incisive taunts at demons and her insightful one-liners to her friends reveal a bravura and maturity far beyond girlhood. Her romantic musings about Angel are short-lived; as he is a vampire who is more than 240 years old, he hardly makes for an appropriate boyfriend, and he breaks up with her just before the prom (to make matters worse, he reverts to his evil, soulless, cursed self just after having sex with her for the first time). In the aftermath of the pre-prom breakup, Giles offers her ice cream, which he has heard is the typical female solace at times like these. Buffy tells him she doesn't need it: "Great thing about being a slayer? Kicking ass is comfort food." She then proceeds to destroy the rabid Hellhounds sent to ravage the prom-goers before pulling her pink dress out of the bag she also uses to carry weapons (fig. 1). At the prom, she is awarded the title of class protector, which she accepts with all the blushing exhilaration of a prom queen. These twists on typically girlish qualities evoke the third wave's insistence that

Fig. 1. Buffy pulls her prom dress out of her bag of weapons, "The Prom," 11 May 1999.

markers of femininity do not define one's identity; Buffy is no less powerful a slayer because she excitedly dons a prom dress and no less feminine a girl because she totes that prom dress around in a bag filled with crossbows and stakes.

Even her choices of clothing that emphasize her femininity and her sexual allure do not simply cite conventional femininity. Her frequently exposed bra straps (a costuming feature common enough in the series' first seasons that fans developed a drinking game around it) are a case in point. Buffy's exposed bra straps announce her girlishness (I have breasts!) but, at the same time, refuse to conform to conventional strictures of femininity. When feminists in the 1960s and 1970s rejected their bras as tools of patriarchal oppression (as in the tossing of bras into a Freedom Trash Can at the protest in 1968 against the Miss America pageant), they were symbolically rejecting conventional feminine style and appearance. In contrast, the trend of the exposed bra strap of the 1990s seemingly embraces conventional feminine style. At the same time, this trend flaunts femininity so as to refuse the rules of propriety that, historically, have attended it. At once modest and immodest, conforming to patriarchal edicts and defying them, Buffy's exposed bra straps can be read as emblematic of the third wave's contradictory understanding of girlie style.

Yet the display of Buffy's body can also be understood as antithetical to a feminist project, as more of a post-feminist opposition to feminism than a contemporary version of feminist concerns. As Rachel Fudge argues in the third-wave 'zine *Bitch*, "Buffy's unreconstructed, over-the-top girliness in the end compromises her feminist potential."[26] In Fudge's reading, the significance of Buffy's girlie-style femininity to the program's premise—"a petite cheerleader being chosen to save the world from evil"—suggests that feminist power is predicated upon feminine attractiveness.[27] This qualified notion of feminist strength, a notion that resonates strongly with versions of the New Woman in series of the 1970s such as *Charlie's Angels*, certainly persists today. Unlike series such as *Charlie's Angels*, however, Buffy's sex appeal plays little to no part in her success as a slayer. She is not dependent on her femininity to achieve "feminist" success in a man's world. If anything, it is the program's effort to take her appearance completely for granted that naturalizes the equation between prettiness and power. Willow's transformation from a shy, awkward, fashion-challenged computer nerd to an outgoing, hip and trendy, occasionally cleavage-baring witch operates similarly. As Willow's feminine physical attractiveness comes to the fore, so do her magical powers and her centrality to the program's premise (see, for example, the prominent place of Alyson Hannigan as Willow in the opening credits of the sixth and seventh seasons). As with Buffy, however, Willow's combination of sex appeal and strength is not the same as, say, the Angels' blend of those qualities. In Willow's case, her lesbian identity has developed alongside her evolution as a witch and her adoption of a more conventionally attractive feminine style. Within the world of the show, Willow's physical appearance is not designed to attract men; it thus challenges patriarchal understandings of the female body and its relationship to feminism.

BUFFY AND FEMINIST ACTIVISM

Buffy's handling of multiply-positioned identities and of conventional feminine style are two key ways the series participates in defining feminism and femininity in contemporary Western culture. We have seen how these two features juggle post-feminist and third-wave feminist conceptions of the New Woman, much as earlier generations of television's fictional New Women (such as Charlie's Angels) juggled ideas about feminism and femininity in their historical moments. But I have also suggested that Buffy is somehow different from these earlier versions of New Women on TV, offering a new version of feminism, one closely linked to the third wave, that takes into account the context of the post-1970s but that also retains some long-standing feminist principles. This is most clearly visible in the show's final season, and in particular in its concluding episode.

In this season, we get resolutions of sorts to the stories of at least two of the series' ongoing female characters, Buffy and Anya. Both characters ultimately reject some of the principles of post-feminist thought in favor of more third-wave feminist conceptions of power, strength, and identity. While the evolution of Buffy as a New Woman is of course more central to the series overall, Anya's turn away from post-feminist notions of women's empowerment provides a more subtle counterpoint.

After being abandoned at the altar by her fiancé, Xander, Anya returns to her life as a vengeance demon. In this occupation, she joins multiple other female demons in literally granting the wishes, however figurative, of women wronged by men. The series always had a certain sense of humor about Anya's work, appreciating many women's very real feelings of hurt and betrayal at the hands of men and allowing viewers to indulge in the fantasy of a cadre of demons designed to make such wrongs right. But in the final season episode "Selfless," we learn the full story of Anya's past and are confronted with the morally troubling nature of the vengeance demons' work. In this episode, Anya has summoned a giant spider to rip out the hearts of a group of fraternity brothers who have subjected one of their girlfriends to a humiliating breakup scene in front of the entire fraternity house. Anya ultimately repents, but she unexpectedly sacrifices the life of her friend and fellow vengeance demon Halfreck in the process. Shaken by these events, Anya tells Xander that she needs to figure out who she is, and she rejects his offer to be with her. She explains that she has always "just clung to whatever came along," that she worries that she is "nobody." The episode ends with Anya walking off-screen on her own, bravely facing what lies ahead.

Anya's comments about not knowing who she is are especially resonant because of flashbacks earlier in the episode. In Sjornjost in 800, in St. Petersburg in 1905, and in Sunnydale in 2001, we see Anya declaring her love for Olaf, her dedication to vengeance, and her hopefulness about her future with Xander, respectively. Through these flashbacks, we see a woman who has swung between caricatured versions of femininity and feminism her entire life. Her saccharine sweetness (including a fondness for bunnies) and her dedication to caring for Olaf mark her excessive femininity in the earliest flashback, as does the intensity of her jealousy at the prospect of Olaf being with another woman. The fact that she turns him into a troll in vengeance (even before she becomes an official vengeance demon) marks her with another stereotypically feminine trait, out-of-control emotion. In the flashback to St. Petersburg, it becomes clear that Anya has turned her capacity for vengeful emotion into a successful career as a vengeance demon. No longer a victim of traditional femininity, she is now its polar opposite. "Vengeance is what I am," she tells Halfreck. Anya is now a caricature of both the career-driven woman and the radical feminist, coldly setting out to help "wronged women" by destroying men. When we see her again in 2001, she has returned to her path of conventional femininity, this time taking it to Disney-fied extremes. Dressed in a 1950s-style pink dress with ribbons tied around her waist and floating down her back, with long, blond curls framing her face, Anya sings her new anthem, "I'm the Mrs." in excited anticipation of her upcoming marriage to Xander (fig. 2a). Her song is cut off only after she transforms into a bride (fig. 2b), wearing her wedding dress as she belts out, "I'll be Mrs./I will be his Mrs.!"

As humorous as these flashbacks are, they all contain an underlying sadness, particularly when juxtaposed with the horrific situation created in the present by Anya's return to her identity as a "feminist" vengeance demon. Thus, when Anya takes responsibility for what she has done, refuses Xander's offer of consolation, and recognizes her pattern of "clinging" alternately to stereotypical versions of femininity and feminism, she undergoes a fundamental change. Rejecting neither feminism nor femininity but instead a post-feminist notion of "choosing" one extreme or the other, Anya tentatively steps toward a new identity as she walks off on her own, one in which her power and her sense of self are not to be found in an either/or choice of being a woman ("feminine") or being a demon ("feminist"), but in finding her own place by refusing such narrow categorizations.

Buffy's development as a New Woman also finds her rejecting television's historic reliance on some kind of "balance" between femininity and feminism, as well as rejecting post-feminist conceptions of identity and power. Instead,

Figs. 2a and b. Anya imagines herself as a fully feminine woman, "Selfless," 22 October 2002.

Buffy embraces a new feminism, one we could call third-wave feminism, inspired by the collective anti-patriarchal stance of earlier feminisms and full of hope for all women. After the character's series-long struggle with her multiply-positioned identity, Buffy becomes a somewhat exaggerated version of a self-righteous, angry feminist in the final season. Her long-winded speeches to the group of potential slayers who have gathered in her home to be protected against the First and to train for the upcoming battle become monotonous and tiring, and her humorless insistence on the girls toughening up becomes grating. She insists that she alone is responsible for saving the world. (As she declares in "Selfless," "There's only me. I am the law.") The "feminist" dimension to Buffy's position is further emphasized with the arrival of Caleb, the demonic preacher sent by the First to torture Buffy and the others. Caleb happens to be a pitch-perfect stereotype of the misogynist, Southern, Christian fundamentalist—a Jerry Falwell in a handsome young actor's body who is prone to uttering dialogue such as, "Ah, now look. Things don't go just exactly your way, so here come the waterworks. Ain't that just like a woman?" Caleb is ultimately killed only when Buffy slices into his body by driving a scythe up through his genitals. As satisfying as it is to see Caleb's sexist menace ended in this way, this "girl power" gesture does not really approach the renewed kind of feminism Buffy achieves later on in the concluding episode.

In "Chosen," Buffy comes up with a plan to rid the world of the First once and for all. The plan is only revealed to the audience as it happens, and the revelation ends the series on a note that both opposes-post-feminism and supports third-wave feminism. Buffy recognizes that her power alone (even with the help of her friends and her fellow slayer, Faith) is not the answer to the world's problems. Instead, she realizes that it is only by turning all of the potentials into slayers, by empowering *all* of the girls, that they can actually make a difference. As she tells the potentials about this plan, asserting that Willow's power as a witch is greater than that of all of the men who instituted the "one girl in all the world" rule about slayers in the first place, she declares, "I say *my* power should be *our* power. . . . From now on, every girl in the world who might be a slayer, *will* be a slayer. Every girl who *could* have the power, *will* have the power. *Can* stand up, *will* stand up. Slayers every one of us. Make your choice. Are you ready to be strong?" With Willow's spell in action, we see a range of girls, all over the world, coming into the power that Buffy envisions for them.

A white preteen, ready to bat in a baseball game, slowly smiles with confidence (fig. 3a); a black teenager leans against a row of high school lockers, feeling her power (fig. 3b); a young white woman picks her head up off a bathroom floor; an Asian girl rises from her family's dining table (fig. 3c); an overweight white girl holds off an ominous male fist. Surrounding these images are those of the potential slayers fighting alongside Buffy, rapturously feeling the power alight within them, as Willow transforms into a white-haired goddess aglow with all of the girls' strength (fig. 3d). It is a utopian vision of feminist empowerment, to be sure, but it is a meaningful one, especially in an early-twenty-first-century context in which post-feminist ideas about the need for feminist activism being long past hold such great sway. By engaging in a collective action instead of an individual one, by turning *her* power into *our* power, Buffy ends the series as a truly new New Woman, one who redefines television's version of feminism and rejects a post-feminist perspective that sees the need for collective action as a thing of the past. Buffy's renewed kind of feminism, a kind closely identified with the third wave, triumphs as the series ends.

CONCLUSION

Television's representations of the New Woman who has been changed by feminism into someone who must achieve a balance between her newfound feminism and her inherent femininity is a simplified, even caricatured, version of the struggles real-world women have faced since at least the 1970s. Despite their distance from "reality," television's portrayals of women in a feminist and post-feminist world help us to imagine ourselves and others in our own encounters with that world. Thus, it is vital to consider television's representations of the New Woman—as so many scholars of the media have done—with an eye to the historical contexts within which those representations are created and received. This chapter has been an attempt to do just that, putting *Buffy* into the context of its post-feminist and third-wave feminist moment.

As a program in keeping with a long tradition of representing the New Woman on TV, *Buffy the Vampire Slayer* carries on many of the traits of those earlier representations, in particular their juggling of traits of feminism and femininity to make their characters appealing to a mass (or even a niche) audience. What makes *Buffy* different from these earlier shows is not so much some more authentically feminist premise, but the specificity of its constructions

Figs. 3a, b, c, and d. The potential slayers are empowered as a result of the goddess Willow's spell, "Chosen," 20 May 2003.

of feminism and femininity to its late-twentieth-century and early-twenty-first century context. The ideas about feminism and femininity produced in *Buffy* resonate as post-feminist, as third wave, as anti-feminist, or as yet-to-be-labeled because we read them during a time in which these categories are up for redefinition, albeit with specific limitations and possibilities. I have argued that the series ultimately defines feminism and femininity in ways more in keeping with third-wave ideals than with post-feminist principles. It remains to be seen whether future series will move further along this path or will re-assert the post-feminist stances that have figured in so many of television's representations of the New Woman.

NOTES

1. See, for example, Bellafante, "Bewitching Teen Heroines."
2. Perhaps the most widely cited popular articulations between *Buffy* (as well as series such as *Ally McBeal* and musical acts such as the Spice Girls) and feminism are Bellafante, "Feminism: It's All about Me!"; and Labi, "Girl Power."
3. See, for example, the first five chapters in South, *"Buffy the Vampire Slayer" and Philosophy*.
4. Both Karp and Stoller, *The BUST Guide to the New Girl Order*: and Baumgardner and Richards, *Manifesta* mention the series as an example of contemporary feminist ideals.
5. "Buffy's No Feminist," *The Gazette* (Montreal), 20 October 1998, B4.
6. Fudge, "The Buffy Effect," 58.
7. Udovitch, "What Makes Buffy Slay?" 65.
8. Levine, *Wallowing in Sex*.
9. Stacey, "Sexism by a Subtler Name?," 8.
10. Bonnie Dow discusses this conception of post-feminism as distinct from a feminist backlash. Dow, *Prime-Time Feminism*, 93–94. Part of the problem with the post-feminist perspec-tive—feminist backlash or not—is that it conceives of feminism in the 1970s as univocal, as being fundamentally centered on issues of workplace equality, gender discrimination, and so forth. Thus, post-feminist discourse typically responds to one key wing of feminism in the 1970s: mainstream, liberal feminism. In so doing, post-feminism denies the breadth and depth of the many different feminisms of the 1970s.
11. Ibid., 209.
12. See, for example, Dow, *Prime-Time Feminism*; Projansky, *Watching Rape*; and Kim, "'Sex and the Single Girl' in Postfeminism."
13. Some scholars, particularly in contexts outside the United States, have tried to conceive of post-feminism not as a rejection of feminism but as a new form of feminism. See Lotz, "Postfeminist Television Criticism" for a defense of post-feminism as a new form of femi-nism. Lotz draws, among others, upon the work of Ann Brooks, a scholar based in New Zealand, to support her argument. Brooks, *Postfeminisms*. I argue that many feminists see post-feminism as too laden with negative connotations for it to be a useful analytical or practical label for this new kind of feminism.
14. "Buffy's No Feminist," *The Gazette* (Montreal), 20 October 1998, B4.

15. Ibid.; and Gloria Goodale, "Television's Superwomen," *Christian Science Monitor*, 5 February 1999, 13.
16. Quoted in Baker and Kline, *The Conversation Begins*, 361.
17. Heywood and Drake, *Third Wave Agenda*, 2.
18. Walker, "Being Real," xxxiii.
19. See Walker, "Being Real"; and Findlen, *Listen Up*.
20. Walker, "Being Real," xxxiv.
21. See, for example, Sandoval, "U.S. Third World Feminism"; and Collins, *Black Feminist Thought*.
22. See the chapter by Cynthia Fuchs for more on the role of race.
23. Projansky, *Watching Rape*, 79.
24. Klein, "Duality and Redefinition," 222–23.
25. Stoller, "Feminists Fatale," 42.
26. Fudge, "The Buffy Effect," 58.
27. Ibid.

BIBLIOGRAPHY

Acland, Charles. *Youth, Murder, Spectacle: The Cultural Politics of "Youth in Crisis."* Boulder, Colo.: Westview Press, 1995.

Adams, Michael. *Slayer Slang: A "Buffy the Vampire Slayer" Lexicon.* Oxford: Oxford University Press, 2005.

Allen, Robert C., ed. *Channels of Discourse, Reassembled: Television and Contemporary Criticism.* 2nd ed. Chapel Hill: University of North Carolina Press, 1992.

Allison, Dorothy. *Skin: Talking about Sex, Class and Literature.* Ithaca, N.Y.: Firebrand Books, 1994.

Ang, Ien. "Melodramatic Identifications: Television Fiction and Women's Fantasy." In *Feminist Television Criticism: A Reader*, edited by Charlotte Brunsdon, Julie D'Acci, and Lynn Spigel, 155–66. Oxford: Oxford University Press, 1997.

Ariès, Philippe. *Centuries of Childhood: A Social History of Family Life.* Translated by Robert Baldick. New York: Alfred A. Knopf, 1962.

Baker, Christina Looper, and Christina Baker Kline. *The Conversation Begins: Mothers and Daughters Talk about Living Feminism.* New York: Bantam Books, 1996.

Baumgardner, Jennifer, and Amy Richards. *Manifesta: Young Women, Feminism, and the Future.* New York: Farrar, Straus and Giroux, 2000.

Bellafante, Ginia. "Bewitching Teen Heroines." *Time*, 5 May 1997, 82–84.

———. "Feminism: It's All about Me!" *Time*, 29 June 1998, 54–60.

Benjamin, Walter. "The Work of Art in the Age of Mechanical Reproduction." In *Illuminations*, edited by Hannah Arendt and translated by Harry Zohn, 217–52. New York: Schocken, 1969.

Bordo, Susan. *The Male Body: A New Look at Men in Public and in Private.* New York: Farrar, Straus and Giroux, 1999.

Brooks, Ann. *Postfeminisms: Feminism, Cultural Theory, and Cultural Forms.* New York: Routledge, 1997.

Brunsdon, Charlotte. *The Feminist, the Housewife, and the Soap Opera.* New York: Oxford University Press, 1992.

————. "What Is the 'Television' in Television Studies?" In *Television: The Critical View*, 6th ed., edited by Horace Newcomb, 609–28. New York: Oxford University Press, 2000.

Brunsdon, Charlotte, Julie D'Acci, and Lynn Spigel, eds. *Feminist Television Criticism: A Reader*. Oxford: Oxford University Press, 1997.

Caldwell, John Thornton. *Televisuality: Style, Crisis, and Authority in American Television*. New Brunswick, N.J.: Rutgers University Press, 1995.

Carrillo, Jenny. "To the Max." *Dreamwatch* 79 (April 2001): 22–26.

Case, Sue-Ellen. "Tracking the Vampire." *differences: A Journal of Feminist Cultural Studies* 3, no. 2 (1991): 1–20.

Clover, Carol. *Men, Women and Chainsaws: Gender in the Modern Horror Film*. Princeton, N.J.: Princeton University Press, 1992.

Cohan, Steve. *Masked Men: Masculinity and the Movies in the Fifties*. Bloomington: Indiana University Press, 1997.

Cohan, Steve, and Ina Rae Harke, eds. *Screening the Male: Exploring Masculinities in Hollywood Cinema*. New York: Routledge, 1993.

Collins, Jim. "Postmodernism and Television." In *Channels of Discourse, Reassembled: Television and Contemporary Criticism*, 2nd ed, edited by Robert C. Allen, 327–53. Chapel Hill: University of North Carolina Press, 1992.

Collins, Patricia Hill. *Black Feminist Thought: Knowledge, Consciousness, and the Politics of Empowerment*. New York: Routledge, 1990.

Cordesman, Anthony H. "Biological Warfare and the 'Buffy Paradigm.'" Washington: Center for Strategic and International Studies, 29 September 2001, http://www.csis.org (accessed 21 June 2003).

Cover, Arthur Byron. *Night of the Living Rerun: Buffy the Vampire Slayer* 4. New York: Pocket Books, 1998.

D'Acci, Julie, ed. "Lifetime: A Cable Network 'For Women.'" Special issue, *Camera Obscura* 33–34 (1994).

Doane, Mary Ann. "Information, Crisis, Catastrophe." In *Logics of Television: Essays in Cultural Criticism*, edited by Patricia Mellencamp, 222–39. Bloomington: Indiana University Press, 1990.

Doherty, Thomas. "Buffy, Vampire Slayer." *Femme Fatales* 7, no. 5 (October 1998): 8–11.

————. "Teenagers and Teenpics, 1955–1957: A Study of Exploitation Filmmaking." In *The Studio System*, edited by Janet Staiger, 298–316. New Brunswick, N.J.: Rutgers University Press, 1995.

Douglas, Mary. *Purity and Danger: An Analysis of Concepts of Pollution and Taboo*. New York: Praeger, 1966.

Dow, Bonnie J. *Prime-Time Feminism: Television, Media Culture, and the Women's Movement Since 1970*. Philadelphia: University of Pennsylvania Press, 1996.

Dyer, Richard. *A Matter of Images*. New York: Routledge, 1993.

Ellis, John. *Visible Fictions: Cinema, Television, Video*. Rev. ed. New York: Routledge, 1992.

Feuer, Jane. "The Concept of Live Television: Ontology as Ideology." In *Regarding Television: Critical Approaches—An Anthology*, edited by E. Ann Kaplan, 12–21. Los Angeles: The American Film Institute, 1983.

————. "Feminism on Lifetime: Yuppie TV for the Nineties." *Camera Obscura* 33–34 (1994): 133–46.

Findlen, Barbara, ed. *Listen Up: Voices from the Next Feminist Generation*. Seattle: Seal Press, 1995.

Frankenberg, Ruth. "Introduction: Local Whitenesses, Localizing Whiteness." In *Displacing Whiteness: Essays in Social and Cultural Criticism*, edited by Ruth Frankenberg, 1–34. Durham, N.C.: Duke University Press, 1997.

Frith, Simon. "Youth/Music/Television." In *Sound and Vision: The Music Video Reader*, edited by Simon Frith, Andrew Goodwin, and Lawrence Grossberg, 67–84. New York: Routledge, 1993.

Fudge, Rachel. "The Buffy Effect." *Bitch* 10 (summer 1999): 18+.

Gallagher, Diana G. *Prime Evil*: *Buffy the Vampire Slayer* 10. New York: Pocket Books, 2000.

Gauntlett, David, and Annette Hill. *TV Living: Television, Culture and Everyday Life*. London: Routledge, 1999.

Ginsberg, Elaine K. "Introduction: The Politics of Passing." In *Passing and the Fictions of Identity*, edited by Elaine K. Ginsberg, 1–18. Durham, N.C.: Duke University Press, 1996.

Giroux, Henry. *Fugitive Cultures: Race, Violence and Youth*. New York: Routledge, 1996.

Gitlin, Todd. *Inside Prime Time*. New York: Pantheon Books, 1985.

Golden, Christopher. *Buffy the Vampire Slayer* 23. Milwaukie, Ore.: Dark Horse Comics, July 2000.

Golden, Christopher, and Nancy Holder. *"Buffy the Vampire Slayer": The Watcher's Guide*. New York: Simon and Schuster, 1998.

Halberstam, Judith. *Skin Shows: Gothic Horror and the Technology of Monsters*. Durham, N.C.: Duke University Press, 1995.

Hansen, Miriam. *Babel and Babylon: Spectatorship in American Silent Film*. Cambridge, Mass.: Harvard University Press, 1991.

Haralovich, Mary Beth, and Lauren Rabinovitz, eds. *Television, History, and American Culture: Feminist Critical Essays*. Durham, N.C.: Duke University Press, 1999.

Harrison, Taylor, Sarah Projansky, Kent A. Ono, and Elyce Rae Helford, eds. *Enterprise Zones: Critical Positions on Star Trek*. Boulder, Colo.: Westview Press, 1996.

Hendershot, Heather. "Nickelodeon's Nautical Nonsense: The Intergenerational Appeal of *SpongeBob SquarePants*." In *Nickelodeon Nation: The History, Politics, and Economics of America's Only TV Channel for Kids*, edited by Heather Hendershot, 182–208. New York: New York University Press, 2004.

Heywood, Leslie, and Jennifer Drake. *Third Wave Agenda: Being Feminist, Doing Feminism*. Minneapolis: University of Minnesota Press, 1997.

Holder, Nancy. *The Evil That Men Do*: *Buffy the Vampire Slayer* 6. New York: Pocket Books, 2000.

Jeffords, Susan. *Hard Bodies: Hollywood Masculinity in the Reagan Era*. New Brunswick, N.J.: Rutgers University Press, 1994.

Jenkins, Henry. "'Do You Enjoy Making the Rest of Us Feel Stupid?': alt.tv.twinpeaks, the Trickster Author, and Viewer Mastery." In *Full of Secrets: Critical Approaches to "Twin Peaks*," edited by David Lavery, 51–69. Detroit: Wayne State University Press, 1995.

———. *Textual Poachers: Television Fans and Participatory Culture*. London: Routledge, 1992.

Joyrich, Lynne. "Critical and Textual Hypermasculinity." In *Logics of Television*, edited by Patricia Mellencamp, 156–72. Bloomington: Indiana University Press, 1990.

Karp, Marcelle, and Debbie Stoller, eds. *The BUST Guide to the New Girl Order*. New York: Penguin Books, 1999.

Kaveney, Roz, ed. *Reading the Vampire Slayer: An Unofficial Critical Companion to "Buffy" and "Angel."* London: I. B. Tauris, 2001.

Kett, Joseph F. *Rites of Passage: Adolescence in America, 1790 to the Present*. New York: Basic Books, 1977.

Kim, L. S. "'Sex and the Single Girl' in Postfeminism: The F Word on Television." *Television and New Media* 2, no. 4 (November 2001): 319–34.

Kincaid, James R. *Child-Loving: The Erotic Child and Victorian Culture*. New York: Routledge, 1992.

Kinder, Marsha. *Playing with Power in Movies, Television, and Video Games*. Berkeley: University of California Press, 1991.

Klein, Melissa. "Duality and Redefinition: Young Feminism and the Alternative Music Community." In *Third Wave Agenda: Being Feminist, Doing Feminism*, edited by Leslie Heywood and Jennifer Drake, 207–25. Minneapolis: University of Minnesota Press, 1997.

Kompare, Derek. *Rerun Nation*. London: Routledge, 2005.

Labi, Nadya. "Girl Power." *Time*, 29 June 1998, 60–62.

Langer, John. "Television's 'Personality System.'" *Media, Culture, and Society* 4 (October 1981): 351–65.

"Last Call." *Buffy the Vampire Slayer Magazine* 2, no. 4 (summer 1999), 21–22.

Lavery, David, ed. *Full of Secrets: Critical Approaches to "Twin Peaks."* Detroit: Wayne State University Press, 1995.

Lavery, David, Angela Hague, and Marla Cartwright, eds. *Deny All Knowledge: Reading "The X-Files."* Syracuse, N.Y.: Syracuse University Press, 1996.

Levine, Elana. *Wallowing in Sex: The New Sexual Culture of 1970s American Television*. Durham, N.C.: Duke University Press, 2007.

Lipsitz, George. *The Possessive Investment in Whiteness*. Philadelphia: Temple University Press, 1998.

Lotz, Amanda D. "Postfeminist Television Criticism: Rehabilitating Critical Terms and Identifying Postfeminist Attributes." *Feminist Media Studies* 1, no. 1 (March 2001): 105–21.

Luckett, Moya. "Girl Watchers: Patty Duke and Teen TV." In *The Revolution Wasn't Televised: Sixties Television and Social Conflict*, edited by Lynn Spigel and Michael Curtin, 95–116. New York: Routledge, 1997.

Marshall, David P. *Celebrity and Power: Fame in Contemporary Culture*. Minneapolis: University of Minnesota Press, 1997.

Mayne, Judith. "*L.A. Law* and Prime-Time Feminism." *Discourse* 10, no. 2 (spring–summer 1988): 30–47.

McCracken, Allison. "Boy Soaps: Liberalism without Women." *Flow* 1, no. 12 (March 2005), http://jot.communication.utexas.edu/flow/?jot=view&id=632 (accessed 12 April 2007).

McRobbie, Angela. *Postmodernism and Popular Culture*. London: Routledge, 1994.

Meaney, Gerardine. "Dead, White and Male: Irishness in *Buffy the Vampire Slayer* and *Angel*." In *The Irish in Us: Irishness, Performativity and Popular Culture*, edited by Diane Negra, 254–81. Durham, N.C.: Duke University Press, 2006.

"Merchants of Cool." *Frontline*. PBS and 10/20 Productions, 2001.

Meyrowitz, Joshua. *No Sense of Place: The Impact of Electronic Media on Social Behavior*. New York: Oxford University Press, 1985.

Mitchell, Penni. "Fans Slay Network." *Herizons* 16, no. 4 (spring 2003): 11.

Modleski, Tania. *Loving with a Vengeance: Mass-Produced Fantasies for Women*. Los Angeles: American Film Institute, 1983.

Mulvey, Laura. "Visual Pleasure and Narrative Cinema." In *Narrative/Apparatus/Ideology*, edited by Philip Rosen, 198–209. New York: Columbia University Press, 1986.

Murray, Susan. "Saving Our So-Called Lives: Girl Fandom, Adolescent Subjectivity, and *My So-Called Life*." In *Kids' Media Culture*, edited by Marsha Kinder, 221–38. Durham, N.C.: Duke University Press, 2000.

———. "'TV Satisfaction Guaranteed!': Nick at Nite and TV Land's 'Adult' Attractions." In *Nickelodeon Nation: The History, Politics, and Economics of America's Only TV Channel for Kids*, edited by Heather Hendershot, 69–84. New York: New York University Press, 2004.

Nash, Melanie, and Martti Lahti. "'Almost Ashamed to Say I Am One of Those Girls': *Titanic*, Leonardo DiCaprio and the Paradoxes of Girls' Fandom." In *Titanic: Anatomy of a Blockbuster*, edited by Kevin S. Sandler and Gaylyn Studlar, 64–88. New Brunswick, N.J.: Rutgers University Press, 1999.

Newcomb, Horace, ed. *Television: The Critical View*. 6th ed. New York: Oxford University Press, 2000.

"Number One with a Bullet." *Buffy the Vampire Slayer Magazine* 3, no. 3 (fall 2000), 14–15.

Parks, Lisa. "Brave New *Buffy*: Rethinking 'TV Violence.'" In *Quality Popular Television*, edited by Mark Jancovich and James Lyon, 118–36. London: British Film Institute, 2003.

Peirce, Kate. "*YM*." In *Women's Periodicals in the United States: Consumer Magazines*, edited by Kathleen L. Endres and Therese L. Lueck, 485–90. Westport, Conn.: Greenwood Press, 1995.

Penley, Constance. *NASA/TREK: Popular Science and Sex in America*. London: Verso, 1997.

Persons, Mitch. "Buffy, Vampire Slayer." *Femme Fatales* 8, no. 3 (August 1999): 12–15.

Peters, John Durham. *Speaking into the Air: A History of the Idea of Communication*. Chicago: University of Chicago Press, 1999.

Phillips, Maxine. "The 'Buffy Paradigm' Revisited: A Superhero and the War on Terror." *Dissent Magazine* (spring 2003), http://www.dissentmagazine.org/article/?article=511 (accessed 12 April 2007).

Postman, Neil. *The Disappearance of Childhood*. New York: Delacorte, 1982.

Projansky, Sarah. *Watching Rape: Film and Television in Postfeminist Culture*. New York: New York University Press, 2001.

Robinson, Sally. *Marked Men: White Masculinity in Crisis*. New York: Columbia University Press, 2000.

Rundle, Lisa B. "Out of Bounds." *Herizons* 17, no. 4 (spring 2004): 31.

Russo, Mary. *Female Grotesques: Risk, Excess and Modernity*. New York: Routledge, 1994.

Sandoval, Chela. "U.S. Third World Feminism: The Theory and Method of Oppositional Consciousness in the Postmodern World." *Genders* 10 (spring 1991): 1–24.

Schatz, Thomas. "The New Hollywood." In *Film Theory Goes to the Movies*, edited by Jim Collins, Hilary Radner, and Ava Preacher Collins, 8–36. New York: Routledge, 1993.

Sconce, Jeffrey. *Haunted Media: Electronic Presence from Telegraphy to Television*. Durham, N.C.: Duke University Press, 2000.

Slayage: The Online International Journal of Buffy Studies, http://slayageonline.com (accessed 12 April 2007).

Smith, Paul. "Eastwood Bound." In *Constructing Masculinity*, edited by Maurice Berger, Brian Wallis, and Simon Watson, 77–97. New York: Routledge, 1995.

South, James B. *"Buffy the Vampire Slayer" and Philosophy: Fear and Trembling in Sunnydale*. Chicago: Open Court, 2003.

Spigel, Lynn, and Michael Curtin, eds. *The Revolution Wasn't Televised: Sixties Television and Social Conflict*. New York: Routledge, 1997.

Stacey, Jackie. *Star Gazing: Hollywood Cinema and Female Spectatorship*. London: Routledge, 1994.

Stacey, Judith. "Sexism by a Subtler Name? Postindustrial Conditions and Post-feminist Consciousness in the Silicon Valley." *Socialist Review* 17 (November/December 1987): 7–28.

Stoller, Debbie. "Feminists Fatale: BUST-ing the Beauty Myth." In *The BUST Guide to the New Girl Order*, edited by Marcelle Karp and Debbie Stoller, 41–47. New York: Penguin Books, 1999.

Studlar, Gaylan. *This Mad Masquerade: Stardom and Masculinity in the Jazz Age*. New York: Columbia University Press, 1996.

Tasker, Yvonne. *Spectacular Bodies: Gender, Genre and the Action Cinema*. New York: Routledge, 1993.

Torres, Sasha, ed. *Living Color: Race and Television in the United States*. Durham, N.C.: Duke University Press, 1998.

Udovitch, Mim. "What Makes Buffy Slay?" *Rolling Stone*, 11 May 2000, 60–66.

Wald, Gayle. *Crossing the Color Line: Racial Passing in Twentieth-Century U.S. Literature and Culture*. Durham, N.C.: Duke University Press, 2000.

Walker, Rebecca. "Being Real: An Introduction." In *To Be Real: Telling the Truth and Changing the Face of Feminism*, edited by Rebecca Walker, xxix–xl. New York: Anchor Books, 1995.

Watson, Andi. *Buffy the Vampire Slayer* 17. Milwaukie, Ore.: Dark Horse Comics, January 2000.

Weber, Samuel. *Mass Mediauras: Essays on Form, Technics and Media*. Edited by Alan Cholodenko. Stanford, Calif.: Stanford University Press, 1996.

Weigman, Robyn. *American Anatomies: Theorizing Race and Gender*. Durham, N.C.: Duke University Press, 1995.

White, Mimi. "Crossing Wavelengths: The Diegetic and Referential Imaginary of American Commercial Television." *Cinema Journal* 25, no. 2 (winter 1986): 51–64.

Wilcox, Rhonda. *Why "Buffy" Matters: The Art of "Buffy the Vampire Slayer."* London: I. B. Tauris, 2005.

Wilcox, Rhonda V., and David Lavery, eds. *Fighting the Forces: What's at Stake in "Buffy the Vampire Slayer."* Lanham, Md.: Rowan and Littlefield, 2002.

Williamson, Judith. "A Piece of the Action: Images of 'Woman' in the Photography of Cindy Sherman." In *Consuming Passions*, 91–114. London: Marion Boyers, 1986.

Wlodarz, Joe. "Maximum Insecurity: Genre Trouble and Closet Erotics in and out of HBO's *Oz*." *Camera Obscura* 58 (June 2005): 59–105.

Wyatt, Justin. *High Concept: Movies and Marketing in Hollywood*. Austin: University of Texas Press, 1994.

Zollo, Peter. *Wise Up to Teens: Insights into Marketing and Advertising to Teenagers*. Ithaca, N.Y.: New Strategist Publications, 1995.

CONTRIBUTORS

Ian Calcutt is a freelance journalist for print and online media specializing in the entertainment and consumer electronics sectors. He has been a regularly published writer on cult TV and films in such magazines as *Starburst*, *Dreamwatch*, *Shivers*, *Cult Times*, and *Film Review*. He has written on home theater and digital broadcasting in outlets such as *What Video & HDTV*, *Home Cinema Choice*, and *T3*. Before moving into journalism he was a research executive for a TV ratings bureau based in the United Kingdom.

Cynthia Fuchs is an associate professor of English, film, and media studies and of African American studies at George Mason University. She is the film, video, and TV editor for the weekly magazine *PopMatters* (www.popmatters.com). She co-edited *Between the Sheets, in the Streets: Queer, Lesbian, and Gay Documentary* (1997).

Amelie Hastie is an associate professor of film and digital media at the University of California, Santa Cruz, and a member of the *Camera Obscura* editorial collective. She is the author of *Cupboards of Curiosity: Women, Recollection, and Film History* (2006), also published by Duke University Press. Her work has also appeared in *Afterimage*, *Camera Obscura*, *Cinema Journal*, *Post Script*, and elsewhere.

Annette Hill is a professor of media and the director of research in the School of Media, Arts, and Design at the University of Westminster. In addition to writing a variety of articles on audiences and popular culture, she is the co-editor (with Robert C. Allen) of *The Television Studies Reader* (2003), the co-author (with David Gauntlett) of *TV Living: Television, Audiences and Everyday Life* (1999), and the author of *Reality TV: Audiences and Popular Factual Television* (2005). Her forthcoming book, *Factual TV*, is on the reception of news and current affairs, and documentary and popular factual television in Britain and Sweden.

Mary Celeste Kearney is an assistant professor in the department of radio-television-film at the University of Texas, Austin. Her research to date has focused on girls' culture, girls' media production, and girls' representations in American film and television. She is the author of *Girls Make Media* (2006).

Elana Levine is an assistant professor in the department of journalism and mass communication at the University of Wisconsin, Milwaukee. She is the author of *Wallowing in Sex: The New Sexual Culture of 1970s American Television* (2007), also published by Duke University Press. Her work has also been published in such journals as *Critical Studies in Media Communication*, *Television and New Media*, and *The Velvet Light Trap*.

Allison McCracken is an assistant professor of American studies at DePaul University. Her book, *Real Men Don't Sing: Crooning and American Culture, 1928–1933*, is forthcoming from Duke University Press.

Jason Middleton is a visiting assistant professor in film and media studies in the English department at the University of Rochester. He has published work on film, television, and popular music in collections from Duke University Press and in journals such as *The Velvet Light Trap* and *Popular Music*. He is the co-editor (with Roger Beebe) of *Music Video/Music Television/MTV* (2007), also published by Duke University Press, and he is currently working on a manuscript titled *Documentary/Genre*, which concerns intersections of documentary films with narrative fiction genre films. He is also an award-winning experimental filmmaker.

Susan Murray is an assistant professor of culture and communication at New York University. She is the author of *Hitch Your Antenna to the Stars! Broadcast Stardom and Early Television* (2005) and the co-editor of *Reality TV: Remaking Television Culture* (2004).

Lisa Parks is an associate professor of film and media studies at the University of California, Santa Barbara. She is the author of *Cultures in Orbit: Satellites and the Televisual* (2005), also published by Duke University Press, and the co-editor of *Planet TV: A Global Television Reader* (2003). She is currently working on a new book called *Mixed Signals: Media Technologies and Cultural Geography*.

INDEX

Academy. *See* Criticism; Scholarship

Aca/fans, 11, 89, 92

Acland, Charles, 98

Action genre, 36, 99, 121, 128, 132, 135, 140, 141 n. 2, 142 n. 5, 143 n. 18, 146; heroines of, 145–48, 151–55, 160–65, 166 n. 11. *See also* Superheroines

Adolescence, 7, 19, 21, 23–24, 102, 104, 160. *See also* Teens

Adults, 19, 21, 106; appeal of *Buffy* to, 31–33, 41 n. 50; fears about youth and, 22; reading down and, 24–25; U.K. television and, 57–58; youth attitude toward, 108; youthful sensibility and, 23–24, 29, 36–38, 98–99, 102

Advertising, 19; aspirational consumerism and, 23; girl power and, 28; mass audience and, 19–20; men represented in, 122; narrowcasting and, 20; reading down and, 25; to teens, 18, 22, 29, 53; youthfulness and, 21, 38. *See also* Marketing

African Americans: as audience, 15 n. 22; representations of, 28, 55 n. 24, 102–3, 143 n. 24

Afterlife: of *Buffy the Vampire Slayer*, 4. *See also* Death

Age, 2; as aspirational, 22; *Buffy* viewers and, 7, 12, 25; identifying across, 21, 36; as identity category, 19, 98–99, 174; representations of, 11, 13; spectatorial identification and, 18–19, 46; target marketing and, 19, 22, 28–29; television viewership and, 18

Alias, 141

All About You, 28

Allen, Robert C., 77–79

Allie, Scott, 151, 154, 165

Allison, Dorothy, 127

All My Children, 50, 55 n. 18

Ally McBeal, 168, 176, 188 n. 2

American Gothic, 62

America Online, 49–50

Ancillary products. *See* Merchandise

Anderson, Pamela, 162–63

Ang, Ien, 31

Angel, 84, 91, 117, 132, 143 n. 19, 144 n. 30; DVD release of, 66–67; homoeroticism of, 131, 133–39, 143 n. 21; masculinism of, 139–40, 143 n. 18; U.K. broadcast of, 12, 56, 58, 59–63, 65–66, 69, 72 n. 4; U.S. broadcast of, 6–7, 9, 15 n. 24, 72 n. 11

Angel (character), 65, 84, 86, 102, 105, 142 n. 5, 142–43 n. 11, 174; Buffy and, 1, 110–11, 118, 119–22, 124, 128–31, 178; as comic

Angel (character) (*continued*)
    spectacle, 134–37; normative masculinity
    and, 13, 128–32, 139–40; as object of
    torture, 13, 116–20, 123–24, 139; passivity
    and, 120–23, 126–27, 137–38; queer body
    of, 117–27, 131–39, 141; readings of, 132;
    sadomasochism and, 13, 119–26, 131–32,
    141, 144 n. 26; as sexual object, 13, 116–18,
    120–22, 132, 137–38, 141 n. 1
Anya, 104, 106, 126–27, 181–83
Aphrodite IX, 149
Ariès, Philippe, 19
Audience: adult, 7; African Americans as, 15
    n. 22, 26; behavior of, 20–21; British tele-
    vision and, 57–58, 63; coalition, 20, 26;
    critics as, 11, 88–90; cult TV and, 58, 63;
    family, 20, 26, 57–59, 69; fragmentation
    of, 19, 20, 38; mass, 19–20, 185; multigen-
    erational, 19, 26, 29, 38; ratings for *Buffy*
    and, 28, 29, 38, 62, 63, 64, 66, 67; target-
    ing of, 12, 19, 20, 58; for teen series, 18, 19,
    45–46, 53; transnational, 57–58, 63–64;
    as viewers vs. watchers, 84–87; viewing
    positions of, 143 n. 14; youth, 7, 11, 12, 18,
    44, 58, 60. *See also* Fans; Spectatorship
Avengers, The, 147

Babylon 5, 62
Baby-Sitters Club, The, 27
Backstreet Boys, The, 44
Barbarella, 147, 164
Barb Wire, 162–63, 165
Batgirl, 166 n. 15
Battlestar Galactica, 61
Baumgardner, Jennifer, 172–73
BBC1, 72 n. 12
BBC2, 57–59, 61, 63–64, 65, 66; *Buffy* message
    boards of, 64–65, 68–69
Beats, 24
Benjamin, Walter, 15 n. 6
Berman, Gail, 28
Beulah, 77
Beverly Hills, 90210, 27, 31, 45, 99, 142 n. 8
Bibb, Bob, 26, 29, 40 n. 33
Bionic Woman, The, 32

Blade Runner, 111
Blake's 7, 72 n. 12
Blossom, 27
Bordo, Susan, 142 n. 8
Boreanaz, David, 135, 136, 142 n. 6, 143 n. 18
Brandy, 43
Brat Pack, 44
Britain. *See* United Kingdom
British Board of Film Classification, 67
Broadcasters' Audience Research Board, 61,
    72 n. 13
Broadcasting Standards Commission, 58–59,
    63, 65, 72 n. 5
Broadcast television, 5, 20, 43; British appear-
    ance of *Buffy* on, 61, 64–65; British regu-
    lation of, 58–60; public service mission
    of, 64–65; target audiences of, 20. *See also*
    UPN; WB, The
Brunsdon, Charlotte, 94 n. 5, 94 n. 7, 95 n. 23
Buffy. *See* Summers, Buffy
Buffy syndrome, 7
Buffy the Vampire Slayer (feature film), 6, 28,
    30, 36
"Buffy the Vampire Slayer" and Philosophy, 10,
    95 n. 18, 95 n. 20, 188 n. 3
Buffy the Vampire Slayer Annual, 152–53
Buffy the Vampire Slayer Pop Quiz, 81–82, 84
*Buffy the Vampire Slayer: The Animated
    Series,* 8
BuffyUK.org, 66, 68–70, 73 n. 36
Buffyverse, 1, 117, 123, 125
BUST magazine, 177

Cable, 27, 54, 58, 60, 76, 78; as competition
    for broadcast networks, 20, 26, 90; media
    convergence and, 43
Caldwell, John T., 20
Caleb, 184
Calendar, Jenny, 129
Camera Obscura, 95 n. 23
Cameron, James, 96, 113
Capitalism, 6, 74–75; *Buffy* and, 81; television
    scholarship as function of, 75–81, 90–92
Carpenter, Charisma, 167 n. 18
Cassidy, David, 44

vision and, 57–58, 61, 62, 72 n. 13; *Buffy*
and, 28, 62, 63, 64, 66, 67; the WB and,
29, 38
Reading the Vampire Slayer: The Unofficial
Critical Companion to "Buffy" and "Angel,"
91, 95 n. 18
Realism, 32
Reception. *See* Audience; Fans
Recirculation: *Buffy the Vampire Slayer* and, 3;
television series and, 4, 5–6
Red Sonja, 147
Regulation of TV content in United King-
dom, 58–59
Reruns. *See* Syndication
Research: *Buffy's* representation of, 83–86, 89.
See also Scholarship
Resurrection: representations of, 4; television
series and, 4, 5
Revolution Wasn't Televised, The, 94 n. 7
Richards, Amy, 173
Right to Reply, 65
Riot Grrrl, 27
Rock music, 36–38
Romeo and Juliet, 44
Rosenberg, Willow, 96, 128, 129, 178; as Final
Girl, 161–62; sexuality of, 1, 10, 33, 34–35,
116–18, 126–27, 167 n. 18, 180, as witch,
69, 104–5, 178, 180, 184–85, 187
Roswell, 6, 53
Rowden, Sam, 61

Sadomasochism, 117–26, 132–33, 137–38, 147
Sassy, 28
Satellite television, 20, 58, 60, 78. *See also*
Cable
Schatz, Thomas, 52
Scheduling: of *Buffy* and *Angel* in United
Kingdom, 61–67, 71–72; U.K. television
and, 56, 58–63
Scholarship: *Buffy* and, 3, 10, 11, 12–13, 74,
89–94, 95 n. 18–19, 145; market demand
and, 74–75, 77–81, 90–94; teen television
and, 18; temporality and, 74–75, 77–81,
90–94, 94 n. 7; vampires and, 123. *See also*
Conferences; Television studies

School violence. *See* Violence
Science fiction, 2, 13, 96, 99, 127, 146, 148,
160; U.K. import of, 58, 60–61. *See also*
Genre
Scooby Doo, 49
Scopophilia, 149, 158–60, 165, 166 n. 8. *See*
also Fetishization; Voyeurism
Scream, 17, 44, 50–51, 104
Scream Queens, 146, 148, 149, 166 n. 6
Secret World of Alex Mack, The, 27
Seinfeld, 95 n. 20
Serenity, 5
Serial narrative, 33, 64, 85, 89, 93, 124, 126,
132, 137, 140, 145–46
Seventeen, 28
Sex: content regulation and, 59, 63; discrimi-
nation and, 125; premarital behaviors and,
23, 40 n. 27; representation of, 105, 110,
114, 127–28; spectatorial identification
and, 18, 36; targeting of audiences and, 20
Sex in the City, 90
Sexuality, 2, 7, 173; challenges to adulthood
and, 24; dangers of, 128–31; girls and,
110–11, 117–19; horror and, 160–62;
lesbianism, 10, 143 n. 15; representations
of, 11, 13, 33, 143 n. 15, 163; spectatorial
identification and, 18, 36; transgressive,
116–19, 126–27
Sexualization, of Buffy, 120, 151–60, 171
Shawshank Redemption, The, 125
Shot selection. *See* Cinematography
Simpsons, The, 60, 61, 95 n. 20
Sisters in Style, 28
Sister, Sister, 27, 28
Six Feet Under, 90
Sky One, 57, 60, 61, 62, 63, 68–69
Slayage, 10
Slayer Slang, 10
Smallville, 6, 140–41
Snyder, Principal, 102
Soap opera, 118, 132, 145–46, 166 n. 2–3;
"boy," 140–41, 144 n. 29
Someone Like Me, 27
Sopranos, The, 90, 95 n. 20
South, James B., 95 n. 18, 95 n. 20, 188 n. 3

Elana Levine is an assistant professor in the department of journalism and mass communication at the University of Wisconsin, Milwaukee. Lisa Parks is an associate professor of film and media studies at the University of California, Santa Barbara.

Library of Congress Cataloging-in-Publication Data
Undead TV: essays on Buffy the vampire slayer / edited by Elana Levine and Lisa Parks.
p. cm.
Includes bibliographical references and index.
ISBN 978-0-8223-4065-2 (cloth: alk. paper) — ISBN 978-0-8223-4043-0 (pbk.: alk. paper)
1. Buffy, the vampire slayer (Television program) I. Levine, Elana, 1970– II. Parks, Lisa.
PN1992.77.B84U53 2007
791.45′72—dc22   2007017113